# Performance Management

## Perspectives on Employee Performance

Richard S Williams
Department of Organizational Psychology,
Birkbeck College, University of London

INTERNATIONAL THOMSON BUSINESS PRESS
I ⊤ P® An International Thomson Publishing Company

London • Bonn • Boston • Johannesburg • Madrid • Melbourne • Mexico City • New York • Paris
Singapore • Tokyo • Toronto • Albany, NY • Belmont, CA • Cincinnati, OH • Detroit, MI

**Performance Management: Perspectives on Employee Performance**

**Copyright © 1998 International Thomson Business Press**

First published by International Thomson Business Press

I(T)P® A division of International Thomson Publishing Inc.
The ITP logo is a trademark under licence

*British Library Cataloguing-in-Publication Data*
A catalogue record for this book is available from the British Library

**First edition 1998**

Typeset by J&L Composition Ltd, Filey, North Yorkshire
Printed in the UK by Clays Ltd, St Ives plc

**ISBN 1–186152–184–7**

International Thomson Business Press
Berkshire House
168–173 High Holborn
London WC1V 7AA
UK

International Thomson Business Press
20 Park Plaza
13th Floor
Boston MA 02116
USA

http://www.itbp.com

# Performance Management

## Perspectives on Employee Performance

*[handwritten] good for Competences & Job analysis*

*[handwritten]*
- defn of mission statem } p33
- defn of culture } p40
- values p41
- defn of evaluation p91
- objectives: what? how?

ESSENTIAL BUSINESS PSYCHOLOGY
Series editor: Clive Fletcher

This series interprets and examines people's work behaviour from the perspective of occupational psychology. Each title focuses on a central issue in management, emphasizing the role of the individual's workplace experience.

Other books in the series:

**Successful Team Management**
*Nicky Hayes*

**The Healthy Organization**
Ethics and Diversity at Work
*Sue Newell*

**Business Leadership**
*Viv Shackleton*

**Impression Management in Organizations**
*Paul Rosenfeld, Robert A. Giacalone and Catherine A. Riordan*

**The Psychology of Personnel Selection**
*Dominic Cooper and Ivan T. Robertson*

**Innovation and Change in Organizations**
*Nigel King and Neil Anderson*

# Contents

# Figures

# — *Tables*

# Boxes

# Series editor's preface

The rapid, far-reaching, and continuing changes of recent years have brought about a situation where understanding the psychology of individuals and teams is of prime importance in work settings. Organizational structures have shifted radically to the point where individual managers and professionals have far greater autonomy, responsibility and accountability. Organizations seek to reduce central control and to 'empower' individual employees. Those employees combine in teams that are frequently cross-functional and project-based rather than hierarchical in their construction. The traditional notion of careers is changing; increasingly, the expectation is that an individual's career is less likely to be within a single organization, which has implications for how organizations will command loyalty and commitment in the future. The full impact of the information technology revolution is finally being felt, with all the consequences this has for the nature of work and the reactions of those doing it.

The capacity of people to cope with the scale and speed of these changes has become a major issue, and the literature on work stress bears testimony to this. The belief in the importance of individuals' cognitive abilities and personality make-up in determining what they achieve and how they can contribute to team work has been demonstrated in the explosive growth in organizations' use of psychometric tests and related procedures. Perhaps more than ever before analysing and understanding the experience of work from a psychological perspective is necessary to achieve the twin goals of effective performance and quality of working life. Unfortunately, it is the latter of these that all too often seems to be overlooked in the concern to create competitive, performance-driven, or customer-focused cultures within companies.

It is no coincidence that the rise in the study of business ethics and increasing concern over issues of fairness paralleled many of the organizational changes of the 1980s and 1990s. Ultimately, an imbalance between the aims and needs of the employees and the aims and needs of the organization is self-defeating. One of the widely recognized needs for the years ahead is for a greater emphasis on innovation rather than on simply reacting to pressures, yet psychological research and theory indicate that innovation is much more likely to take place where individuals feel secure enough to take the risks involved, and where organizational reward systems encourage experimentation and exploration – which they have singly failed to do in the last decade. Seeking to help organizations realize the potential of their work-force in mutually enhancing ways is the business challenge psychology has to meet.

The aim of the *Essential Business Psychology* series is to interpret and explain people's work behaviour in the context of a continually evolving pattern of change, and to do so from the perspective of occupational and organizational psychology. The books draw together academic research and practitioner experience, relying on empirical studies, practical examples, and case studies to communicate their ideas. Hopefully, the reader will find that they provide a succinct summary of accumulated knowledge and how it can be applied. The themes of some of the books cover traditional areas of occupational psychology, while others will focus on topics that cut across some of those boundaries, tackling subjects that are of growing interest and prominence. The intended readership of the series is quite broad; whilst they are most directly relevant for practitioners, consultants, and students in HR and occupational psychology, much of what they deal with is increasingly the concern of managers and students of management more generally. Although the books share a common aim and series heading, they have not been forced into a rigid stylistic format. In keeping with the times, the authors have had a good deal of autonomy in deciding how to organize and present their work. I think all of them have done an excellent job; I hope you think so too.

*Clive Fletcher*

# 1   *What is performance management?*

The idea of performance management is far from new – it has long been recognized that performance needs to be managed. This is true whether we are concerned with performance at the organizational level, the individual level, or any level in between. And over the years we have seen many practices, techniques, tools, systems and philosophies which have as their aim the management of performance. Indeed, the term performance management itself may be seen as yet another philosophy or system, and as such it came to particular prominence in the late 1980s/early 1990s. But its precise nature remains indistinct: as I shall go on to show, there are a number of perspectives on performance management.

So, performance management is no single thing. That said, one main interpretation has come to dominate in practice – one which focuses on the individual and which, for the most part, is essentially an evolutionary extension of traditional appraisal practice. But this has many deficiencies, not least of which is that it clings on to outmoded values about employees, their motivation and performance. By contrast, the models that are advocated in the textbooks on this subject – both the practitioner-oriented literature and that of a more academic kind – are broader in their scope. And they promulgate rather different values, such as participation, a philosophy of improvement and concern for employee well-being.

If we accept these values then we might expect to see a different approach not just to performance management itself but also to the way in which systems are designed and developed. So, for example, an involving approach to design and implementation might mean that systems will better meet the needs and interests of those most directly affected by performance management. It is said that performance management should be owned and driven by the line – if this is so then we might expect to see line managers being brought into the development process as a way of helping to bring about their acceptance of the system. A participative approach is one way of showing that employees are valued and trusted.

Going hand in hand with participation is the need for diagnosis and analysis. This theme is clear in much of the writing on performance management that we have seen over the past decade or so. Emphasis is also placed on the need to maintain, monitor and manage performance management systems. Though evaluation is often seen as something that is tacked on afterwards, it is a necessary part of the plan–do–check–act cycle.

We would expect an improvement philosophy to show itself in a developmental approach to performance management rather than the excessive emphasis on control and external reward that characterizes so much of contemporary practice. The latter are important but they need to be balanced by more of a concern for the employee – their well-being, fairness of treatment. And for the sceptics who see such thinking as unduly altruistic, there is increasing evidence to indicate that organizational benefits are to be obtained.

For the most part, however, it is not concern for the employee that has driven the introduction of performance management. Indeed, as might be expected, no single force was responsible; rather, there were a number of interrelated influencing factors. They are as germane today as they were a few years ago. So, by way of background, let me first briefly examine these influences. I'll then go on to look at the nature of performance management.

## FACTORS INFLUENCING THE INTRODUCTION OF PERFORMANCE MANAGEMENT

### Market conditions

The increasingly competitive environment of the 1980s, which continued throughout the recessionary early 1990s and remains a dominant factor today, has been identified by many commentators (e.g. Connock 1991; Storey and Sisson 1993) as a major influence leading to increased concern for performance improvement. Some (e.g. Lawler 1995) go so far as to say that the nature of competition is the 'most significant difference' about the business environment of the 1990s:

> Many businesses have become global, and as a result, success requires much higher levels of performance in three areas: the quality of goods and services produced, the cost at which they are produced, and the speed with which the producers innovate and get new products and services to the market.
>
> (Lawler 1995: 52)

In some sectors new market conditions have been created, particularly in the public sector; for example amongst schools, hospitals and other units within the health service, executive agencies within central government, and within local authorities through compulsory competitive tendering. All this has led to a much sharper focus in the public sector on performance and performance management.

The competitiveness theme is widespread in recent literature on organizational and employee performance, as the extracts in Table 1.1 show. However, important though it is, competitiveness is only one element in the drive to increase productivity and performance. In the same way that there are several forces pressing on organizations, so too there is a range of responses available to organizations. The sources quoted in Box 1.1 represent just a few of the perspectives from which the 'problem' of performance and productivity management has been approached. For example, Flood and Olian (1996) and Fay (1995) take a human resource management perspective, Peppard and Preece (1995) and Bredrup (1995a) emphasize the business process, and Bounds et al. (1994) are concerned with total quality management (TQM). These represent three overall approaches for managing performance which continue to be important in the 1990s.

## Box 1.1    Competitiveness and organizational performance

'The world of business has become a struggle to gain competitive advantage in a much larger and more demanding marketplace. Markets now stretch across international boundaries, trade barriers have crumbled and distribution channels have become more efficient. State intervention in many markets has diminished and organizations now confront an unequalled number of competitors. Consumer preferences have been ratcheted up, with increasingly demanding calls for higher quality products and services, delivered faster, and at a lower price.'

(Flood and Olian 1996: 5)

'Managers of today are under increasing pressure to improve the competitive position of their organization, either to steal a march on their competitors or to simply keep up with the ever accelerating pace of competition. . . . At a macro level, it is easy to discern the changes taking place in the environment and the consequential demands and challenges which such developments place on organizations. Globalization of markets, commodization of products and services, and intense competition all challenge the way that organizations traditionally compete. New information and communication technologies are changing the very nature of business itself.'

(Peppard and Preece 1995: 157)

'A clear trend . . . is that competition will increase due to more globalization and more demanding customers. As customers are exposed to better products and services their expectations for better quality, service and value will increase. Higher expectations have to be met by improved performance to obtain customer satisfaction.'

(Bredrup 1995a: 61)

'The changes that are affecting organizations and work design include the increasing intensity and scope of international competition, a drive by American organizations to cut costs (in part to meet foreign competition relying on lower labour costs), a continued move toward automation of production processes, a reliance on more sophisticated information processing technologies, and greater use of communication technology in place of face-to-face interactions.'

(Fay 1995: 23)

'Over time, managers have faced a growing intensity of global competition and pervasive change. . . . Relentless advances in technology open and close markets as products rapidly move through ever-shorter life cycles. . . . Better communications and logistical innovations have increased accessibility to even the remotest corners of the earth. As technological and economic development continues, the number of global competitors will continue to increase. Customers now expect more because competitors offer more.'

(Bounds *et al.* 1994: 5)

Today's concern for competitiveness may be seen as a continuation or development of the long-standing search for greater productivity. There have been many 'productivity improvement programmes' (e.g., Lawlor 1985; Prokopenko 1987) but some authorities (e.g., Heap 1992) have seen the traditional UK approach to improving productivity as being overly concerned with cost-cutting. Productivity has risen in the short term, but at what long-term expense? Increasingly, then, we have seen arguments for a broadening of the productivity concept, with greater emphasis being placed on the 'top-line' or performance element (e.g., Heap 1992; Andersen 1995).

## Management theories and movements: excellence and quality

Also influential have been changes in thinking about the nature of the management of organizations and about performance. Two particular examples of this are the 'search for excellence' movement and the concern for quality. The latter has been especially

*Table 1.1* Characteristics of 'excellent' companies
(source: Peters and Waterman 1982)

---

- A bias for action
- Close to the customer
- Autonomy and entrepreneurship
- Productivity through people
- Hands-on, value-driven
- Stick to knitting
- Simple form, lean staff
- Simultaneous loose–tight properties

---

influential because it has reshaped the way in which we think about performance and because of the changes to manufacturing and service delivery processes that have resulted.

Though the research carried out by Peters and Waterman (1982) has come to be questioned (e.g., Hitt and Ireland 1987), there is no doubt that their eight principles of excellence (Table 1.1) have been influential. For example, the ideas of getting close to the customer and finding out what the customer wants so as to identify and meet changing consumer demand and expectations/requirements are now widely accepted (Lawler 1995). They have been reinforced in the public sector, for example, by many of the changes pushed through by central Government. Similarly, 'sticking to the knitting' is an idea that we see reflected in the notion of the 'core competence' of an organization (Prahalad and Hamel 1990). And the case for productivity or competitiveness through people has been argued by many (e.g., Pfeffer 1994).

## Technological developments

From one point of view technology is part of performance management, one of the tools, that is, for managing performance. Product and process technology have been identified by Pfeffer (1994), for example, as one of the traditional bases of competitive success. And, indeed, technology, especially information technology, has been in many cases a solution to a performance problem which has led to that business gaining competitive advantage: American Airlines and their SABRE system is a particular case in point (McKenney 1995). Others in the industry then were left to catch up, often doing so with a comparable technological solution of their own.

Over the years we have seen many technological developments which have led organizations to make changes to their systems for managing performance, that is, their manufacturing process or the service delivery process. Examples include automation, computer-aided design (CAD), computer-aided manufacturing (CAM), just in time (JIT), and lean production, and business process re-engineering (BPR) typically will involve the application of information technology (IT). All of these have their implications for the people expected to operate them.

## Organizational restructuring and change

Like technology, organizational restructuring may be seen as part of performance management. Much restructuring seems to have been as a response to the prevailing economic conditions and we have seen many different manifestations: '"de-layering", "down-sizing", "flexibility", "team-working", "service level agreements", "high performance work systems", "strategic business units", "core and periphery", "teleworking", "franchising"' (Storey and Sisson 1993: 80) are many of the terms which illustrate the different forms of restructuring that we have come to see. In addition there have been changes of ownership and mergers. All these developments have been seen in both the private and public sectors.

Though the sorts of structural changes listed above may cut costs (and so boost productivity) they do not necessarily do anything to increase performance, at whatever level and however defined. Potentially, they offer an opportunity for doing so: for example, Fletcher and Williams point out that 'Delayering might be seen as facilitating performance management, in that it places more power to determine organizational performance in the hands of individual managers' (Institute of Personnel Management 1992: 82). Extending this still further we have ideas like 'empowerment' and 'control through involvement' (Lawler 1995) which seek, amongst other things, to push authority lower down the hierarchy (where there still is a hierarchy, that is!). But such structural changes might be seen very differently by employees who remain in the organization, as in the negative consequences of 'down-sizing' (Cascio 1993; Feldman 1995).

One consequence claimed for such restructuring as delayering and decentralization has been an alteration in the **role of the line manager** – the quote from Fletcher and Williams above gives one example. But there may have been other changes as well, such as having more extensive personnel management and employee development responsibilities for larger numbers of staff. In other words, the **management** role comes to be emphasized more than the technical aspects of managers' jobs.

## Government policies

Certain of these have had a particular impact on the public sector, as in the creation of new markets mentioned above. Other legislative changes – local management of schools (LMS), care in the community, and many others – have already affected service provision and will continue to do so. This is true also of other legislative changes which have affected organizations more generally, namely those bearing on employment and industrial relations.

**Industrial relations changes**
As Fletcher and Williams comment:

> The 1980s saw a number of legislative changes, which together with other factors (including high unemployment) made inroads into traditional collective bargaining. One result of this has been to facilitate the movement towards dispensing rewards on a more individual, rather than collective, basis, and to allocate more of those rewards on the basis of merit.
>
> (Institute of Personnel Management 1992: 84)

Here again, the employment-related legislation now in force seems set to remain. Performance management as typically practised is wholly consistent with this individualization of the employment relationship – goal-setting, appraisal, and performance-related pay all operate, for the most part, on an individual basis.

## The inadequacies of performance appraisal

A final influencing factor is the claim that performance appraisal is deficient as a tool for managing employee performance. This argument is particularly evident in the North American literature on performance management (e.g., Schneier *et al.* 1986; Heisler *et al.* 1988), although there are examples of it elsewhere (e.g., South Africa – Spangenberg 1994). Table 1.2 summarizes the problems which continue to be potential pitfalls for performance management.

At one level, then, performance management may be seen as a reaction against performance appraisal. Indeed, much more generally, performance management policies and practices appear very much to be a **response** to the sorts of pressures and influences summarized above. And organizations have responded in many different ways: thus, it is clear that there is no single approach to performance management. Evidence from surveys of practice support this view, as do the writings of academics and practitioners.

## PERSPECTIVES ON PERFORMANCE MANAGEMENT

One of the things that writers on performance management agree about is that performance management is difficult to define – this is true, of course, of many other initiatives, such as total quality management (TQM) and business process re-engineering (BPR). None the less, it seems possible to discern three main perspectives or types of model:

- performance management as a system for managing organizational performance;
- performance management as a system for managing employee performance;
- performance management as a system for integrating the management of organizational and employee performance.

What are the main features of these perspectives? I'll set these out first before going on to identify some underlying themes.

### Performance management as a system for managing organizational performance

A good illustration of this view is found in Rogers (1990), who writes about corporate, authority-wide systems of performance management in local government:

The characteristics of such systems are that they are corporate systems which include the following processes as part of an annual integrated cycle of management:

*Table 1.2* Sources of performance appraisal problems (source: Spangenberg 1994: 3)

1  CONTEXT
   1.1  Organizational characteristics
      • Emphasis on the past clashes with managerial preference for current information
      • No commitment to appraisal
      • Conducting of appraisals not reinforced, e.g. no rewards for conscientious appraisals
      • Performance appraisals not declared an important managerial function
      • Redundant in democratic participative climate
   1.2  Position characteristics
      • Inability to observe performance

2  SYSTEM CHARACTERISTICS
   2.1  Implementation
      • No user participation in system development
      • Failure to develop performance measures from job analysis
      • Rating systems administered subjectively
      • Results used to discriminate on the basis of race, sex, etc.
   2.2  Performance appraisal policies
      • No standard policy regarding rater's tasks/roles in appraisal
      • No standard policy regarding frequency of appraisals

3  PERFORMANCE APPRAISAL ELEMENTS
   3.1  Rater and rating process
      *Observation*
      • Lack of knowledge of ratee's job
      • Possession of erroneous or incomplete information
      • Differing expectations because of level in hierarchy and role
      *Judgement*
      • Bias and errors in human judgement
      • Stereotypes and prejudices
   3.2  Performance appraisal instrument
      *Performance measures (criteria)*
      • Ambiguity of performance measures: incompleteness
      • Lack of specificity and behaviour-based language
      • Irrelevant performance criteria
      • Criteria not communicated explicitly to ratees
      *Performance appraisal system*
      • Inability of system to reflect dynamic nature of jobs and organizational context
      • Credibility loss from outdated systems

4   PERFORMANCE APPRAISAL OUTCOMES
>    *Evaluation*
>    • Failure to recognize excellent performance
>    • Promotional decision errors
>    • Staffing jobs with inadequate skills mix
>    *Guidance and development*
>    • Failure to recognize potential
>    • Failure to build skills through training
>    *Motivation*
>    • Grievances because of subjectivity and bias

---

>    • setting corporate policy and resource aims and guidelines
>    • specifying, within the framework provided by (1) above, a detailed set of plans, budgets, objectives, targets and standards of performance
>    • regularly and systematically reviewing the performance of all services.
>
>    (Rogers 1990: 29)

Another illustration of this conception is presented by Bredrup (1995), who sees performance management as comprising three main processes – planning, improving and reviewing. Of course, these three processes could be taken as applying to the management of performance at whatever level of analysis one chooses – organization-wide, business unit, department, team, individual, etc. (Mabey and Salaman 1995). But Bredrup's schematic representation (see Figure 1.1) of his model shows rather more clearly the organizational perspective.

Thus, in this model **performance planning** is concerned with such activities as formulating the organization's vision and strategy and defining what is meant by performance. **Performance improvement** takes a process perspective, that is, including such activities as business process re-engineering, continuous process improvement, benchmarking, and total quality management. **Performance review** embraces performance measurement and evaluation.

One of the reasons why this model is of particular interest is because it incorporates many of the management ideas, philosophies, practices, etc. that have emerged in the 1980s and 1990s.

*Figure 1.1* Performance management: planning, improvement and review (source: Bredrup 1995a)

This is true also of other, recent portrayals of performance management: an illustration of this comes from the Institute of Personnel and Development's (IPD) latest book on performance management, as shown in Table 1.3.

Performance management of the kind depicted so far hardly is new and perhaps is more familiar to us as strategic/business planning, operations management and the like. In other words, the focus of this model is on the determination of the organization's strategy and the implementation of that strategy through the organization's structure, technology, business systems and procedures, etc. Employees are **not** the primary focus, although they will be affected by changes in technology, structure, operating systems, etc.

## Performance management as a system for managing employee performance

There are several variants of this model, with performance management commonly being represented as a cycle. Here are a few examples. Ainsworth and Smith (1993) have a three-step cycle, as in Figure 1.2. Guinn (1987) also proposes a three-step process:

*Table 1.3* Components of effective performance management (source: Lawson 1995: 12–13)

---

Effective performance management means:

- articulating your company's vision
- establishing key results, objectives and measures at key business unit level
- identifying business process objectives and the key indicators of performance for those processes
- identifying and installing effective departmental measures
- monitoring and controlling four key performance measures
  1 quality
  2 delivery
  3 cycle time
  4 waste
- managing the continuous improvement of performance in those key areas – 'benchmarking' your performance against the best
- being prepared to aim for 'breakthrough' improvements in performance when this is required by a significant shortfall in your performance measured against the performance of your major competitors

---

*Figure 1.2* Performance management: planning, assessment and feedback (source: Ainsworth and Smith 1993)

*Table 1.4* Elements in the performance management system (source: (a) Guinn 1987, cited in Heiser *et al.* 1988: 151 (b) Heiser *et al.* 1988: 156)

(a)

| *Planning* | *Managing* | *Appraising* |
|---|---|---|
| Establish performance targets | Monitor behaviour and objectives | Formal meeting of employee and manager |
| Identify job behaviours | Reinforce desired behaviours and objective attainment | Written record |
| Identify basis for measuring performance | Redirect inappropriate behaviours | Focus on future and employee's development |
| Provide direction, initial energizing of behaviour | Provide control | Provide for replanning and new objective establishment |

(b)

| *Direct* | *Energize* | *Control* | *Reward* |
|---|---|---|---|
| Key result areas | Set goals | Monitor | Evaluate |
| Performance indicators | Establish behavioural expectations | Provide feedback | Reinforce |
| Required behaviours | | Redirect | |
| | | Develop | |

planning, managing and appraising, as shown in the upper half of Table 1.4. Torrington and Hall (1995) likewise have three: planning, supporting and reviewing performance. Common in much of this writing is the idea that manager and managed should have a shared view of what is expected of the employee; involvement and participation of a direct kind are typically advocated as the means by which this shared view may be arrived at. Supporting performance is seen as a responsibility of the line manager who also has a particular part to play in reviewing performance. Here again we have an activity that often is presented as being shared between manager and managed – that is, performance review is a joint activity in which the responsibility rests with the job holder as much as with the manager. Moreover, review is seen as an ongoing activity rather than as something that happens just once or twice a year.

Heisler *et al.* (1988) have four elements in their performance management process: directing, energizing, controlling and rewarding (shown in the lower half of Table 1.4). Schneier *et al.* (1987) give us five: planning, managing, reviewing, rewarding and developing. Table 1.4 illustrates the employee focus of this conception of performance management by its reference to behaviours and the motivational language that is used, e.g. providing direction, energizing.

## Performance management as a system for integrating the management of organizational and employee performance

This model may be regarded as a combination of the first two, although this perhaps is rather too simple a view as there are variations on the basic theme. This variation reflects the two main models identified above, that is, the extent to which there is an emphasis on organizational as compared to employee performance.

In the second category of model described above the stress is firmly on employee performance; that said, several of the particular models within that category recognize that the management of employee performance takes place within a framework of organizational goals. But there is a sense in which this framework is taken as given. For example, in presenting their employee-focused view of performance management Ainsworth and Smith make certain assumptions:

This assumes that the important corporate issues of 'mission' and the setting of corporate goals have been addressed and resolved. It assumes that objectives for the sub-sections of the organization (the departments, divisions or business units) have been set within the key results areas, and that the senior management group has identified just where the competitive advantage and value added dimensions of the business lie. It further assumes that all of this has been communicated to and understood by those involved.

(Ainsworth and Smith 1993: 5–6)

In other models which present performance management as an integrative system the organizational framework is made even more explicit. The performance management cycles presented by McAfee and Champagne (1993) and Storey and Sisson (1993) – shown in Figure 1.3 – represent illustrations. Rather more elaborate versions of this sub-type are to be found, as illustrated in Table 1.5. Though they are intended to enhance organizational performance, what characterizes all these models is their emphasis on employee-focused interventions:

Performance management supports a company's or organization's overall business goals by linking the work of each individual employee or manager to the overall mission of the work unit.

(Costello 1994: 3)

The central aim of performance management is to develop the potential of staff, improve their performance and, through linking an employee's individual objectives to business strategies, improve the company's performance.

(Incomes Data Services 1992: 1)

[Performance management] is about directing and supporting employees to work as effectively and efficiently as possible *in line with the needs of the organization*.

(Walters 1995: x)

Rather different are those models which, while claiming to be integrative, place more emphasis on managing organizational performance. For example, Rogers puts forward an elaboration of his corporate model which adds the management of employee performance:

corporate systems . . . include the following processes as part of an annual integrated cycle of management:

- setting corporate policy and resource aims and guidelines
- specifying, within the framework provided by (1) above, a detailed set of plans, budgets, objectives, targets and standards of performance
- regularly and systematically reviewing the performance of all services.

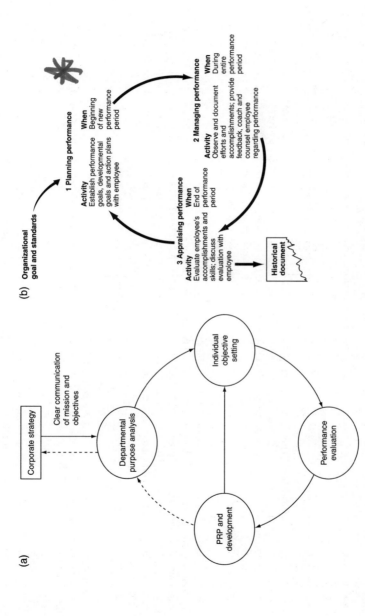

(b) Organizational goal and standards

**1 Planning performance**

**When**
Beginning of new performance period

**Activity**
Establish performance goals, developmental goals and action plans with employee

**2 Managing performance**

**When**
During entire performance period

**Activity**
Observe and document efforts and accomplishments; provide feedback, coach and counsel employee regarding performance

**3 Appraising performance**

**When**
End of performance period

**Activity**
Evaluate employee's accomplishments and skills; discuss evaluation with employee

Historical document

(a)

Corporate strategy

Clear communication of mission and objectives

Departmental purpose analysis

Individual objective setting

Performance evaluation

PRP and development

*Figure 1.3* Performance management cycles (source: (a) Storey and Sisson 1993; (b) McAfee and Champagne 1993)

Table 1.5 Integrative models of performance management (source: Bevan and Thompson 1991; Fletcher 1993, 1994; Lockett 1992; Audit Commission 1995a)

| A 'textbook' performance management system | The main building blocks of performance management | Requirements of the performance management process | Improving the performance of the organization and the contribution of staff |
|---|---|---|---|
| The organization has a shared vision of its objectives, or a mission statement, which it communicates to all its employees. | The development of the organization's mission statement and objectives. | A clear statement of the organization's mission – i.e. what the organization needs to do to compete and survive in its current business environment. | In order to maximize performance, focus the efforts of the organization on explicit, challenging and realistic aims and objectives. |
| The organization sets individual performance management targets which are related both to operating-unit and wider organizational objectives. | Associated with this, the development of the business plan (business being interpreted in the broadest sense of the word). | A mechanism to enable the performance of individuals within the organization to be aligned with that mission statement and a way of adjusting performance requirements to meet new challenges which may arise. | Target and improve the understanding, commitment and contribution of individual staff in the delivery of those objectives. |
| It conducts a regular, formal review of progress towards these targets. | Enhancing communications within the organization, so that employees are not only aware of the objectives and the business plan but can contribute to their formulation. | A set of human resource management policies which support the organization's strategic aims and which give individuals an incentive to work towards their own personal objectives. | Support the delegation of responsibility to front-line staff by using management through objectives. |

This involves creating an environment where high performance is actively encouraged and human resource policies are in tune with corporate goals.

A clear statement of the organization's future goals – their vision and the direction in which they intend to move.

A process which enables the critical capability factors within the organization to be developed as part of the performance management process. This is particularly relevant with regard to the development of people – their competence, skills and knowledge need to be a critical part of the development of capability.

Provide quantitative and qualitative standards for judging individual and organizational performance.

Provide feedback to the organization and to individual staff about their actual performance.

Identify and implement training and other actions necessary to improve individual performance.

Clarifying individual responsibilities and accountabilities (which means, amongst other things, having job descriptions, clear role definitions, and so on, and being willing to be held accountable).

Defining and measuring individual performance (with the emphasis on being measured against one's own objectives rather than being compared with others).

Implementing appropriate reward strategies.

Developing staff to further improve performance, and their career progression, in the future.

It uses the review process to identify training, development and reward outcomes.

It evaluates the effectiveness of the whole process and its contribution to overall organizational performance to allow changes and improvements to be made.

. . . systems which integrate the procedures for managing organizational performance with those for managing the performance of individuals . . . have the following additional characteristics:

• Procedures and systems for planning, monitoring and appraising the performance of individuals which are integrated with those for managing organizational performance.

Some, though not all . . . have a fifth characteristic:

• Systems, such as performance related pay, for rewarding individual achievements.

(Rogers 1990: 29–30)

What's being said in all of this, of course, is that there is a need to manage performance at several levels: this is made explicit in a number of models. Thus, Rummler and Brache (1995) specify three interdependent levels of performance: organization, process and job/performer. Spangenberg (1994), drawing on Mohrman (1990) and Rummler and Brache, presents one of the most comprehensive of the integrated models and identifies three levels of performance: organization, process/function and team/individual. And at each level he envisages a five-step annual performance cycle, as illustrated in Table 1.6.

## PERFORMANCE MANAGEMENT: SOME UNDERLYING THEMES

A number of interrelated themes run through these several perspectives on performance management. I will introduce these themes here before returning to them in later chapters.

The first is indicated by the way in which the different models have been categorized, that is, the level at which performance management operates (Mabey and Salaman 1995). At the one extreme we have models which are concerned with managing organizational performance; at the other extreme are those which define performance management as being the management of employee performance. Some of the latter explicitly recognize the organizational context within which employee performance must be located. Some commentators (e.g., Storey and Sisson 1993) have argued that in these models the management of

*Table 1.6* Spangenberg's integrated model of performance (source: Spangenberg 1994: 30–1)

| *Organization* | *Process/function* | *Team/individual* |
| --- | --- | --- |
| **1 PERFORMANCE PLANNING** | | |
| • Vision<br>• Mission<br>• Strategy<br>• Organizational goals set and communicated | • Goals for key processes linked to organizational and customer needs | • Team mission, goals, values and performance strategies defined<br>• Individual goals, responsibilities, and work-planning aligned with process/function goals |
| **2 DESIGN** | | |
| • Organization design ensures structure supports strategy | • Process design facilitates efficient goal achievement | • Teams are formed to achieve process/function goals<br>• Job design ensures process requirements reflected in jobs; jobs logically constructed in ergonomically sound environment |
| **3 MANAGING PERFORMANCE (AND IMPROVEMENT)** | | |
| • Continual organization development and change efforts<br>• Functional goals (in support of organizational goals) managed, reviewed and adapted quarterly<br>• Sufficient resources allocated<br>• Interfaces between functions managed | • Appropriate sub-goals set; process performance managed and regularly reviewed<br>• Sufficient resources allocated<br>• Interfaces between process steps managed | • Active team-building efforts, feedback, co-ordination and adjustment<br>• Developing individual understanding and skills; providing feedback<br>• Sufficient resources allocated |

*Table 1.6* Continued

| Organization | Process/function | Team/individual |
|---|---|---|
| **4 REVIEWING PERFORMANCE** | | |
| • Annual review, input into strategic planning | • Annual review | • Annual review |
| **5 REWARDING PERFORMANCE** | | |
| • Financial performance of organization | • Function rewards commensurate with value of organizational performance and function contribution | • Rewards commensurate with value of organization performance, and: for team – function and team contribution; for individual – function/team performance and individual contribution |

employee performance comes to be given heightened, strategic importance. The more comprehensive of the models present performance management as being concerned with the management of performance at all levels – organizational, individual and everything in between. Related to this is the theme of **integration** and **linking**; many of the models present performance management as an **holistic** process.

Implied by many models is a view of the **nature of organizations** – essentially a 'rationalistic, directive view of the organization' (Mabey and Salaman, 1995: 186). An element of this theme is the need for an organization to have a vision and strategy and a statement of goals and objectives. Related to this theme is one to do with the **nature of performance** – in other words, what is performance? For ease of illustration let me confine myself to the two extremes – organizational performance and individual performance. At the organizational level a goal-oriented perspective seems to be dominant. But other conceptions of organizations and organizational performance are to be found, for example ones which emphasize process and adaptation/learning.

These same points apply to individual performance, which is primarily seen in terms of outputs/results. But the idea that performance can be equated with behaviour is also evident. Defining individual performance – both conceptually and operationally – must surely be one of the key issues in performance management. There is also the related question of what **causes** performance.

What is performance management for, especially in relation to the management of individual performance? In broad terms the overall purpose is to contribute to the achievement of organizational performance. But performance management systems typically have many elements to them and what remains a controversial issue is the balance between development and reward purposes. Also, what's in it for the worker? Where do job satisfaction, employee well-being and the like fit within performance management systems? As I will go on to show, employee interests are not especially evident in performance management practice.

One theme that is especially clear is the **importance of communication**. One aspect of this might be termed **organizational communication**, and in many of the models this is seen as essentially downward, although some do recognize the value of upward communication. The second aspect is the day-to-day **interpersonal communication** that takes place between manager and managed. Indeed, and this is another theme, the line manager takes on particular importance in the employee-focused models of performance management both as an agent of communication and as **owner** of the performance management process. And in many of the models there is a recognition of mutuality – for example, manager and managed should jointly set employee goals. Hence, in much of the advocacy one sees a particular set of values, those stressing **participation** and **involvement**.

Models vary in the extent to which they are **prescriptive** of what organizations should do and how they should do it (Mabey and Salaman 1995). The tendency in most of the models referred to earlier is towards prescription, at least to the extent of prescribing **what** should be done. Some go further and prescribe **how**. However, the models generally are unsatisfactory as descriptions of practice since the reality of what happens falls short in many respects of what the textbooks and popular literature advocate.

Another theme is that there is variation in the **nature** and **scope** of the policies/practices that are implied or specified. This relates to the earlier theme concerning the level at which performance management operates. Models emphasizing the management of organizational performance tend to give more prominence to the business process, and performance management interventions will often be of a structural or technological kind. There are, of course, implications for employees but these typically will be consequential rather than policies being directed specifically at them. But where the concern is with employee performance the sorts of interventions are those which are generally taken as falling within the ambit of personnel management or human resource management (HRM). And the scope may be broad or narrow, that is, all of HRM or just a sub-set (Storey and Sisson 1993). The former would, for example, include recruitment and selection as performance management activities on the grounds, say, that these offer the first opportunity to convey expectations of what performance will be required from the employee. The narrowest conception embraces results-oriented appraisal and, probably, appraisal-related pay – control would seem to be the main underlying intent here.

The importance of organizational culture features in many models. Two points of view may be distinguished – that performance management must fit the organization's culture and that performance management is an instrument of culture change. The latter perspective in essence involves the imposition of top management's values on the rest of the organization – a **unitarist** view which ignores the plurality of interests that we would expect to find in an organization.

## What consensus is there about the components of performance management?

The weight of opinion amongst British writers seems to view performance management as an essentially employee-centered set of interventions. It aims to harness the contribution of individual employee performance to organizational performance. Thus, at the heart of performance management we find a cycle of activity which includes policies and procedures for some or all of the following aspects of individual performance:

- directing/planning;
- managing/supporting;

- reviewing/appraising;
- developing/rewarding.

The consensus position recognizes also that these activities take place within a given organizational context, two facets of which are afforded particular emphasis:

- the organization's mission, objectives, and business plan;
- communication about that mission etc.

All this seems very reasonable, sensible and rational. We decide where the organization is heading and what it is trying to do, we communicate that to all our employees, and we have systems for planning the work of individuals so that their efforts can be appropriately directed. This is easier said than done, of course; and when we look at the survey evidence about performance management practice it seems that it isn't happening.

## PERFORMANCE MANAGEMENT IN PRACTICE: SURVEY EVIDENCE

Though now a few years old (and consequently out of date in at least some respects), still the most informative survey is the large-scale postal study carried out by the then Institute of Manpower Studies (IMS; now Institute for Employment Studies) for the Institute of Personnel Management (IPM) as it was at the time (now Institute of Personnel and Development – IPD). This was extended by a smaller, more qualitative investigation by Fletcher and Williams (Institute of Personnel Management 1992) into twenty-six organizations, nine of which provided attitude survey data about employee experience of performance management. Also of some interest is a later survey carried out by the Industrial Society (1994). The following account will draw mostly on these two surveys. However, in addition there are various case study reports and other accounts of practice, e.g. by Incomes Data Services (1992), Rogers (1990), Local Government Management Board (1993) and the Audit Commission (1995a, 1995e, 1995b), the last including some survey evidence about employees' attitudes towards performance management.

## Who was surveyed?

The IMS sent its questionnaire to 1,863 private- and public-sector organizations of varying sizes and industrial sector. (Fuller details are given in the research report; Institute of Personnel Management 1992.) The usable response rate was 46 per cent. The survey was carried out between March and June 1991. The Industrial Society carried out its postal survey in April 1994, sending a questionnaire to 4,351 personnel and human resource managers. These were drawn randomly from the Industrial Society's database. The response rate was 23.6 per cent.

Unfortunately, not enough facts about the nature of the Industrial Society's sample are reported to allow the exact make-up of the two samples to be compared. Similarly, the content of the two surveys (as will be shown below) was not exactly the same. Consequently, we are not comparing like with like and the two surveys are probably best regarded as two snapshots taken at different points in time.

## What did the surveys ask about?

The IMS survey was clearly organized around a particular conception of performance management – harnessing the contribution of employee performance in the pursuit of organizational performance. It asked about seven main aspects of performance management. By contrast, the Industrial Society survey takes a narrower view; it appears to be essentially a survey of appraisal and appraisal-related pay practice rather than of performance management more broadly defined. (This does, however, accurately reflect the core of performance management practice in the UK.) Table 1.7 summarizes the main content areas of the two surveys.

## What did the surveys find?

To sketch an overall picture only the main findings will be summarized here, with others being given in later chapters. The two reports, especially that of the IPM survey, give much more detail.

### How many organizations have policies and practices aimed at managing employee performance?

According to the IMS survey, 'Just under 20 per cent of respondents had a 'formal performance management programme', 66 per cent had other types of policies to manage employee performance

*Table 1.7* The IMS and Industrial Society performance management surveys: what they were about (source: Institute of Personnel Management 1992; Industrial Society 1994: 5)

---

*The IMS survey*
- communicating organizational strategy
- defining jobs and tasks
- performance requirements
- performance review
- outcomes of performance review
- performance and pay
- monitoring the management of performance

---

*The Industrial Society survey*
- main **aims** of performance management systems
- **changes** to systems in the last two years
- how **extensively** performance management is used
- which **groups** of employees systems typically cover
- key **components** of the typical performance management system
- how frequently post-appraisal performance is **reviewed**
- how many appraisers are **trained** for appraisal
- performance **indicators** most used in appraisal
- **completion** rate of appraisals, and the role of the appraiser's manager
- top **benefits** from performance management
- links between appraisal and the individual's **pay**

---

and 14 per cent had no polices at all' (Institute of Personnel Management 1992: 17).

### Which employees?
The two surveys are broadly agreed in reporting that performance management applies more to managerial levels than to manual staff. This is one respect in which the Industrial Society survey is slightly more informative that the one by the IMS. Figure 1.4 shows the Industrial Society's findings.

### Aims of performance management
The IMS survey identified improving organizational effectiveness, motivating employees, and improving training and development as the three main reasons for introducing performance management. In similar vein, the Industrial Society discovered the identification of individual training needs to be a main purpose of

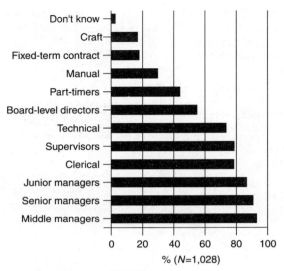

*Figure 1.4* Employee groups where a large majority is covered by performance management (source: Industrial Society 1994)

schemes. Other purposes included setting objectives/targets and providing feedback on performance; changing the organizational culture and linking pay to productivity were also important reasons amongst organizations with formal performance management systems.

### Do organizations have mission statements and do they communicate them to employees?

From the IMS survey we learn that there is a difference between organizations which have formal performance management policies and those which don't: this is clearly illustrated in Figure 1.5. Having a mission statement is one thing; but telling all employees what it is seems to be something else! It would appear that mission statements are not universally communicated, even by organizations which claim to have performance management policies. Figure 1.6 shows that communication is even less likely in organizations without performance management policies.

### Communicating requirements and performance review

Amongst organizations having performance management systems performance requirements, and their measurement criteria, are

*Figure 1.5* Organizations with mission statements (source: Institute of Personnel Management 1992)

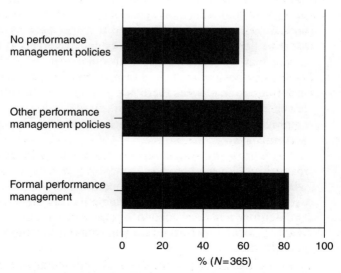

*Figure 1.6* Communication of mission statements (source: Institute of Personnel Management 1992)

commonly expressed in objective, output-based terms; this is particularly the case for managers.

Generally speaking, line management is the most commonly used channel of communication, followed by the appraisal process. For both, the incidence of use is less for those organizations which do not have performance management policies.

How is performance reviewed, and by whom? Amongst organizations having formal performance management or some other policies a 'joint discussion between employee and line manager' was by far the most common approach to performance review. For those organizations with no performance management policies the most common approach was 'no review'! According to the IMS survey self-, peer and upward appraisal all seem to be rare, although review findings are commonly seen by a third party in organizations which have performance management policies. The Industrial Society survey reports a surprisingly high incidence, of 71 per cent, for self-appraisal.

## Performance and pay

How directly is pay linked to performance? This varies according to level of employee and the presence of formal performance management. For senior managers, over half the organizations with formal systems maintain a direct link between the achievement of performance requirements and pay. This is significantly higher than in organizations with other sorts of policies (39 per cent) and those with no policies at all (20 per cent). For other white-collar employees there is a similar overall pattern, but with fewer organizations reporting a direct link. And for manual employees there is still less of a tendency to link pay directly to performance.

The type of pay system linking pay and performance varies. For manual employees bonus schemes are the most common but for white-collar staff appraisal-related pay is the most frequently used, with the incidence of use rising with the level of employee. In addition, appraisal-related pay is more likely to be used by formal performance management organizations than by other organizations.

## A CONCLUDING COMMENT: DOES PERFORMANCE MANAGEMENT EXIST?

From their findings the IMS researchers concluded that 'There was no consistent definition of performance management among those professing to operate it' (Institute of Personnel Management 1992: 5). That said, the sophistication of their survey allowed them to identify a number of characteristics which distinguished formal performance management organizations from those having other policies for managing employee performance. These characteristics are shown in Table 1.8. Though organizations professing to have formal performance management policies *tended* to engage in practices and activities of the kind advocated in the textbooks, the IMS researchers were able to identify only 3 per cent of organizations (out of the 856 respondents) which closely matched their textbook model.

From the survey evidence presented in this chapter it is clear that formal employee performance management of the holistic, comprehensive, integrative kind that is advocated in much of the literature is rare. The dominant approach to managing employee performance still rests on appraisal, probably supplemented with appraisal-related pay. To this extent, then, the reality of contemporary performance management practice is probably best seen as

*Table 1.8* Distinguishing characteristics of formal performance management organizations (source: Institute of Personnel Management 1992: 5)

---

Performance management organizations were more likely to:
- have mission statements which are communicated to all employees;
- regularly communicate information on business plans and progress towards achieving these plans;
- implement policies such as total quality management (TQM) and performance related pay (PRP);
- focus on senior managers' performance rather than other manual and white-collar employees;
- express performance targets in terms of measurable outputs, accountabilities and training/learning targets;
- use formal appraisal processes and CEO presentations as ways of communicating performance requirements;
- set performance requirements on a regular basis;
- link performance requirements to pay, particularly for senior managers.

---

'a logical progression in the history of the development of appraisal systems' (Lundy and Cowling 1996: 307).

To this extent, then, much of today's practice is merely an extension of what has gone before. That systems evolve is understandable, but perhaps we also need to see signs of revolution. There is evidence of some changes in thinking – for example a broader perspective on the nature of performance. At the organizational level, I look at this in Chapters 2 and 3, which focus on the organizational context for performance management. I then shift attention to the individual level and examine employee performance and its determinants, in Chapters 4, 5 and 6. The key role of the line manager in reviewing, supporting and rewarding performance is developed in Chapters 7 and 8. Finally, in Chapters 9 and 10, I turn to design, development and management. Throughout these chapters I emphasize themes of diagnosis, analysis and participation and the need to recognize and balance the goals of the several groups who have an interest in performance management.

# 2 *The organizational context I*
## *Vision, mission and strategy*

In this and the following chapter I will examine the organizational context within which employee-centered performance management exists. As shown in the previous chapter, there is widespread agreement in the performance management literature that organizations should have a vision, mission and strategy. I will consider what these terms mean and the implications for performance management.

In Chapter 3 I will go on to consider the nature of organizational performance, as it is clear that a central purpose of performance management, even as an employee-focused intervention, is to contribute to the delivery of performance at the organizational level.

## VISION, MISSION AND STRATEGY

Advocacy of the need for vision, mission and strategy is by no means confined to the performance management literature. As we would expect it is particularly prevalent in texts on strategic management (e.g. Luffman *et al.* 1996), but it is also found widely elsewhere in writings on various aspects of management and organization, for example Bounds *et al.* (1994) on quality management, Torrington and Hall (1995) on personnel management, and Wild (1995) on operations management.

What do we mean by the terms *vision, mission* and *strategy*? Table 2.1 gives some definitions. As can be seen, the terms are partly overlapping and by no means clearly distinguished – these variations reflect company practice, as Campbell and Yeung (1991a) discovered in their research among forty-two organizations. So, though not all writers distinguish between vision and mission Campbell and Yeung (1991b) suggest that the former term denotes some desired future state, whereas the latter is more concerned with the present and may be a more enduring statement about an organization's intent. The term strategy may be interpreted in two senses – *content* or *process* – as implied in Brown's definition in Box 2.1. In some models, strategy content is seen as part of mission; for example, Campbell and Yeung see a strong mission as having the following four linked elements working together in a mutually reinforcing way:

- **purpose**: why the organization exists;
- **strategy**: the competitive position and distinctive competence;
- **values**: what the company believes in;
- **behaviour standards**: the policies and behaviour patterns that underpin the distinctive competence and the value system.

---

Box 2.1    **Definitions of vision, mission and strategy**

**Vision**

'A vision indicates what the company is aiming at in the future. It serves as the long-term road map for the company.'

(Bredrup 1995d: 92)

'A *vision* statement outlines what purposes managers want the organization to serve over the long term and what the organization should become.'

(Bounds *et al.* 1994: 218)

'Vision is the term used to describe a picture of a relatively remote future in which business has developed under the best possible conditions and in accordance with the hopes and dreams of the owner or chief executive. A vision provides a benchmark for what one hopes to achieve in business, and can be a guide to the level of ambition of strategic planning.'

(Karlöf 1993: 150–1)

## Mission

'A mission defines the scope of the business activities the company pursues. . . . A mission answers the question: "What business should the company be in?"'

(Bredrup 1995d: 94–5)

'The *mission* should describe the organization's current purpose in terms of what the organization will do over the near term. This statement should set the organization apart from those serving the same customer need.'

(Bounds *et al.* 1994: 218)

'Mission is an organization's character, identity and reason for existence. It can be divided into four inter-relating parts: purpose, strategy, behaviour standards and values. Purpose addresses why an organization is in being: for whose benefit is all this effort being put in? Strategy considers the nature of the business, the desired positioning vs other companies and the source of competititve advantage. Behaviour standards are the norms and rules of "the way we do things around here". Values are the beliefs and moral principles that lie behind the behaviour standards, beliefs that have normally been formulated within the organization by a founding dynasty or a dominant management team.'

(Campbell and Yeung 1991b: 145)

## Strategy

'The MEANS by which organizations meet, or seek to meet, OBJECTIVES. There can be a strategy for each product or service, and an overall strategy for the organization.'

(Thompson 1990: x)

'According to some, strategy refers to a plan for interacting with the competitive environment in order to achieve organizational goals. Such plans are generally characterized as formal, explicit, devised by senior executives, long-termist, and have a significant effect on how the organization behaves in its environment. . . . An alternative view of strategy suggests that it can be less structured, and more informal and implicit in its formulation. The idea here is that strategy is something intrinsic to the process of leading and managing. Rather than being a set plan, strategy is a set of principles or heuristics for managing that are encoded in a system of management and which allow for considerabe flexibility and adaptability in dealing with the exigencies of a changing environment.'

(Brown 1995: 167)

Collectively the terms vision, mission and strategy are a series of statements about the direction in which an organization wishes to head in the future and the means by which it wishes to get there. We can see these features in the examples shown in Boxes 2.2 and 2.3.

Box 2.2   **Example of a mission statement**

**The Co-operative bank**
We, The Co-operative Bank Group, will continue to develop a successful and innovative financial institution by providing our customers with high quality financial and related services whilst promoting the underlying principles of co-operation which are:

- **Quality and Excellence**
  To offer all our customers consistent high quality and good value services and strive for excellence in all that we do.
- **Participation**
  To introduce and promote the concept of full participation by welcoming the views and concerns of our custo-

- mers and by encouraging our staff to take an active role within the local community.
- **Freedom of Association**
  To be non-partisan in all social, political, racial and religious matters.
- **Education and Training**
  To act as a caring and responsible employer encouraging the development and training of all our staff and encouraging commitment and pride in each other and the Group.
- **Co-operation**
  To develop a close affinity with organizations which promote fellowship between workers, customers, members and employers.
- **Quality of Life**
  To be a responsible member of society by promoting an environment where the needs of local communities can be met now and in the future.
- **Retentions**
  To manage the business effectively and efficiently, attracting investment and maintaining sufficient surplus funds within the business to ensure the continued development of the Group.
- **Integrity**
  To act at all times with honesty and integrity and within legislative and regulatory requirements.
                    (source: *Strength in Numbers*, a Co-operative
                           Bank promotional document, p. 7)

---

Box 2.3   **Example of a strategy statement**

**Universities Superannuation Scheme (USS) Ltd
Corporate Aim**
To carry out the duties of trusteeship and the administration of USS for the benefit of members, pensioners and participating institutions in an efficient and cost-effective manner in accordance with quality management principles.

**Strategic Objective One: Trusteeship** – *To exercise the powers and duties conferred by the USS trust deed and rules in a lawful and fair manner.*

- We undertake to act within the powers provided by the trust deed and rules, with UK and EC legislation and in accordance with all relevant regulations, guidelines and codes of practice.
- We will exercise discretion fairly and consistently in the interests of the scheme membership as a whole.
- We will ensure that the directors and staff of USS Ltd are fully trained and are aware of their duties and obligations. We will control investment managers and the officers to whom they delegate responsibility and receive full and regular reports from them.
- We will make sure that there are resources to meet the benefits promised, taking appropriate professional advice where necessary.
- We will maintain communication with members. We will keep members' guide up-to-date and provide this to all members. Reports of actuarial valuations and annual reports and accounts will be available for members to view.
- We will seek to maintain and develop good working relationships with participating employers, with the aim of constant improvement.

**Strategic Objective Two: Administration** – *To strive constantly for higher standards of scheme administration and service at an acceptable cost.*

- We will demonstrate a high level of operational efficiency, committing ourselves to quality management principles and always aiming to increase cost-effectiveness.
- We will take into account the best practices in other organizations and the availability of new equipment and technology. We will develop and improve our own procedures and maintain comprehensive up-to-date procedure notes and work instructions.

**Strategic Objective Three: Investment** – *To maximize the long-term investment return on assets consistent with the liabilities of the scheme.*

- We will set demanding but realistic targets for all managers and monitor investment performance.

**Strategic Objective Four: Company Management** – *To strive constantly for improved management of the trustee company at an acceptable cost and in accordance with the company's Memorandum and Articles of Association and quality management principles.*

- We will develop and maintain employment policies and practices consistent with being a fair and considerate employer.
- We will adopt quality management principles, and in that light will take account of best practice elsewhere and our own experience to improve our systems and procedures.

(Objectives 2, 3 and 4 have been abbreviated.)

(Source: abstracted from *Corporate Aims and Objectives*, a USS Ltd Company leaflet)

These examples also illustrate certain other features of such statements over which there also is some measure of agreement:

- the **values** which guide the organization;
- the **distinctive features** that characterize the organization;
- the interests of all **stakeholders**.

## VALUES

What do we mean by values? Ravlin defines values as 'a set of core beliefs held by individuals concerning how they should or ought to behave over broad ranges of situations' (1995: 598). We all have values which develop through the process of socialization that we experience across the life-span. But in the present context values are being regarded as a property of the organization, in that all the employees are expected to subscribe to a particular set of values which have been articulated by the organization's leadership. Bringing about a congruence of individual values with organizational values is what Campbell and Yeung (1991a) refer to as creating a **sense of mission** – that is, employees' personal commitment to the organization's mission.

However, there exists the possibility of disagreement or even conflict should the values of individuals be at odds with those set out in the mission statement. Also, day-to-day business pressures may conflict with the espoused values. For example, Stiles *et al.* (1997) studied the performance management activities of a distribution company, a telecommunications company and a bank, all three of which had introduced values statements. But managers at the sharp end saw short-term demands to satisfy budgetary and financial targets as continuing to drive their activity, not the 'worthier' corporate values.

In the organizational context the term values is commonly associated with the term **organization** (or **organizational**) **culture**. This remains an elusive concept, with Brown listing fifteen definitions, his own preference being as follows:

> Organizational culture refers to the pattern of beliefs, values and learned ways of coping with experience that have developed during the course of an organization's history, and which tend to be manifested in its material arrangements and in the behaviours of its members.
>
> (Brown 1995: 8)

Within this definition is the idea that there are **levels of culture**, as exemplified by Schein (1992) and Kotter and Heskett (1992), and illustrated in Figure 2.1. In these conceptions actual behaviours and organizational practices and procedures are the outward manifestations of more deep-seated values (the root of organizational culture) and learned norms and rules (the behaviour standards that guide what people do).

The notion of organizational culture may be important for performance management in at least two ways, depending on which elements of the definition of culture we choose to emphasize. First, if we stress the values/behaviour standards aspects then culture provides the moral principles and behavioural guidelines that regulate employees' performance – quality, excellence, ethics etc. in the case of The Co-operative Bank. Related to this is the

Invisible     Harder to change

**Shared values:** important concerns and goals that are shared by most of the people in a group, that tend to shape group behaviour, and that often persist over time even with changes in group memberships
**Examples:** the managers care about customers; executives like long-term debt

**Group behaviour norms:** common or pervasive ways of acting that are found in a group and that persist because group members tend to behave in ways that teach these practices (as well as their shared values) to new members, rewarding those who fit in and sanctioning those who do not
**Examples:** the employees are quick to respond to requests from customers; the managers often involve lower-level employees in decision-making

Visible     Easier to change

(b)

Visible organizational structures and processes (hard to decipher)

Strategies, goals, philosophies (espoused justifications)

Unconscious, taken-for-granted beliefs, perceptions, thoughts and feelings (ultimate source of values and action)

Artifacts

Espoused values

Basic underlying assumptions

*Figure 2.1* Levels of organizational culture (source: (a) Kotter and Heskett 1992; (b) Schein 1992) view that culture and organizational performance are causally related. I shall come on to explore this proposition in just a moment.

Second, if we stress the artifact aspects, then performance management may be seen as part of an organization's culture – that is, part of 'the way we do things around here'. From this point of view performance management may be an instrument for maintaining culture (reinforcing norms of behaviour and values) or possibly for modifying it (inculcating new values). I will return to this second theme later.

## Culture and organizational performance

The core themes in the argument that organizational culture affects organizational performance have been summarized in Box 2.4. In other words, a particular kind of culture – a 'strong' corporate culture – facilitates goal alignment and engenders high levels of employee motivation, and 'is better able to learn from its past' (Brown 1995: 185). At the centre of this argument is what is termed the **integration perspective** on organizational culture:

> Integration studies of culture implicitly assume that a 'strong' culture is characterized by consistency, organization-wide consensus, and clarity. According to Integration studies, consistency occurs because people at the higher levels of an organization articulate a set of espoused values, sometimes in the form of a philosophy of management or mission statement; these values are then reinforced by a variety of cultural manifestations which presumably generate organization-wide value consensus. In Integration studies, there is clarity concerning what the organizational values are and should be, what behaviours are preferable. . . . Organizational members apparently know what they are to do and they agree why it is worthwhile to do it.
>
> (Martin 1995: 377)

Martin notes that this perspective 'has gained wide acceptance, in part because such a harmonious and clear environment is attractive, particularly to managers who would like to think that they could create a vision and enact a culture that would inspire such consensus' (1995: 378). The appeal of this view of culture as a means of 'social control' (O'Reilly 1989) is thus readily apparent. But what is wrong with this integration perspective?

---

Box 2.4   **Organizational culture and organizational performance**

[The] argument of the corporate-culture school is:

- That organizations have cultures.
- That they become more effective when they develop the right 'strong' cultures (which need careful definition).
- That these cultures create consensus and unity and motivate staff.
- That cultures have an effect on corporate performance.
- That when necessary, cultures can be – and should be – changed.
- That it is the responsibility of senior managers to change them.

The corporate-culture approach presumes that organizational cultures can be assessed, managed, constructed and manipulated in the pursuit of enhanced organizational effectiveness. Employees' norms, beliefs and values can (and when necessary should be changed so that they can contribute the appropriate behaviour, commit themselves to the organization, support management and strategy. This prevalent view holds that the norms and values shared by members of the organization create consensus, induce unity and when appropriate generate appropriate behaviour. Cultures integrate the organization (Meek 1988).

(source: Mabey and Salaman 1995: 283)

---

The fundamental criticism is that it is based on the assumption that an organization has a single culture. Drawing on Meek (1988), Mabey and Salaman state that 'managerialist approaches to corporate culture tend to ignore systemic conflicts within the organization, ignore structures of power and interest, ignore structures of hierarchy and inequality, and ignore difference and differentiation of groups and of cultures' (1995: 291). Many of these issues were evident in the three companies studied by Stiles *et al.* (1997) – in all three, objective-setting was intended to support the corporate strategy and values. However, objectives were set top-down without negotiation, so that they ended up being seen as imposed. Added to this, restructuring (downsizing) had diminished career opportunities leaving managers doubtful that achieving their objectives was going to be in their interests – advancement opportunities were reduced and good performance did not guarantee job security.

A more realistic alternative is the 'differentiation' perspective in which organizations are viewed as 'composed of overlapping, nested subcultures that coexist in relationships of intergroup harmony, conflict, or indifference' (Martin 1995: 378). In other words, we have here a view of organizational culture which is anything but consensual, unifying, unitarist and managerialist.

A second difficulty is the assumption that a strong culture is in some sense(s) a 'good thing'. This assumption has been challenged in several recent commentaries (e.g., Legge 1995; Mabey and Salaman 1995), and Brown (1995) gives us four reasons why the assumption might not hold true, as shown in Box 2.5.

---

Box 2.5    **Reasons to doubt the 'strong culture equals high performance' equation**

1 A strong culture may facilitate goal alignment, but the goals set by a culture may not always be positive in two senses: they may not be ethical, and they might not encourage good economic performance. In the first case we can imagine an organization such as a political or religious sect that brainwashes its members into pursuing violent ends, or an economic organization that pursues environmentally catastrophic objectives. An example of the second case would be an organization with a culture which dictated that care for employees was of greater value than profitability or market share, with the result that economic objectives were made subservient to human resource objectives.

2 It cannot be assumed that all strong cultures are associated with high levels of employee motivation. The point is that strong cultures may encourage many different attitudes towards the organization and to work other

than the purely positive. As regards motivation, therefore, strong cultures can work both ways.

3 It is probably true that an organization which appreciates its past and which encodes information about past decisions in stories and anecdotes is advantaged compared with similarly placed organizations which do not. However, it is also true that organizations can become too wrapped up in the past and fail to focus on the present and future. It is also possible for organizations to reapply lessons learned in the past to current situations when the old rules no longer apply, perhaps because of technological innovation or increased competition. In other words, there is a thin dividing line between being able to learn from the past and being a prisoner of the past.

4 There are in fact quite a few well-known examples of organizations with both strong cultures and strong economic performances. Yet even these companies do not necessarily lend credence to the strong culture argument. The reason for this is the problem of determining causality. After all, it may be that good economic performance is the cause of a strong culture rather than a strong culture being responsible for high performance. Organizational success often consolidates cultural beliefs and values. It therefore seems more than reasonable to suggest that economic success can strengthen a culture.

(Source: abstracted from Brown 1995: 186–7)

A third area of difficulty is that the evidence we have of a positive association between culture and performance is far from compelling. Of particular importance in this regard is the work of Kotter and Heskett, who claim that 'Corporate culture can have a significant impact on a firm's long-term economic performance' (1992: 11). What is the basis for their claim?

### Dysfunctional cultures
Kotter and Heskett carried out two studies. The essence of the first was to associate a 'culture strength' index with a number of

measures of economic performance for a 'large and diverse sample of companies' in the US. The culture strength index was derived from a questionnaire sent to the top six officers in the selected companies; economic performance was assessed using a range of measures (e.g. return on investment (RoI), increase in share price) over a twelve-year period. They concluded that 'There is a positive correlation between corporate culture and long-term economic performance but . . . not a very strong one' (Kotter and Heskett 1992: 20–1). Kotter and Heskett went on to add: 'The statement "Strong cultures create excellent performance" appears to be just plain wrong' (1992: 21). In so concluding they recognized the possibility that strong cultures may be **dysfunctional** for an organization.

This idea is also evident in some British work, that by Bate (1984). Bate's interest was in the impact of culture on organizational problem-solving. Based on interviews and discussions in three companies, he identified six characteristics or aspects of culture (which he called 'cultural orientations'), as shown in Box 2.6. Though these orientations are of interest in themselves, their apparently adverse consequences for organizational problem-solving are of more significance for the present discussion.

So, if we assume that there is such a thing as 'strong' culture we apparently have evidence which indicates that it isn't necessarily the good thing that so much of the literature contends. Kotter and Heskett (1992) were not, however, deterred by their initial finding and proceeded to a further study. They concentrated on twenty-two organizations and the core of their data-gathering was to seek opinions from financial analysts on the nature of those organization's cultures. These opinions were supplemented with findings from employees and managers in seventeen of the twenty-two companies.

## Adaptive cultures

In this further research Kotter and Heskett claim to have found support for their hypothesis that 'a culture is good only if it "fits" its context, whether one means by context the objective conditions of its industry, that segment of its industry specified by a firm's strategy, or the business strategy itself' (1992: 28). Furthermore, they contend that 'only cultures that can help organizations anticipate and adapt to environmental change will be associated with

**Box 2.6    Cultural Orientations**

*Unemotionality:* '*Avoid showing or sharing feelings or emotions*'
*Depersonalization of issues:* '*Never point the finger at anyone in particular*'
*Subordination:* '*Never challenge those in authority and always wait for them to take the initiative in resolving your problems*'
*Conservatism:* '*Better the devil you know*'
*Isolationism:* '*Do your own thing and avoid treading on other people's toes*'
*Antipathy:* '*On most things people will be opponents rather than allies*'

The data show that the six cultural associations discussed appear to be linked with the following range of problematic predispositions: a low commitment to and involvement in the change process; a disowning of problems and an abdication of responsibility for the search for solutions; a lack of openness in confronting and dealing jointly with issues; avoidance of data-gathering on the causes of problems; overcaution and a lack of decisiveness and creativity in problem-solving; erection of barriers to change; and a taking of adversary positions on all issues regardless of whether any potential measure of agreement between the parties exists.

(source: Bate 1984: 64)

superior performance over long periods of time' (1992: 44). As to the nature of adaptive cultures, Table 2.1 sets out the core values and common behaviour identified by Kotter and Heskett.

Brown describes the findings of Kotter and Heskett (1992) as 'truly stunning' (1995: 189), but rightly points to the methodological difficulties in the research. For example, a rather narrow view is taken of organizational performance – namely, economic performance; yet, as we shall see later the multi-faceted nature of performance is given greater emphasis today. Moreover, the

*Table 2.1* Adaptive v. unadaptive corporate cultures (source: Kotter and Heskett 1992: 51)

|  | *Adaptive corporate cultures* | *Unadaptive corporate cultures* |
|---|---|---|
| *Core values* | Most managers care deeply about customers, stockholders and employees. They also strongly value people and processes that can create useful change (e.g. leadership up and down the management hierarchy). | Most managers care mainly about themselves, their immediate work group or some product (or technology) associated with that work group. They value the orderly and risk-reducing management process much more highly than leadership initiatives. |
| *Common behaviour* | Managers pay close attention to all their constituencies, especially customers, and initiate change when necessary to serve their legitimate interests, even if that entails taking some risks. | Managers tend to behave somewhat insularly, politically and bureaucratically. As a result, they do not change their strategies quickly to adjust to or take advantage of changes in their business environments. |

underlying premise that certain cultures *cause* high performance is very likely to be far too simplistic – as Brown implies (Box 2.5), causality may work the other way. Though we can't dismiss the possible importance of organizational culture for performance we are very far from understanding what the relationship is.

## THE ORGANIZATION'S DISTINCTIVE FEATURES

The literature on strategic management typically advocates the analysis of strengths, weaknesses, opportunities, and threats **(SWOT analysis)** as a key element in the process of developing a strategy. Many tools exist for this, some being more concerned with the organization's environment (opportunities and threats), whilst others are internally directed and in essence are concerned with the question 'What is the organization is good at?'

In much of the 1990s writing on strategy and competitiveness emphasis has been placed on the importance of an organization's strengths as a source of advantage. Of particular interest is the concept of **core competence** (Prahalad and Hamel 1990). Hubbard (1995) points out that this term is not clearly defined and identifies other, similar terms, namely **distinctive competence** (Selznick 1957) and **capabilities**, but what they together signify is a concern for the internal features of organizations; this lies at the heart of **resource theory** (or **resource-based theory**):

> At its simplest level, the resource view is based around a number of linked or sequential questions: what is the firm good at? Does this derive from a unique set of resources and/ or a particular set of capabilities? Can the firm utilize its resources more effectively than its competitors? Can these strengths be easily copied by others? (In which case there is little competitive advantage to be obtained.) Is the firm able to keep its resources from depreciating rapidly? Is it able to reproduce and develop resource strengths and capabilities for future benefit?
>
> (Purcell 1995: 81–2)

Resources and capabilities may be tangible or intangible and certainly include the people (their skills, abilities, etc.) of an organization. Indeed, some have argued that traditional sources of competitive success such as technology have become less important, whereas employees and the way they work remain a 'crucial, differentiating factor' (Pfeffer 1994: 14). This echoes the view put by Storey and Sisson about the management of employee performance, namely that it 'is elevated to a higher plane: it comes to be regarded as an issue of strategic importance' (1993: 132).

## STAKEHOLDERS

Stakeholders are those who have some interest or stake in an organization's success. As Figure 2.2 illustrates, an organization is likely to have several stakeholders and these will vary in nature and importance from organization to organization and over time according to such factors as the values that top management places on particular stakeholders, the organization's environment, its activities and so forth. The examples in Boxes 2.2 and 2.3 give illustrations of the various stakeholders which these two organizations apparently regard as especially important.

A stakeholder to whom considerable importance has been attached in recent years is the customer. The excellence literature particularly influenced this, as did the emphasis on quality. Bounds *et al.*, for example, present a strategic management model 'driven by customer needs' (1994: 211). Their argument is that 'managers and employees put customers first on the list of stakeholders, because the value perceived by customers is the ultimate source of all opportunities to create new wealth' (1994: 224).

Important though the customer is, there is today the view that an effective/successful organization seeks to meet the interests not of just one stakeholder deemed to have superior importance but rather of several stakeholders. Illustrative of this view is the work of Kotter and Heskett (1992) mentioned earlier: they see customers, shareholders and employees as key stakeholders. Likewise, Schein writes of the need to maintain 'good relationships with the major stakeholders of the organization' and to keep their needs 'in some kind of balance' (1992: 53). He includes: '(1) the investors and stockholders, (2) the suppliers of the materials needed to produce, (3) the managers and employees, (4) the community and government, and last but not least, (5) the customers willing to pay for the good or service' (1992: 53).

The analysis of stakeholder needs and interests is of particular importance for performance management as different stakeholders

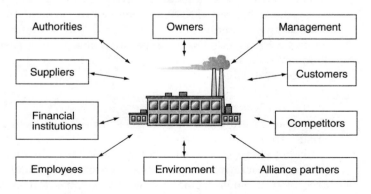

*Figure 2.2* The stakeholder model (source: Bredrup 1995b)

have different views of the nature of performance and of standards of performance that are expected. Numerous approaches to stakeholder analysis may be found in the literature – e.g. Beer *et al.* (1995) offer a model of organizational effectiveness which is focused on meeting stakeholder needs; and Bredrup and Bredrup (1995) apply stakeholder analysis to the determination of organizational performance requirements, a theme that I will come back to in the next chapter.

## A CONCLUDING COMMENT

Helpful though stakeholder analysis may be, it is not without its difficulties. Though it may reveal commonalities of interest it is likely also to reveal conflicts – over the direction in which the organization should be going, the means of getting there, etc. And very often these conflicts will reveal ethical dilemmas (Newell 1995). Some balance among the several interests therefore needs to be achieved – that is, stakeholder analysis itself isn't enough, we need stakeholder **synthesis** as well (Winstanley and Stuart-Smith 1996). In other words, an organization needs to incorporate stakeholder requirements within mission and strategy, and this particular aspect of organizational decision-making is only partly rational – it is as much a political process.

If the mission/strategy statement is to provide direction and serve as a basis for action, to promote particular values and act as a guide to behaviour and such like it seems only reasonable that those who will be affected by it should have some say in shaping its content. Some research (Brabet and Klemm 1994) indicates that an involving approach can be effective in developing a shared strategy and in gaining employee commitment; in other words, this may help to produce not just the mission statement but also the **sense of mission**. In the next chapter I will give some examples of how a participative approach has been used in defining organizational performance.

# 3 *The organizational context II*
## *Performance*

The importance of vision, mission and strategy as the framework for performance management is strongly emphasized in much of the practitioner-oriented literature (as we saw in Table 1.5, page 18). Taken together they set out what the organization is to become in the long term and how that desired position is to be arrived at. They state the purpose(s) of the organization and what it is to achieve – at least in general terms, then, they offer some statement of the organizational performance that is wanted. Also,  a framework for guiding the performance of individual employees is provided – by stating the overall goal(s) and by specifying the values and standards that govern behaviour.

This, then, brings me on to consider the nature of organizational performance, and related terms like **productivity** and **effectiveness**. None of these terms is straightforward to define, whether conceptually or operationally. Indeed, Mansfield described this whole area as a 'nightmare of ambiguity and contradictions' (1986: 21). In considering how performance is defined in operational terms, we necessarily have to pay some attention to performance measures and their place in performance management.

In years past a book like this probably would have had the word productivity in the title somewhere. More recently, there has been a shift in emphasis – as we saw in Chapter 1, there is today a much broader concern for competitiveness. This is not to say that interest in productivity has disappeared altogether – far from it – so let me look first at this and how it fits within contemporary conceptions of organizational performance.

## PRODUCTIVITY

Reiterating Guzzo's claim that 'productivity may mean different things to different people'(1988: 63), Pritchard has recently noted the wide range of meanings attaching to the term productivity:

> The term has been used to refer to individuals, groups, organizational units, entire organizations, industries, and nations. It has been used as a synonym for output, efficiency, motivation, individual performance, organizational effectiveness, production, profitability, cost/effectiveness, competitiveness, and work quality.
>
> (Pritchard 1995: 448)

That said, Campbell and Campbell earlier suggested that 'there is a clear consensus that it is useful to reserve the term productivity for efficiency indices' (1988: 83). If we accept this view then we find that there is some agreement over a common core: 'This common core is the ratio of outputs to inputs, a ratio that reflects the efficiency with which resources are transformed into outputs' (Guzzo 1988: 63). Expressed in these terms, productivity clearly is a systems concept: inputs are subject to some conversion process(es) which lead to the production of outputs.

So, in seeking to measure productivity we are basically concerned with the question of how well (how efficiently) available inputs are converted into outputs. The answer to this question may be expressed in terms of a whole host of indicators; Table 3.1 gives some examples.

### Inputs and outputs

Table 3.1 also illustrates some of the many ways in which inputs and outputs may be operationalized, and a few more examples are provided in Table 3.2.

**Inputs**

In a general sense, by **inputs** we mean all the resources, employees, raw materials, energy, buildings, equipment, etc. that are required to manufacture a product or deliver a service. Reducing

*Table 3.1* Examples of productivity indices

- GNP/Population, i.e. labour productivity at the national level
- Yield of crop per acre of land cultivated
- Output per worker employed, e.g. number of units produced/number of hours worked; £ value of units produced/number of employees
- Number of calls per salesperson per day
- Average revenue per call
- Number of revenue passenger miles generated/available passenger miles (i.e. passenger load factor for an airline)
- Train miles per member of staff
- Number of criminal offences cleared up per police officer
- Average number of patients treated per general surgery bed per year
- Sales per square foot
- Return on investment
- Return on sales

*Table 3.2* Examples of input and output indices

*Inputs*
- Number of employees
- Hours worked
- Staff costs
- Area of sales space available
- Units/cost of energy used
- Amount/cost of raw materials used

*Outputs*
- Number of passengers carried
- Number of surgical operations carried out
- Number of units sold
- £ value of units sold
- Number of users of a local authority leisure centre
- Quantity/value of goods carried by a delivery company
- Number of benefits paid through the Social Security system

inputs – essentially, cutting costs – for the same (or greater) levels of output is commonly adopted as a means of increasing productivity (Heap 1992). Structural change such as downsizing would be an example of this. However, though short-term productivity may improve, long-term gains are not to be guaranteed: output may not go up, and could even go down – thereby reducing the productivity gains. For example, we know that downsizing can adversely affect the morale of staff, not just while the cuts are taking place but also for some time afterwards – the survivors remain affected. One example of this comes from the study by Stiles *et al.* (1997) mentioned in Chapter 2. They investigated performance management systems in three companies, all of which had experienced undesirable consequences following job losses – Box 3.1 summarizes some of the main findings.

---

**Box 3.1   Improving productivity? Negative effects of downsizing on performance management**

[There] was evidence that downsizing and delayering had a significant effect on employees attempting to reach their objectives. Restructuring had impacted severely on job security and career ladders, and motivation to reach targets was affected by employees' perceptions that:

(i)   there was little benefit, in terms of advancement, of achieving one's objectives (though fear of losing one's job was obviously a strong counterbalance),

(ii)  fulfilling one's objectives entailed . . . that the objectives or targets would be raised substantially the following year, and

(iii) achieving good performance did not necessarily entail that an employee's job was safe.

(Source: Stiles *et al.* 1997: 61)

---

**Output as quantity**

Output is typically taken to mean what an organization produces or the service it delivers. Though outputs are part of productivity, the two terms clearly cannot be regarded as one and the same. By contrast, the terms output and production may be taken as synonyms. Output has traditionally been measured in quantitative terms as the examples in Tables 3.1 and 3.2 show. But such global measures will often be disaggregated into different types. For example, an airline may wish to break down the number of passengers carried according to class of travel – first, business and economy – further subdividing according to the type of ticket sold. An insurance company is likely to be interested in the numbers sold of each of the different types of policy that it provides. Police forces will be interested in the clear-up rates for different crimes.

One particular kind of output is referred to as a **throughput** – 'a special sort of output that is intended for internal consumption' (Brinkerhoff and Dressler 1990: 30). As already noted, productivity is a systems concept. When we apply the systems idea to an organization we discover that any organization as a system is likely to comprise a number of subsystems. The output from one subsystem will be an input to another subsystem (or subsystems) – the latter being an internal customer of the former, in other words. Managing the performance of the organization as a whole is, of course, as much about the management of throughputs as it is about the management of the product or service that eventually gets delivered to the external customer.

Though producing more output without an increase in inputs is one general strategy for improving productivity, greater output in itself doesn't necessarily mean a rise in productivity. If inputs have increased correspondingly or, worse, at a greater rate, then productivity will at best have remained stable and may even have deteriorated.

### Output as quality

As well as the quantitative aspect of output there also is a **quality** dimension. In recent years quality has become a central feature of organizational performance in both the private and public sector (Cameron 1995; Kirkpatrick and Lucio 1995; Wilkinson and Willmott 1995a). Wilkinson and Willmott, for example, note that 'quality initiatives are reportedly occurring in three-quarters of companies in the United States and the United Kingdom' (1995b: 1).

Though the management of quality is apparently widespread, the nature of the concept remains open to several interpretations. Reeves and Bednar (1994) identify four main types of definition, each of which has its own strengths and weaknesses: these are summarized in Table 3.3. In the view of Reeves and Bednar it is the last of the four which is the most prevalent today. As the table

*Table 3.3* Strengths and weaknesses of quality definitions (source: Reeves and Bednar 1994: 437)

| Definition | Strengths | Weaknesses |
|---|---|---|
| **Excellence** | Strong marketing and human resource benefits<br>Universally recognizable – mark of uncompromising standards and high achievement | Provides little practical guidance to practitioners<br>Measurement difficulties<br>Attributes of excellence may change dramatically and rapidly<br>Sufficient number of customers must be willing to pay for excellence |
| **Value** | Concept of value incorporates multiple attributes<br>Focuses attention on a firm's internal efficiency and external effectiveness<br>Allows for comparisons across disparate objects and experiences | Difficulty extracting individual components of value judgement<br>Questionable inclusiveness<br>Quality and value are different constructs |
| **Conformance to specifications** | Facilitates precise measurement<br>Leads to increased efficiency<br>Necessary for global strategy<br>Should force disaggregation of consumer needs<br>Most parsimonious and appropriate definition for some customers | Consumers do not know or care about internal specifications<br>Inappropriate for services<br>Potentially reduces organizational adaptability<br>Specifications may quickly become obsolete in rapidly changing markets<br>Internally focused |
| **Meeting and/ or exceeding expectations** | Evaluates from customer's perspective<br>Applicable across industries<br>Responsive to market changes<br>All-encompassing definition | Most complex definition<br>Difficult to measure<br>Customers may not know expectations<br>Idiosyncratic reactions<br>Pre-purchase attitudes affect subsequent judgements<br>Short-term and long-term evaluations may differ<br>Confusion between customer service and customer satisfaction |

shows, many of the definitions include the **customer**, typically interpreted in both the **external** and the **internal** sense. Indeed, the development of a customer perspective has come about hand in hand with the rise in the importance of quality. The table shows how definitions of quality have broadened over time: application of the term has extend from manufacturing to service, from being concerned narrowly with attributes of the product (or service) – the **what** of quality – to include the **how** of quality, and from internally (company) defined attributes to a customer perspective.

## Transformation processes

Viewing productivity as a systems concept tells us that inputs are converted into outputs via some transformation process or processes. Similarly, an organization, as a system, comprises many subsystems and it is these which are concerned, directly or indirectly, with the transformation processes that convert inputs to outputs. Numerous writers have proposed categorizations of generic organizational subsystems: for example, Katz and Kahn (1978) and Mullins (1996) each identify five subsystems, as shown in Box 3.2. Though the two schemes depict different ways of viewing an organization, their relevance here is that they highlight the several aspects of organizations which are related to organizational productivity and performance and which need to be managed.

---

Box 3.2    **Organizational subsystems**

Production or technical subsystem:   The production system is concerned with the throughput, the energic or informational transformation whose cycles of activity comprise the major functions of the system.

Supportive subsystems:   Supportive subsystems carry on the environmental transactions of procuring the input or disposing of the output or aiding in these processes. Some transactions are a direct extension of the production activities of the organization, importing the material to be worked on or exporting the finished product. Others are indirectly related to the production cycle but supportive of

---

it, maintaining a favourable environment for the operation of the system.

Maintenance subsystems: Maintenance activities are not directed at the material being worked on but at the equipment for getting the work done. . . . Whereas the supportive systems of procurement and disposal are concerned with insuring production inputs, that is, materials and resources for the work of the organization, the maintenance system is concerned with inputs for preserving the system either through appropriate selection of personnel or adequate rewarding of the personnel selected.

Adaptive subsystems: Nothing in the production, supportive and maintenance subsystems would suffice to ensure organizational survival in a changing environment. Except for the functions of procurement and disposal, these subsystems face inward; . . . In most formal organizations there arise, therefore, structures that are specifically concerned with sensing relevant changes in the outside world and translating the meaning of those changes for the organization. There may be structures that devote their energies wholly to the anticipation of such changes. All these comprise the adaptive subsystem of the organization and bear such names as product research, market research, long-range planning, research and development, and the like.

Managerial subsystems: These systems comprise the organized activities for controlling, co-ordinating, and directing the many subsystems of the structure.

(source: Katz and Kahn 1978: 52, 52–3, 54–5, 55)

---

Task – the goals and objectives of the organization. The nature of inputs and outputs, and the work activities to be carried out in the transformation or conversion process.

Technology – the manner in which the tasks of the organization are carried out and the nature of work performance. The materials, systems and procedures, and equipment used in the transformation or conversion process.

Structure – patterns of organization, lines of authority, formal relationships and channels of communication among members. The division of work and co-ordination of tasks by which the series of activities are carried out.

People – the nature of the members undertaking the series of activities: such as their attitudes, skills and attitudes; needs and expectations; interpersonal relations and patterns of behaviour; group functioning and behaviour; informal organization and styles of leadership.

Management – co-ordination of task, technology, structure and people, and policies and procedures for the execution of work. Corporate strategy, direction of the activities of the organization as a whole and its interactions with the external environment.

(source: Mullins 1996: 85)

Much of the effort to improve organizational productivity has focused on the organization's transformation processes, very often with the aim of reducing costs (Heap 1992). Modern-day approaches, and their associated tools and techniques, include total quality management (TQM), new wave manufacturing, and business process re-engineering (BPR). The boundaries of these approaches are by no means hard and fast, with many of the tools and techniques falling into more than one of them. For example, just-in-time is sometimes presented as a key element in quality management (e.g., Dale 1994) and sometimes as a new wave manufacturing strategy (e.g., Harrison 1994). Similarly, benchmarking is presented as an important measurement tool in its own right (Andersen 1995) as well as in the context of both TQM (Dale and Boaden 1994) and BPR (Peppard and Rowland 1995).

## FROM PRODUCTIVITY TO PERFORMANCE

One of the factors that has contributed to the multiplicity of productivity definitions that we have is that different disciplines have brought their particular perspectives to bear on the concept, as Table 3.4 shows. As is clear from the table, the notion of

*Table 3.4* Different disciplines' perspectives on productivity (source: Pritchard 1992: 448–9)

*The Economist*
The economist sees productivity as the ratio of outputs over their associated inputs. . . . Put another way, productivity is the efficiency of the transformation of inputs into outputs.

*The Accountant*
Approaches to productivity based on an accounting perspective attempt to describe and improve the financial performance of the organization. This is done through the construction of a series of financial ratios, such as dollars of sales divided by the cost of labour or dollars of profit divided by the capital employment to produce it. Most of these measures have an output/input format and are thus a type of efficiency measure, but they are focused primarily on financial efficiency. Typically, multiple measures are constructed to get an overall picture of organizational functioning.

*The Industrial Engineer*
The industrial engineer views productivity as the efficiency of throughput as measured by output to input ratios. It is based on the model of a machine, where productivity is the ratio of useful work (the output) divided by the energy used to produce the work (input). . . . Measurement is typically focused on the operational units within the organization rather than the total organization and usually attempts to assess the functioning of a 'man-machine' system.

*The Psychologist*
[This] focuses primarily on the aspects of productivity that the individual can control, that is, behaviour. The assumption is that by changing individuals' behaviour, productivity will be changed.

*The Manager*
The broadest but least precisely indentifiable perspective is that of the manager. In this perspective, productivity includes all aspects of the organization seen as important to effective organizational functioning. It includes efficiency and effectiveness, but also includes quality of output, work disruptions, absenteeism, turnover, and customer satisfaction. No one specific definition of what productivity is nor how it should be measured are specified. Anything that should make the organization function better ipso facto deals with productivity.

efficiency remains central to conceptualizations of productivity, but it is equally clear that the term has come to have broader interpretations, perhaps so broad that the term lost some of its meaning. This in part stems from the changed view of what we mean by output – the importance of the quality dimension is afforded greater emphasis *and* we need to consider what the customer wants. In other words, productivity is more than efficient production; it is also about producing a quality product or providing a quality service that is wanted, considerations that a narrow definition of productivity ignore. This has led some (e.g., Lawlor 1985; Pritchard 1992) to argue that the concept of productivity needs to combine ideas of efficiency and **effectiveness**. That is, the conception of productivity comes to be so broad that it is like the managerial perspective shown in Table 3.4.

Arguably, however, broadening the term in this way is unhelpful – if it includes so much it loses its meaning and usefulness. Others, therefore, have sought to present this widening of the productivity concept in terms of a paradigm shift. One such is Andersen, who writes of a new productivity paradigm:

> The key to the new productivity paradigm is to accept that productivity, in the sense of efficiency, is only one of several important dimensions of the organization that must be measured and improved. We need to move on to include in the equation both effectiveness as well as some of the softer and more intangible dimensions. The new productivity paradigm is actually the performance paradigm, where we actually measure the entire performance, including productivity, of the organization.
>
> (Anderson 1995: 12)

Bredrup regards effectiveness and efficiency as two of three dimensions of organizational performance, the integration of which 'will ultimately decide the competitiveness of a company.' (1995a: 85):

- effectiveness – to what extent are customer needs met;
- efficiency – how economically are the resources of the company utilized;
- changeability – to what extent is the company prepared for future changes.

## ORGANIZATIONAL PERFORMANCE: A MULTIDIMENSIONAL CONCEPT

Though popular today, this view that organizational performance should be broadly defined is not exactly new. If we look back at academic (and other) writings on organizational performance and effectiveness we find that they reflect the now widely accepted idea that performance is multi-faceted. This is well illustrated by the list of thirty criterion measures identified by Campbell (1977) and shown in Table 3.5. So performance is measured in terms of output (inappropriately referred to as productivity in the table) and outcome, profit, internal processes and procedures, organizational structures, employee attitudes, organizational responsiveness to the environment, and so on. The picture is a confusing one: can organizational performance be all of these things?

## The paradox of organizational performance and effectiveness

The paradoxical and confusing nature of organizational performance has been noted by numerous writers:

> We want our organizations to be adaptable and flexible, but we also want them to be stable and controlled. We want growth, resource acquisition, and external support, but we also want tight information management and formal communication. We want an emphasis on the value of human resources, but we also want an emphasis on planning and goal setting.
>
> (Quinn *et al.* 1996)

Theoreticians (e.g., Cameron 1986, 1995; Meyer and Gupta 1994) have attempted to capture these contradictions in their models. Hall, for example, offers four central principles (1996: 275, 277):

1 Organizations face multiple and conflicting environmental constraints.
2 Organizations have multiple and conflicting goals.
3 Organizations have multiple and conflicting internal and external constituencies.
4 Organizations have multiple and conflicting time frames.

All this isn't simply of theoretical interest; it also is of practical significance for measuring performance and evaluating effectiveness, as Dawson notes:

> [Practitioners] need to note that when they are trying to assess the performance of an organization they need to adopt a variety of approaches. Performance is multifaceted and thus a variety of assessment methods are required in order to construct a profile of an organization's performance. Only in this way can its members gauge those things that are being done well and those things that are being done badly.
>
> (Dawson 1996: 50)

*Table 3.5* Criteria of organizational effectiveness (source: Campbell 1977: 36–9)

1  *Overall effectiveness.* The general evaluation that takes into account as many criteria facets as possible. It is usually measured by combining archival performance records or by obtaining overall ratings or judgements from persons thought to be knowledgeable about the organization.

2  *Productivity.* Usually defined as the quantity or volume of the major product or service that the organization provides. It can be measured at three levels: individual, group and total organization via either archival records or ratings, or both.

3  *Efficiency.* A ratio that reflects a comparison of some aspect of unit performance to the costs incurred for that performance.

4  *Profit.* The amount of revenue from sales left after all costs and obligations are met. Per cent return on investments and per cent return on total sales are sometimes used as alternative definitions.

5  *Quality.* The quality of the primary service or product provided by the organization may take many operational forms, which are largely determined by the kind of product or service provided by the organization.

6  *Accidents.* The frequency of on-the-job accidents resulting in lost time.

7  *Growth.* Represented by an increase in such variables as total manpower, plant capacity, assets, sales, profits, market share and number of innovations. It implies a comparison of an organization's present state with its own past state.

8  *Absenteeism.* The usual definition stipulates unexcused absences, but even within this constraint there are a number of alternative definitions (for example, total time absence versus frequency of occurence).

9  *Turnover.* Some measure of the relative number of voluntary terminations, which is almost always assessed via archival records.

10  *Job satisfaction.* Has been conceptualized in many ways but the modal view might define it as the individual's satisfaction with the amount of various job outcomes he or she is receiving.

11  *Motivation.* In general, the strength of the predisposition of an individual to engage in goal-directed action or activity on the job. It is not a feeling of relative satisfaction with various job outcomes but is more akin to a readiness or willingness to work at accomplishing the job's goals. As an organizational index, it must be summed across people.

12  *Morale.* It is often difficult to define or understand how organizational theortists and researchers are using this concept. The modal definition seems to view morale as a group phenomenon involving extra effort, goal communality, commitment and feelings of belonging. Groups have some degree of morale, whereas individuals have some degree of motivation (and satisfaction).

13  *Control.* The degree of, and distribution of, management control that exists within an organization for influencing and directing the behaviour of organization members.

14  *Conflict/cohesion.* Defined at the cohesion end by an organization in which the members like one another, work well together, communicate fully and openly, and co-ordinate their work efforts. At the other end lies the organization with verbal and physical clashes, poor co-ordination, and ineffective communication.

15  *Flexibility/adaptation.* (Adaptation/Innovation). Refers to the ability of an organization to change its standard operating procedures in response to environmental changes.

16  *Planning and goal-setting.* The degree to which an organization systematically plans its future steps and engages in explicit goal-setting behaviour.

17  *Goal consensus.* Distinct from actual commitment to the organization's goals, consensus refers to the degree to which all individuals perceive the same goals for the organization.

18  *Internalization of organizational goals.* Refers to the acceptance of the organization's goals. It includes their belief that the organization's goals are right and proper. It is *not* the extent to which goals are clear or agreed upon by the organization members (goal clarity and goal consensus, respectively).

19  *Role and norm congruence.* The degree to which the members of an organization are in agreement on such things as desirable supervisory attitudes, performance expectations, morale, role requirements and so on.

20  *Managerial interpersonal skills.* The level of skill with which managers deal with superiors, subordinates and peers in terms of giving support, facilitating constructive interaction, and generating enthusiasm for meeting goals and achieving excellent performance. It includes such things as consideration, employee centredness and so on.

21  *Managerial task skills.* The overall level of skills with which the organization's managers, commanding officers or group leaders perform work-centred tasks, tasks centred on work to be done, and not the skills employed when interacting with other organizational members.

22  *Information management communication.* Completeness, efficiency and accuracy in analysis and distribution of information critical to organizational effectiveness.

23  *Readiness.* An overall judgement concerning the probability that the organization could successfully perform some specified task if asked to do so.

24  *Utilization of environment.* The extent to which the organization successfully interacts with its environment and acquires scarce and valued resources necessary to its effective operation.

25  *Evaluations by external entities.* Evaluations of the organization, or unit, by the individuals and organizations in its environment with which it interacts. Loyalty to, confidence in and support given the organization by such groups as suppliers, customers, shareholders, enforcement agencies and the general public would fall under this label.

26  *Stability.* The maintenance of structure, function and resources through time and, more particularly, through periods of stress.

27  *Value of human resources.* A composite criterion that refers to the total value worth of the individual members, in an accounting or balance sheet sense, to the organization.

*Table 3.5* continued

28 *Participation and shared influence.* The degree to which individuals in the organization participate in making the decisions that directly affect them.
29 *Training and development emphasis.* The amount of effort the organization devotes to developing its human resources.
30 *Achievement emphasis.* An analogue to the indivdual need for achievement referring to the degree to which the organization appears to place a high value on achieving major new goals.

## PERFORMANCE MEASUREMENT

### The need for performance measurement

If performance measurement simply means the retrospective collection of historical results it is likely that little useful purpose will be served from the point of view of performance management (Bredrup 1995c; Zairi 1994). Many commentators (e.g., Chakravarthy 1986; Eccles 1991) have noted that commonly used indicators, especially accounting-based ones, paint a picture of the past. But if measurement is to be useful in performance management it has to be forward-looking and concerned with performance improvement. Bredrup (1995c), for example, suggests eight important reasons that might be served by a measurement system, as shown in Table 3.6.

### Multiple performance indicators

The consequence of all of the above is that for any organization we need a range of indicators if we are to measure performance and make judgements about effectiveness. Thus, we would expect to see measures of outcome, output, throughput, internal functioning, etc., including the five main areas suggested by Walters (1995: 172):

- contribution to the achievement of strategic objectives;
- measures of quality;
- measures of quantity and volume;
- measures of efficiency and value for money;
- measures of external and internal customer satisfaction.

*Table 3.6* Important purposes for a performance measurement system (source: Bredrup 1995c: 172)

- *Decision support.* Ideally measurement should indicate where to act perhaps how to act and hopefully monitor the effect of the action. Decisions should be based on knowledge and measurement plays an important role to provide information.
- *Monitor effect of strategic plans.* Implementation of strategic plans has to be monitored to make necessary corrections to ensure achievement of long-term goals. Indicators have to be chosen to monitor consequences and achievements.
- *Performance evaluation.* Evaluation is required for a number of reasons, such as tracking improvement potentials, setting new yardsticks, satisfying requirements from stakeholders, distributing incentives, etc.
- *Diagnosis.* A company needs indicators with a diagnostic purpose. If business achievements are decreasing, the performance measurement systems should be able to give some warnings in advance and provide input to a search for reasons. However, it is difficult to isolate the cause/effect relationship.
- *Management of a continuous improvement process.* A continuous improvement process often provides stepwise 'blue savings' like released capacity, reduced future costs or increased value for the customer. Measurement is important to justify further investments and effort in the process, to manage the process and ensure consistency with strategy and to transform improvements into business achievements.
- *Motivation.* Measuring progress is necessary to justify further effort in the improvement process. Resistance against change is considerable in most organizations and lacking progress is enough ammunition to kill a project or a process.
- *Comparison.* Evaluation of performance and performance planning depends on a reference to identify performance gaps. Comparative benchmarking is possible to identify these gaps.
- *Record development.* Documentation of development could be demanded by stakeholders like customers, authorities, alliance partners, etc. or used actively as a marketing tool. Measurement to monitor and record supplier performance to give input to their improvement processes could result in productivity improvement.

## The balanced scorecard

One approach which has become popular in recent years which attempts to capture some of the contradictory nature of organizational performance is termed the balanced scorecard (Kaplan and Norton 1992, 1993, 1996). This aims to measure performance in terms of four sets of indicators, each taking a different perspective (Kaplan and Norton 1996: 76):

- **Financial**: to succeed financially, how should we appear to our shareholders?
- **Customer**: to achieve our vision, how should we appear to our customers?
- **Internal business process**: to satisfy our shareholders and customers, what business processes must we excel at?
- **Learning and growth**: to achieve our vision, how will we sustain our ability to change and improve?

One application of the balanced scorecard is shown in Table 3.7; the Europe/Middle East/Africa (EMEA) region of AT&T used it to help determine the objectives required to implement their

*Table 3.7* An application of the business scorecard (source: Letza 1996)

| Perspective | Strategic objectives to make the vision a reality |
|---|---|
| *Financial*<br>To our EMEA<br>shareholders | Pursue economic value-added opportunities<br>Improve gross profit margin<br>Reduce manufacturing and purchase costs |
| *Customer*<br>How we differ from<br>customers | Develop customer partnerships based on trust,<br>    professionalism and shared values<br>Become preferred supplier<br>Out perform other best suppliers<br>Improve responsiveness and reliability in supply of<br>    products and services |
| *Internal processes*<br>How we must excel | Increase effectiveness of salesforce<br>Improve delivery performance<br>Improve responsiveness to opportunities in the<br>    marketplace<br>Build technological capabilities close to the customer |
| *Growth and innovation*<br>How we can continue to<br>improve and create value | Build skills and offer a portfolio for creative solutions<br>Enter CATV, mobile and LD markets<br>Create customer- and project-focused teams<br>Build capability to differentiate on software and<br>    service provision |

vision. Though it is practically useful and helpful in terms of recognizing some of the complexity of organizational performance, critics have said that the approach does not go far enough. For example, Atkinson *et al.* (1997) point to a number of weaknesses, including the failure to pay sufficient attention to employees and suppliers or to the broader community within which the organization operates. Consistent with the stakeholder argument set out in the previous chapter, Atkinson and his colleagues highlight the need to incorporate a much wider range of stakeholders. As an example, they show how the Bank of Montreal has defined different classes of performance measures with reference to different stakeholder groups (Table 3.8).

*Table 3.8* Primary and secondary measures for stakeholder groups at the Bank of Montreal (source: Atkinson *et al.* 1997: 35)

| Stakeholder group | Primary measures | Secondary measures |
| --- | --- | --- |
| Shareholders | Return on common shareholders' investment | Revenue growth Expense growth Productivity Capital ratios Liquidity ratios Asset quality ratios |
| Customers | Customer satisfaction and quality of service | Customer surveys for different market/product requests |
| Employees | Employee commitment Employee competence Employee productivity | Different elements of employee opinion survey Different elements of customer service index (re. employee competence) Financial ratios of employee costs to revenues by different classifications |
| Community | Public image | Different external surveys |

## A CONCLUDING COMMENT

Concern for organizational productivity hasn't disappeared but it has been overtaken by a wider-ranging desire to improve all aspects of the organization's performance and maintain competitiveness. Today, we see the concept of performance as embracing productivity (efficiency) as well as effectiveness, adaptability and responsiveness. It is clear, then, that organizational performance is far from being a simple concept. When we talk about *the* performance of an organization we are not talking about some unitary thing.

Consequently, performance has come to be measured by using multiple indicators. Some are 'hard', and include financial and non-financial metrics. Others are of a 'softer' kind, concerning quality, employee attitudes and the like. Hence, we see measures both of results and of processes. Moreover, our measures need to accommodate the perspectives of the several stakeholder groups – both internal and external – who have an interest in the effectiveness or success of the organization. For any one facet of performance, different stakeholders may have different, perhaps conflicting, expectations. It may be unrealistic to suppose that all stakeholders' expectations can be satisfied all of the time – perhaps the most that we can hope for is that they can be maintained in some state of balance.

# 4   *Individual performance*
## *Outputs and results*

As we saw in Chapter 1, the predominant conception of performance management in the UK is that it is an intervention (or set of
interventions) targeted at individual employees with the aim of
directing and enhancing their performance so as to improve organizational performance. At the heart of performance management
we have a cycle of activity which starts with defining/planning
employee performance requirements, managing/supporting performance, reviewing it, and providing for development and
reward.

In this and the next two chapters I will explore the nature of
individual performance and the causes of performance. As well as
considering performance as a concept I will review how it is
operationalized in practice. There are two main perspectives –
outputs and behaviours. I will start with outputs in this chapter and
in the next deal with the behavioural view. Then, in Chapter 6, I
will go on to consider theories which seek to explain, or at least
describe, the causes or determinants of performance.

## EXPRESSING PERFORMANCE REQUIREMENTS: WHAT HAPPENS IN PRACTICE?

We know from surveys of appraisal practice (Gill 1977; Long
1986) that a results-orientation has come to be the dominant
approach in the UK for expressing performance requirements.
An associated trend has been a shift away from trait-oriented

appraisal. The move towards results was confirmed by the IMS survey of performance management that I referred to in Chapter 1 (Institute of Personnel Management 1992). The IMS asked about the six means of expressing performance requirements listed in Table 4.1.

The level of the job is a significant factor influencing not just the nature of the method used to express performance requirements but also the incidence of use. Amongst organizations having formal performance management policies **clear and measurable accountabilities**, **objectives/targets**, **main job activities and tasks**, and **lists of competences** tended to be used to express performance requirements for senior managers. For other white-collar employees **clear and measurable accountabilities** were used less than **main job activities and tasks** and **written job descriptions**. For manual employees the most frequently used methods were **main job activities and tasks** and **written job descriptions**, but all of the means (listed in Table 4.1) were less frequently used for these categories of staff than for managers. These findings imply a preference for objective rather than subjective standards (such as managerial judgement) so it is hardly surprising that commonly used indicators are 'output-based measures' and 'objectives' (whether or not agreed with the employee).

*Table 4.1* Means of expressing performance requirements (source: Institute of Personnel Management 1992: 5)

- Clear and measurable accountabilities: reflecting approaches to setting unambiguous targets linked to measurable outcomes for which the jobholder is explicitly answerable
- Broad responsibilities and roles: including descriptions of the key elements of jobs expressed as areas of obligation and functional responsibility in general terms
- Objectives/targets: reflecting the aims of the job and the main outputs expected of a competent performer
- Main job activities and tasks: describing the important components of jobs in terms of activity areas and duties
- Written job descriptions: explaining core responsibilities and lines of accountability
- Lists of competences: statements of performance outcomes, often expressed in behavioural or output terms

## PERFORMANCE AS OUTPUT: SOME DEFINITIONS

As the evidence from practice shows, a wide range of terms is used to denote performance as output. The language used includes:

- accountabilities;
- key result areas;
- results;
- duties, tasks and activities;
- objectives;
- goals;
- outputs;
- targets;
- critical success factors;
- competences and standards.

Illustrative definitions of various of these terms are shown in Box 4.1 from which it is clear that performance is being conceptualized, in effect, as a property of the job. Also clear is that there is a high degree of conceptual overlap and redundancy among the several terms. Like Locke and Latham (1984), I will take the view that they can be used synonymously but organizations may find some pragmatic value in drawing distinctions amongst them where it suits their purposes. For example, Legal & General (Life and Pensions) distinguish between principal accountabilities and objectives. Cambridgeshire County Council make a similar distinction:

> **Accountabilities**: These describe the principal purposes for  which each job exists. They do not change from year to year unless the job changes. There are normally about eight per job, covering all aspects of the job.
> **Goals**: These reflect the immediate priorities of the job. They  indicate specific measurable levels of achievement expected within a given period of time. They can be related to standards and used to influence how a job holder meets particular accountabilities.
>
> (Audit Commission 1995c: 5.62)

Also, as we saw above, different terminology (and approaches for expressing performance requirements) may be used for different types or levels of job.

Box 4.1    **Conceptions of performance as output**

**Accountabilities**: 'Principal accountabilities define the key result areas of the job. * . . . The list of principal accountabilities should cover all the key aspects of the job which together contribute to achieving its overall prupose' (Armstrong 1994: 49). The terms '**main tasks**' or '**main duties**' may be used as synonyms.

**Key result areas**: important areas of activity in which achievement determines or indicates success (Ainsworth and Smith 1993: 7).

**Targets**: 'Targets are often known by other names such as objectives and goals but really these terms all describe the same thing. Targets explain what should be achieved at the end of an activity – a point to be hit or a desired result. The emphasis in this definition is important because the focus is on output rather than input or effort' (Hale 1993: 64).

**Goals**: A *goal* is what an employee is trying to accomplish on the job. It is the object or aim of an action. There are many familiar concepts that are similar in meaning to that of goal; e.g., *task*: a piece of work to be accomplished; *performance standard*: a measuring rod for evaluating performance (usually referring to a minimum acceptable amount or quality); *quota*: an assigned amount of work or production; *work norm*: a standard of acceptable conduct as defined by a work group; *objective*: the ultimate aim of an action; *deadline*: a time limit for accomplishing some task; and *budget*: a spending limit for an individual, project department, or organization

'In most instances, the distinctions between these concepts are not of great importance; thus we use the word goal as an umbrella term. No distinction is made, for example, between the terms goal and objective. This is because both of these concepts have the same two elements in common: they imply or specify a *direction* for action to take, and they imply a specified *amount* or quality of work to be accomplished' (Locke and Latham 1984: 5).

> **Compentences and standards**: standards state in terms of outcome what is expected of an individual performing a particular occupational role. They do not look at the underlying abilities or traits of the individual – they describe the expectations which the individual is required to meet. A standard is expressed in two parts:
>
> - an element of competence;
> - its associated performance criteria.
>
> The element describes something which the individual should be able to do. Performance criteria describe the standards of performance required for the successful achievement of that element (Management Charter Initiative 1990: 3).

Though this output-oriented interpretation of performance is especially evident in the practitioner literature (e.g., Ainsworth and Smith 1993; Armstrong 1994; Lockett 1992), we also find it in academic writings. Drawing on earlier work by Kane (1986), one example comes from Bernardin *et al.*:

> Performance is defined as: The *record of outcomes* produced on a *specified job function* or activity during a *specified time period*. . . . Performance on the job as a whole would be equal to the sum (or average) of performance on the critical or essential job functions. The functions have to do with the work which is performed and *not* with the characteristics of the person performing.
>
> (Bernardin *et al.* 1995: 470–1)

Bernardin and his colleagues argue that a focus on results should be the preferred approach to performance management as it takes a customer perspective and enables individuals' efforts to be linked to organizational goals.

A similar example comes from the work of Pritchard and his colleagues (Pritchard *et al.* 1988, 1989; Pritchard 1990a, 1990b). They developed what they termed a Productivity Measurement and Enhancement System (ProMES). Fundamental to this system is the identification of important job outputs, called *products*:

'Products are activities or objectives that an organizational unit is expected to accomplish' (Pritchard 1990a: 80). Though defined in terms of unit accomplishments, these products are intended to provide a focus for individuals' action. Another feature of ProMES that is of particular interest is the involving way in which the system operates. This is described in Box 4.2.

---

**Box 4.2    Pritchard's Productivity Measurement and Enhancement System (ProMES)**

The first step in the development of ProMES is to identify what are called *products*. Products are activities or objectives that an organizational unit is expected to accomplish.

To identify products, a team of supervisors and representative incumbents is formed and led by a facilitator to identify the salient products. This design team would make a listing of these products and discuss and refine it until consensus was reached.

A typical unit would have from three to five products. This list is then reviewed by higher levels of supervision and management for completeness and accuracy. Any disagreements are discussed with the originating group and resolved. At this point, a set of products have been identified and agreed on by multiple levels of the organization.

Once the products have been determined, the next step is to develop *indicators* to these products. An indicator is a measure of how well the organization is generating the product in question. To identify the indicators, the design team is asked to think of things they would use to show how well they are generating their products. There may be one or several indicators for each product.

As with the products, the group works on the indicators until the members are satisfied that the list comprehensively covers all the products and represents valid measures of the products. Great care must be exercised at this point to ensure that good indicators are generated. It is easy to end up with indicators that are incomplete or that tap easily measured aspects of the product rather than what is really important but more difficult to measure. It is also important that the

---

indicator be consistent with the product in the sense that generating a large amount of the indicator does in fact achieve the product. This issue needs much more care than it might at first seem. Once the members of the group have finalized the indicators, the process of approval up the organizational hierarchy is done as it was with the products.

Typically, there will be a total of from eight to fifteen indicators for a given unit.

Once the products and indicators are identified and approved, the next step is to establish *contingencies*. A contingency is a graphic function representing the relationship between the amount of an indicator and the degree of contribution that amount of the indicator makes to overall productivity. (See Pritchard *et al.* 1989 for a fuller description of how contingencies are developed.)

Once the contingencies are completed and approved by management, the last step is to put the system together. This would be accomplished by first collecting the indicator data for a given period of time. Assume that the time period selected was a month-long period. The data for the different indicators would be collected at the end of the month. Then, based on the contingencies, effectiveness scores would be determined for each indicator. . . . Once the effectiveness value for each indicator is determined, they can be summed to get the overall effectiveness of the unit.

This information is then put into a regularly occurring, formal productivity feedback report that is circulated to the members of the unit and their management. They then meet to discuss the report and assess reasons for increases and decreases in their productivity and plan changes that will improve their productivity.

(source: summarized from Pritchard 1990a, 1990b)

Pritchard and his colleagues note several benefits for their approach. One is that it helps to make clear to employees what is required – their unit's objectives, how attainment will be measured and the level of attainment that is expected. Indeed, clarity about expectations is intended to be an outcome of all of the means of expressing performance as goals, results, competences, etc., and some recent British research (Winterton and Winterton 1996) reports that adoption of the MCI National Standards can lead to this outcome as well as various other performance-related benefits, e.g. increased commitment and motivation.

However, for Pritchard and his colleagues it is not just the statement of the products themselves which is important but also the **involving** process of system development. One further benefit that this brings is acceptance of the measurement system on the part of those to whom it applies. As noted in Chapter 1, the participation theme is widespread in the performance management literature and many benefits are claimed for involving employees. For example, an authoritative review (Rodgers and Hunter 1991) of management by objectives (MbO) suggests considerable benefits for employee participation in setting their goals:

Participation in decision making promotes understanding throughout the organization. Managers who rely on only their own ideas are more like a one-person orchestra than a conductor of musicians. But with participatory input from lower levels, useful information that is known to subordinates is made known to top management. Awareness of alternative courses of action is increased and knowledge of the consequences of decisions is enhanced. Problems are found with the design of the work process and the methods necessary to attain work objectives. Periodic changes to work methods result: job responsibilities are reallocated, lines of authority are redrawn, and technical systems are restructured. Subordinates are made aware of top management's objectives, and top managers are made aware of problems involved with implementing the objectives they see as important.

(Rodgers and Hunter 1991: 323)

These sorts of benefits – the enhancement of communication, improvements in the structure and operation of the work system – are all consistent with the outcomes desired of performance management, and in evaluating the operation of a performance management system we would want to gather information about such processes as organizational communication, the extent to which participation/involvement is provided for and the extent to which it is perceived by job holders as having happened.

Unfortunately, the survey evidence that we have provides us with only a few clues about the extent of employee participation in determining job content and performance requirements. So, we know that there is a higher incidence of agreeing performance objectives with employees in formal performance management organizations than in those with other policies or with no policies. But of all organizations responding to the IMS performance management survey, fewer than half report such participation taking place for the majority of their employees. That said, within performance management organizations the expression of performance requirements by some means or other is the norm. Though it does not extend to all hierarchical levels/types of job it is clear that for the most part the preferred approach is one which emphasizes targets, results, accountabilities, etc. – in other words, an overall philosophy that might loosely be labelled **goal-setting**.

## DEFINING PERFORMANCE BY SETTING GOALS

Goal-setting is much advocated in the literature, particularly that which is practice-oriented (e.g., Ainsworth and Smith 1993; Armstrong 1994, 1995; Costello 1994; LGMB 1993; Lockett 1992; Moores 1994), and it has a strong theoretical underpinning. What is typically proposed is a cascading process, very reminiscent of management by objectives (MbO) – Figure 4.1, taken from Moores, provides one illustration. This cascading process is commonly seen as the means by which individual goals and objectives are aligned with organizational goals. For example, in Hewlett-Packard individuals have to achieve key job-relevant results, with these key result areas being related to the overall business objectives: these are expressed in a performance plan. Performance planning is widely advocated and typically happens once a year as part of a joint discussion between job holder and manager.

In keeping with today's interest in business processes, many (e.g., Rummler and Brache 1995) advocate that individual goals must be consistent not just with departmental or functional goals, but also with process goals. To the extent that processes may be seen in horizontal terms in organizations, this then implies both horizontal and vertical integration of goals.

Though organizational goals may serve many functions (as

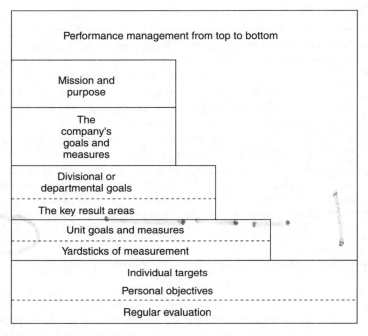

*Figure 4.1* Cascading goals (source: Moores 1994)

Table 4.2 illustrates) the approach is far from being trouble-free. The mission statement may contain a statement of the organization's goals, perhaps in rather vague and general terms. Indeed, the mission statement may contain several goals and in an ideal world these will be wholly consistent with one another: but this will not always be the case, especially as different stakeholders have different expectations of performance – the discussion of the balanced scorecard in Chapter 3 illustrated this. Moreover, the deeper we dig within an organization the more we are likely to find several and different goals across its subunits. Lower-level goals, according to the theory of performance management, ought to be consistent with those set at the top – Rummler and Brache (1995) refer to this as a 'performance logic' – but such goal consistency cannot be assumed. In setting goals members of departments, work teams and so on may set goals consistent with their interests as they see them. Ensuring consistency of

*Table 4.2* Functions of goals (source: Mullins 1996: 293)

- Goals provide a standard of performance. They focus attention on the activities of the organization and the direction of the efforts of its members.
- Goals provide a basis for planning and management control related to the activities of the organization.
- Goals provide guidelines for decision-making and justification for actions taken. They reduce uncertainty in decision-making and give a defence against possible criticism.
- Goals influence the structure of the organization and help determine the nature of techology employed. The manner in which the organization is structured will affect what it will attempt to achieve.
- Goals help to develop commitment of individuals and groups to the activities of the organization. They focus attention on purposeful behaviour and provide a basis for motivation and reward systems.
- Goals give an indication of what the organization is really like, its true nature and character both for members and for people outside the organization.
- Goals serve as a basis for the evaluation of change and organization development.
- Goals are the basis for objectives and policies of the organization.

goals thus becomes one of the main challenges for performance management systems – a participative and involving approach may help to bring this about.

Goal-setting often is presented in the literature as a top-down process and seems commonly to be practised as such. For example, Swale Borough Council has an objectives-based system of performance management. It starts at council level, passing down through committees and services and on to sections and individuals. Each service or function will have between three and seven main objectives each year, as well as specific performance targets (Audit Commission 1995c).

Whilst these sorts of structures and systems provide the framework for individual performance management, line management and the appraisal process are the key means by which performance requirements are communicated, and this communication is more commonly one-way (downwards) rather than the two-way communication that often is advocated. Though some writers see a place for a bottom-up contribution to goal-setting, in practice it seems likely that the extent of employee **involvement** or **participation** is limited to reaching **shared agreement** about their own particular job goals. An illustration is provided by the Royal Borough of Windsor and Maidenhead:

> Within the broad framework set by the corporate plan and by more specific unit business plans, every employee is asked to identify the core elements of his/her job. The outcome is identification of 'key accountabilities' for each post-holder; based on these accountabilities, performance objectives are determined for all members of staff. This is done by post-holders in collaboration with their managers. This way, each employee has 'ownership' of the performance management process, since they are all involved in establishing their own individual objectives.
>
> (Audit Commission 1995c: 5.74)

The absence of such ownership was found to be a barrier in the three performance management systems examined by Stiles *et al.* (1997) – targets were seen as being imposed.

What is agreed often finds expression in some sort of written **action plan**, sometimes referred to as a **performance agreement** (Armstrong 1994) or **performance contract** (Lockett 1992), as described in Box 4.3. Such a statement communicates both the **what** and the **how well** of performance (Rummler and Brache 1995).

---

**Box 4.3   The performance agreement or contract**

A performance agreement, also known as a performance contract, defines expectations – the work to be done, the results to be attained and the attributes (skills, knowledge and expertise) and competences required to achieve these results. It also identifies the measures used to monitor, review and assess performance (Armstrong 1994: 46).

The contract is between two parties and consists of two elements – the clarification of performance requirements and the agreement of the corresponding support in terms of resources, training and direction from the manager. . . . *The performance requirements in a performance contract are for the whole job and not just selected parts of it.* (Lockett 1992: 42).

---

In Mercury Communications the Performance Contract is a mandatory part of their 'Contribution Management' approach to performance management. Amongst other things it includes a statement of the job purpose, what sort of inputs (skills and abilities) the employee brings to the job, how the employee will contribute to Mercury values, agreed accountabilities (outputs to be achieved), as well as details of the review process (such as when reviews will take place) and what Mercury will contribute (e.g., by way of training).

In Zeneca Pharmaceuticals they have a 'performance management discussion record' which covers the following four areas:

- **Business role**: ensures that the job description reflects business objectives.
- **Performance planning**: targets are set by joint agreement between the employee and the appraising manager.
- **Performance development**: define that skills, knowledge and experience needed and plans the required training.
- **Performance measurement**: evaluates performance against targets.

As noted at the start of this chapter, we also find that the term 'goal' is typically defined broadly – task, objective, etc. In addition, different types of goals are distinguished in the literature. For example, it is common to find at least two types of goals, namely **work objectives** (relating to the main task areas of the job and results expected) and **developmental objectives** (personal learning objectives for improving skills and job performance) (e.g., Armstrong 1995). The Zeneca example in Box 4.3 provides one illustration. Others include Mercury Communications, where employees have a personal development plan which specifies how an employee's future career is expected to develop – both short- and medium-term training plans are included. At Standard Life a development plan supports the performance plan by setting out the development or training needed by job holders to produce their outputs.

Some writers take a still broader view. Thus, Spangenberg

*Table 4.3* Types of objectives (source: Warrick and Zawacki 1987, cited in Spangenberg 1994: 85)

1 **Routine objectives**, which represent regular duties and responsibilities that are part of a job.
2 **Problem-solving objectives**, which are related to specific problems.
3 **Innovative objectives**, which pertain to new ideas, services or ways of doing things.
4 **Personal development objectives**, which are related to an individual's personal and professional development and growth.
5 **Organizational development objectives**, which are objectives for the development of the entire organization or a specific department.

(1994) cites the five types of objectives identified by Warrick and Zawacki (1987), as shown in Table 4.3. The inclusion of developmental goals is certainly consistent with the developmental orientation that is claimed for many performance management systems. Moreover, we would expect that development goals would be related to business needs as well as being for the benefit of the individual, as shown by the examples given. However, as I will discuss further in the final chapter, UK practice seems predominantly to be reward- rather than development-driven.

## Characteristics of work goals

The incorporation of individual goals within some system of performance management is hardly a new idea, so we should expect that by now there is some consensus about the characteristics of 'good' work goals. This is indeed the case, and McConkie (1979), analysing the views of nearly forty authorities on MbO, identified near-universal agreement on three aspects of goals within the context of MbO:

- goals and objectives should be specific;
- they should be defined in terms of measureable results;
- individual and organizational goals should be linked one to another.

On other aspects of goals there was rather less agreement, but half or more of authorities agreed on the following points:

- Objectives should be reviewed periodically.
- The time period for goal accomplishment should be specified.
- Wherever possible, the indicator of the results should be quantifiable; otherwise, it should be at least verifiable.
- Objectives should be flexible; changed as conditions warrant.
- Objectives should have an accompanying plan of action for accomplishing the results.
- Objectives should be assigned priority weightings.

These principles are reflected in much of today's conventional wisdom about goals, as in '**SMART**' goals, for example. Box 4.4 illustrates several variations on this basic theme.

---

Box 4.4   **SMART goals**

**S**pecific or **S**tretching
**M**easureable
**A**ttainable or **A**chievable or **A**greed or **A**cceptable or **A**ssignable
**R**esults-oriented or **R**ealistic or **R**elevant
**T**ime-bound

For example, in Legal & General (Life and Pensions) **SMART** means:
**S**pecific – define the work involved precisely
**M**easureable – to assess achievement
**A**greed – both parties committed
**R**ealistic – an acceptable but stretching challenge
**T**imed – specify the deadline and review date

A variation on this theme is **FRAME** (Whetten *et al.* 1994):
**F**ew
**R**ealistic
**A**greed
**M**easured
**E**xplicit

---

## The functions of work goals

One of the most robust of research findings in the behavioural sciences is that goal-setting has a beneficial effect on employees' work performance (Locke and Latham 1990). Positive findings have been reported from real-life studies in the workplace and from experimental studies in the laboratory. Studies have been carried out on a range of jobs and into quality as well as quantity goals. The main findings of the research are as follows:

- Difficult, challenging goals lead to higher performance than do easy goals, **provided that** the job holder accepts and is committed to the goals. In simple terms, the harder the goal, the higher the performance (given goal acceptance).
- Specific goals lead to higher performance than do vague, general 'do your best goals' or no goals at all.

These benefits derive, in part, from clarity over what is expected of employees, a point stressed by Ainsworth and Smith: 'Each person knows what is expected of him or her' and 'Everybody knows how they fit into the bigger picture' (1993: 17). Indeed, such clarity may be seen as a requirement for performance management to work, and may help to avoid the 'activity trap' – that is, losing sight of what job activities are for. This was seen to be a major benefit of a new performance management system introduced in the London Borough of Haringey's Housing Services – the aim was to create a new perception of effectiveness, one based on results rather than completion of tasks (Harris 1995). In this way, goals do provide one basis for measurement, although this is not without problems, as I shall come on to consider in just a moment. Goals may also serve to increase task interest and relieve boredom (Locke and Latham 1990). And in evaluating the operation of a performance management system we might ask employees about these aspects of role clarity.

## How do goals and goal-setting work?

According to the theory of goal-setting (Locke and Latham 1990), it seems likely that goals work through several mechanisms:

- By directing the job holder's attention and action towards the desired end result – the acceptable level of performance: this is more likely to be the case when goals are specific rather than vague as a specific goal makes clear to the job holder what is meant by effective performance; vague goals, on the other hand, allow the individual to interpret pretty well any performance as effective. The mechanism involved here is one that has been described as **orientation** (Robertson *et al.* 1992).

- By mobilizing effort, in other words energizing the job holder; this is likely to be the consequence of a challenging rather than easy goal. Put simply, people try harder when faced with a task that is more rather than less difficult.
- By encouraging persistence over time; people seem more likely to stick at a hard rather than easy goal.

The above mechanisms all are believed to operate in a more or less automatic fashion (Locke and Latham 1990). But effort, action and persistence may not always be sufficient to bring about goal-accomplishment. When faced with a complex or novel task the individual will need to develop ways of (strategies for) achieving the goal(s). Furthermore, it is clear that feedback is also required.

Feedback (knowledge of results) is necessary in order to heighten the performance enhancing effect of goals. Feedback can serve to keep people on track; it provides a signal that a particular goal is still important (which may be particularly critical in cases of under-achievement) and may help to guide the individual towards ways of achieving the goal – in other words, it has **informational** and **learning** value. And when the goal is achieved feedback provides recognition.

## Aspects of the goal-setting process

### Gaining commitment

As we have seen, in order for goals to have the performance effects desired of them job holders have to accept and be committed to the goals. There are a number of aspects to commitment (Naylor and Ilgen 1984; Locke and Latham 1990; Earley and Shalley 1991): the job holder's attachment to the goal; its significance or importance in the eyes of the job holder; its perceived achievability/attainability (including controllability by the individual and difficulty); and the individual's determination and perseverance in achieving it, particularly when faced with obstructions and setbacks. It seems probable that more highly committed people will actually do what they say they will do.

Goal-commitment is taken to be a *sine qua non* so far as performance is concerned. The effect is particularly marked for hard goals, as the less committed job holder is more likely to give up such goals in favour of easier ones. Given this, what then can be done to enhance goal commitment? Two things would seem to be necessary: convincing job holders that it is possible for them to achieve the goal; and convincing them that the goal is important or appropriate.

**Supervisor authority, support and explanation**. Job holders may accept a goal out of deference to the authority of the supervisor. However, it should not be assumed that the use of authority guarantees acceptance and commitment. Various supervisor behaviours, such as providing support, can help to persuade job holders of the importance and attainability of goals. Moreover, explanation, both of why the goal/task is important and perhaps of how it might be done, contributes to goal accomplishment. Such behaviours all help to create a good impression of the manager/ supervisor in the eyes of the job-holder (Huber *et al.* 1989).

**Participation**. The role of employee participation in the goal-setting process remains controversial. Some authorities (e.g., Locke and Latham 1990) are of the view that it is not an absolutely necessary condition to bring about goal acceptance; explanation may be sufficient for this. Yet various case reports – the study of three performance management systems by Stiles *et al.* (1997), for example – continue to indicate that top-down goals are received as imposed rather than owned. However, it may be that participation is important where the task is complex (Wood and Locke 1990), in which case employee participation does seem to enhance acceptance of the goal. And this seems particularly to be so if the goal has initially been rejected by the employee on the grounds that it is unreasonable or too difficult. However, the value of participation seems to be less to do with goal acceptance than, as we saw earlier, with a range of broader benefits.

**Peer influence**. The supervisor isn't the only source of persuasive influence: peers, like supervisors, can serve as role models. Moreover, the power of peers and the work group to set norms of behaviour has long been recognized, as, for example, in the Hawthorne studies (Roethlisberger and Dickson 1939), which revealed, amongst other things, the existence of group norms about acceptable levels of production – typically below management's desired level and below the level that the workers were capable of delivering. Thus, it is important to recognize that co-workers have expectations of what a given employee should do.

- **Incentives and rewards**. Money may have a part to play here provided that the amount on offer is large enough and provided that the goal is not too difficult. If the goal is seen as impossible to achieve, the prospect of monetary reward, such as a bonus, is unlikely to bring about commitment because the reward is likely to be seen as unattainable (Locke and Latham 1990). This, of course, has important implications for appraisal-related pay, an issue that I will come back to later.

### Expectancy, self-efficacy and ability

This last point introduces the notion of expectancy, or **subjective probability of success** (SPS): does the individual expect to succeed in achieving the goal? This rather depends on the difficulty of the goal. Robertson *et al.* sum up the position in these terms:

> In situations where goals are easy it seems likely that SPS is high for all performers, and therefore a link between SPS [and performance] is unlikely to appear. When goals are difficult, as predicted by expectancy-valency theory, there should be, and is, a relationship between SPS and performance.
>
> (Robertson *et al.* 1992: 43)

Expectancy is closely related to another important psychological concept – self-efficacy. The latter is the broader concept and 'may be defined as the belief that one can perform successfully the behaviour required to produce designated types of performance' (Sadri and Robertson 1993: 139). In a review of studies Sadri and Robertson found a positive, albeit modest, relationship between self-efficacy and performance.

Self-efficacy, then, is perceptual – that is, the individual's perception of their ability. But it is not enough for people to perceive themselves as being able to accomplish the goal; they must actually have the requisite ability. Once the limit of an individual's ability has been reached, his or her performance is likely to level off, perhaps even decline (Locke and Latham 1990). Hence, the goal-setting process needs to have regard for individuals' capabilities and, more broadly, performance management needs to be concerned with the management of self-efficacy (Huber *et al.* 1989).

Another factor which influences perceived performance capability is past experience. Job holders' past experience of goals may have an impact on subsequent goal-setting. If previous goals were easy to achieve, employees seem to be prepared to choose more difficult goals the next time around. But if the goals were difficult to achieve on the previous occasion, then next time the job holder seems likely to choose an easier goal (Locke and Latham 1990). (The organization, on the other hand, might see goal accomplishment in one year as a reason for setting higher goals the next.)

## Problems and difficulties with goals and goal-setting

Though there is considerable evidence pointing to the value of goals and the goal-setting process, there are, not surprisingly, a number of problems, including practical difficulties and theoretical weaknesses.

First, the notion that individual goals should be integrated with organizational and unit-level goals requires that such higher-level goals have in fact been established. But as we saw earlier, there are difficulties with the organizational goal-setting process. It doesn't necessarily proceed in the rational, ordered way that is often advocated, and where higher-level goals are set out there also is the possibility of conflict amongst them – a problem that the balanced scorecard attempts to tackle. But all this does mean that the framework of organizational goals/objectives can be very complex. The integration idea also requires that the higher-level goals be communicated, and, as we saw in Chapter 1, not all organizations, including those professing to practise performance management, actually communicate their mission statement etc.

Second, there is a problem of **subjectivity**. It may seem strange to identify this as a problem with goals as these are typically regarded as substantially more objective than subjective. However, the process of setting individual goals is a very subjective one, as is the process of **interpreting** goal accomplishment. This is true whatever level of analysis we are concerned with, from the individual right up to the organizational. As Campbell puts it:

> an objective criterion is a subjective criterion once removed. For example, one might think that the number of units produced is an objective measure of an automobile assembly plant's effectiveness. However, a specific volume of production means

nothing until some metric or standard is applied that informs us what numbers are good and what numbers are bad. Many sub-jective judgements go into the development of such standards

(Campbell 1977: 45)

This highlights the distinction between measurement (as a count-ing activity) and evaluation, which involves making **judgements** about effectiveness.

Furthermore, much of the writing on goals advocates the setting of a relatively small number of goals, and this necessarily involves choice.

> Often to choose and emphasize a limited number of perfor-mance dimensions is to fail to appreciate the subtlety of orga-nizational life, and to risk shattering subtle structures of tacit but critical employee commitment by substituting a simplistic set of objectives. It carries the danger that if the system does 'work', in the sense that people focus on those elements of performance that have been selected and highlighted by the organization, the results may be not at all desirable: a pre-existing pride in skill and work may be replaced by a contrac-tual focus on the rules.
>
> (Mabey and Salaman 1995: 193)

Third, as Macdonell asks, 'Is "joint" goal-setting between a manager and subordinate ever going to be a practical possibility?' (1989: 706). Macdonell is alluding here to the boss–judge/friend–helper dilemma. There's also the added difficulty that stems from others', for example co-workers', expectations. Thus, there is the prospect of conflict amongst an individual's goals, suggesting that the idea of the balanced scorecard may be relevant at the indivi-dual level as it is at the organizational.

Fourth, there is the problem of turbulence. Mabey and Salaman describe this difficulty:

> Identifying desirable aspects of performance which will be measured and rewarded may be possible in an organization which enjoys a relatively stable internal and external environ-ment, but where greater turbulence is experienced it is possible that objectives and hence performance dimensions targeted today may be inapplicable tomorrow.
>
> (Mabey and Salaman 1995: 194)

In similar vein Macdonell asks, 'How do you recognize when conditions are changing and what account needs to be taken of them?' (1989: 706).

Fifth, the effects of goal-setting seem to be weaker for complex tasks than they are for easier tasks – paradoxically, though, the goals-based approach is more common for complex jobs.

Finally, there must surely be the temptation (to which both manager and managed may be susceptible) to focus on that which is measured easily and to express required performance levels as minimum standards but with the consequent risk that these become the maximum levels, which are attained but not exceeded. There may also be the related temptation to concentrate on the easily accomplished. Then there's the difficulty that not all aspects of jobs may be specified in terms of goals, certainly not relatively objective, quantitative ones. Those measures that are used thus become deficient as performance indicators (for the whole job) and employees' attention may become misdirected on the measurable at the expense of other important aspects of performance. In other words, in the same way that there is the problem of the 'activity trap', so there is this problem of 'goal deception' (Henderson 1984).

## A CONCLUDING COMMENT

The output-oriented conception of performance tends to view jobs as collections of tasks to be completed to meet defined objectives/ goals. Compelling though the evidence is about work goals, we certainly should not see goal-setting as a panacea. As noted above, there are a number of practical difficulties.

There's also the issue of how much of an individual's output is actually attributable to the particular performer. I will develop this point further in Chapter 6, but for the present it is sufficient to note that output may in some part be determined by factors that are outside the individual's control. This is one consideration that has led some writers to prefer a behavioural conception of performance. Moreover, as implied above, undue concentration on results – on the **what** – may lead to insufficient attention being paid to the **how** of performance. I will take up these points in the next chapter.

# 5 *Individual performance*
## *Behaviour and competencies*

The view that performance should be equated with task accomplishment, goal achievement, results, outputs, etc. is one that has been challenged in much of the psychological literature. Common today is a behavioural view of performance, one of the themes in which is that performance is *not* output or results. This is not to say that there is no place for goals in such a behavioural conception, as Murphy's definition makes clear: '*The performance domain is defined . . . as the set of behaviours that are relevant to the goals of the organization or the organizational unit in which a person works*' (1990: 162; italics in original). Other examples of this approach are shown in Box 5.1.

Central to the argument that we should not regard performance as task accomplishment or goal achievement is the fact that for many jobs results aren't necessarily the product of what individual employees do – there may be other contributory factors that are nothing to do with the person doing the job (Cardy and Dobbins 1994; Murphy and Cleveland 1995). Moreover, workers do not have equal opportunity to perform, nor is everything that people do whilst at work necessarily task-related (Murphy 1989). There are also the points, alluded to in the previous chapter, that an over-concentration on outputs ignores important processual and inter-personal factors and undue focus on outputs may misdirect employees as to what is required.

Thus, we have two different views of performance – results/outputs and behaviours. Defining performance as both, particularly at the same time, would seem to be unhelpful. One of the reasons for this is that doing so confounds the relationship between behaviours and outputs. Typically (e.g. Cardy and Dobbins 1994; Waldman 1994), behaviour is regarded as one of the *causes* of output, with output being one of the means by which the *effectiveness* of performance (that is, behaviour) may be judged. In other words we make judgements about the effectiveness of employees with reference to what they accomplish – the results they achieve, the output they produce. An illustration of this is provided by Campbell *et al.*: '*Effectiveness* refers to the evaluation of the results of performance' (1993: 41). And Ilgen and Schneider write in similar terms: 'Performance is what the person or system does. Performance measurement is the quantification of what was done, and performance evaluation is the attachment of a judgment of the value or quality of the quantified performance measurement' (1991: 73). All three are, of course, needed in performance management: the necessary first step is the expression of performance requirements.

---

**Box 5.1   Conceptions of performance as behaviour**

Performance is what the person or system does (Ilgen and Schneider 1991: 73).

A performance consists of a *performer* engaging in *behaviour* in a *situation* to achieve *results* (Mohrman *et al.* 1989: 48).

Performance is . . . defined as synonymous with behaviour. It is something that people actually do and can be observed. By definition, it includes only those actions or behaviours that are relevant to the organization's goals and that can be scaled (measured) in terms of each individual's proficiency (that is, level of contribution). Performance is what the organization hires one to do, and do well. Performance is *not* the consequence or result of action, it is the action itself. . . . performance consists of goal-relevant actions that are under the control of the individual, regardless of whether they are cognitive, motor, psychomotor, or interpersonal (Campbell *et al.* 1993: 40).

In everyday practice, however, the term performance tends to be used in a loose way to embrace both outputs and behaviour. This may be a convenient shorthand, but from a practical point of view it is likely to be more useful to be precise about what is meant as managing performance as outputs may require different interventions from the management of performance as behaviours. For example, the production of output may well involve many factors beyond the individual's control, such as the design of the work system. Behaviour, on the other hand, though not free from extraneous influence, might be expected to be much more within the direct control of the individual.

## PERFORMANCE IS BEHAVIOUR, BUT IS *ALL* BEHAVIOUR PERFORMANCE?

What is implied in these behavioural views (and in some cases is explicit) is the idea that whilst performance is behaviour not all behaviour is performance – only behaviour that is goal-relevant counts as performance. However, some writers have drawn a distinction between the aspects of jobs that are formally required and expected and those expectations which arise, perhaps as part of the **psychological contract**, in a more informal way. Thus, Borman and Motowidlo (1993) distinguish between **task performance** (the formally defined aspects of a job) and **contextual performance**. Some examples of what they mean by the latter are given in Table 5.1. This class of behaviours also has been referred to as **organizational citizenship behaviour** (e.g. Bateman and Organ 1983), **prosocial organizational behaviour** (Brief and Motowidlo 1986), **organizational spontaneity** (George and Brief 1992) or **extra-role behaviours** (Van Dyne *et al.* 1995). It is important to recognize that though these behaviours are to the benefit of the organization they are not a formal part of the job and to that extent they are much more heavily volitional or discretionary than are formally prescribed behaviours (Van Dyne *et al.* 1995).

Of course, we might hope that all employees would help and cooperate with others, endorse the organization's objectives, and so on, but the point that is being made here is that these sorts of behaviours are not normally expressed formally as a part of the

*Table 5.1* Examples of contextual performance and organizational spontaneity (source: Borman and Motowidlo 1993: 73; George and Brief 1992)

*Contextual performance*
- Volunteering to carry out task activities that are not formally a part of the job.
- Persisting with extra enthusiasm or effort when necessary to complete own task activities successfully.
- Helping and cooperating with others.
- Following organizational rules and procedures even when personally inconvenient.
- Endorsing, supporting and defending organizational objectives.

*Organizational spontaneity*
- Helping co-workers.
- Protecting the organization.
- Making constructive suggestions.
- Developing oneself.
- Spreading goodwill.

job. That said, the shift in emphasis towards quality and service may mean that for many jobs such behaviours are more explicitly expected these days (Waldman 1994). Indeed, some North American research (MacKenzie *et al.* 1991, 1993) indicates that managers of sales personnel attach great weight to organizational citizenship behaviours (OCBs) when making performance evaluations. They examined such OCBs as altruism (voluntarily helping others), civic virtue (e.g. attending meetings that aren't formally required as part of the job) and conscientiousness, and concluded that 'a salesperson's overall performance evaluation was determined more by his or her citizenship behaviour – including altruistic acts . . . and conscientiousness – than by his or her actual sales success' (MacKenzie *et al.* 1993: 78).

One of the interesting questions raised by these findings is whether the sales agents concerned were aware that OCBs were influencing their performance evaluations. If not, then this might be one factor which would help to explain perceptual differences in performance – sales staff seeing themselves as doing well because of a high volume of sales but getting a lower than expected evaluation from their managers because the latter have also been taking OCBs into account. Moreover, under such circumstances we might regard the managers' evaluations as at least unfair, if not downright dishonest.

This discussion of extra-role behaviours indicates one of the difficulties with the performance-as-behaviour view, namely mapping the behavioural domain. One attempt to do this has been made by Campbell (Campbell 1990; Campbell *et al.* 1993; Campbell *et al.* 1996) in his theory of performance. He presents a factor model of the components of performance and speculates that job performance can be described in terms of eight general factors, as shown in Table 5.2, with each factor containing a number of sub-factors.

Campbell argues that 'three of the factors – core task proficiency, demonstrated effort, and maintenance of personal discipline – are major performance components of *every* job' (Campbell *et al.* 1993: 49), although the others vary in the extent to which they apply to different jobs. Campbell suggests that other behavioural models can be accommodated within this framework – forms of organizational spontaneity and OCBs fit within various of the factors, for example (although they would, of course, cease to be voluntary behaviours if they were formally required). Also, much of the research on job behaviour can be related to the model. That said, the model remains speculative because, as yet, specific empirical tests are rare. However, from a practitioner point of view the eight factors may have value in serving as a kind of general framework to ensure that important aspects of job performance are not overlooked. For example, in designing a behaviourally based performance management system the dimensions that are identified might be compared with the Campbell framework to check that all important aspects are represented.

## Positive and negative behaviours

In their fifth factor (maintaining personal discipline) Campbell and his colleagues refer to the avoidance of certain kinds of negative behaviours. The idea of negative behaviours features rather more prominently in another performance-as-behaviour model (Murphy 1989, 1990; Murphy and Cleveland 1995), which identifies four main clusters of behaviours:

- task-orientated behaviours;
- maintaining interpersonal relations;

*Table 5.2* A taxonomy of major performance components (source: Campbell *et al.* 1993: 46–8)

1 *Job-specific task proficiency.* The first factor reflects the degree to which the individual can perform the core substantive or technical tasks that are central to the job. They are the job-specific performance behaviours that distinguish the substantive content of one job from another. . . .

2 *Non-job-specific task proficiency.* This factor reflects the situation that in virtually every organization, but perhaps not all, individuals are required to perform tasks or execute performance behaviours that are not specific to their particular job. . . .

3 *Written and oral communication task proficiency.* Many jobs in the workforce require the individual to make formal oral or written presentations to audiences that may vary from one to tens of thousands. For those jobs the proficiency with which one can write or speak, independent of the correctness of the subject matter, is a critical component of performance.

4 *Demonstrating effort.* The fourth factor is meant to be a direct reflection of the consistency of an individual's effort day by day, the frequency with which people will expend extra effort when required, and the willingness to keep working under adverse conditions. It is a reflection of the degree to which individuals commit themselves to all job tasks, work at a high level of intensity, and keep workng when it is cold, wet, or late.

5 *Maintaining personal discipline.* The fifth component is characterized by the degree to which negative behaviour such as alcohol and substance abuse at work, law or rules infractions, and excessive absenteeism are avoided.

6 *Facilitating peer and team performance.* Factor six is defined as the degree to which the individual supports his or her peers, helps them with job problems, and acts as a de facto trainer. It also encompasses how well an individual facilitates group functioning by being a good model, keeping the group goal-directed, and reinforcing participation by other group members. . . .

7 *Supervision/leadership.* Proficiency in the supervisory component includes all the behaviours directed at influencing the performance of subordinates through face-to-face interpersonal interaction and influence. Supervisors set goals for subordinates, they teach them more effective methods, they model the appropriate behaviours, and they reward or punish in appropriate ways. The distinction between this factor and the previous one is a distinction between peer leadership and supervisory leadership. Although modelling, goal-setting, coaching and providing reinforcement are elements in both factors, the belief here is that peer versus supervisor leadership implies significantly different determinants.

8 *Management/administration.* The eighth and last factor is intended to include the major elements in management that are distinct from direct supervision. It includes the performance behaviours directed at articulating goals for the unit or enterprise, organizing people and resources to work on them, monitoring progress, helping to solve problems or overcome crises that stand in the way of goal accomplishment, controlling expenditures, obtaining additional resources and representing the unit in dealing with other units.

- down-time behaviours (e.g. absenteeism, alcohol and drug abuse);
- destructive/hazardous behaviours (e.g. safety violations, sabotage).

The last two categories clearly comprise counter-productive behaviours that are to be avoided. Other kinds of (possibly) negative behaviour that need to be considered are identified by Van Dyne *et al.* (1995) in their discussion of extra-role behaviours. These are **whistle-blowing** and **principled organizational dissent**, the latter being defined as 'a protest and/or effort to change the organizational status quo because of a conscientious objection to current policy or practice' (Graham 1986; cited in Van Dyne *et al.* 1995: 228).

Recognition of these sorts of behaviours immediately points to one of the flaws with the conceptualizations of performance so far advanced, namely that they view performance solely through the eyes of the organization. In the same way that it is possible to adopt a stakeholder approach to considering organizational performance, one can see individual performance through many different sets of eyes. In recognition of this Ilgen and Hollenbeck (1991) refer to **job elements** (formally defined) and **role elements**. The latter arise out of negotiation/discussion/interaction between the job holder and another stakeholder (or stakeholders), such as a colleague or customer. The point here is that a job incumbent will be at the centre of a particular role set and it should not be assumed that the members of that role set will have the same expectations of the job holder's performance. This is a consideration to be borne in mind in using 360° feedback instruments – different evaluations of performance may be the result of differing expectations of what is required, not just different perceptions of what was done.

## COMPETENCES AND COMPETENCIES

In Britain we have come to associate job behaviours with competencies. There is much confusion about this term, and competences, mentioned in the previous chapter. As accounts (e.g. Tuxworth 1989) of the origins of the two terms show, this confusion seems to have been there right from the early days and it has been compounded by lack of definitional rigour (Collin 1989) and by loose use of terminology in much of the literature. This has been further exacerbated by the use of such terms as **core competence** and **distinctive competence** as properties of the organization, as discussed in Chapter 2 (see also Sparrow 1994, 1996).

So, we find the term **competences** being used to refer to distinctive features of the organization and to properties of jobs. Thus, in the UK we have come to associate competences with National Vocational Qualifications (NVQs) and the Management Charter Initiative (MCI) National Standards. The term **competencies**, on the other hand, more usually is interpreted in a person-related sense – but still with substantial disagreement. There seem to be two main conceptualizations.

## Competencies as behaviours

In contemporary UK practice a popular interpretation of a competency is that it is 'a dimension of overt, manifest behaviour that allows a person to perform competently' (Woodruffe 1992: 17). Some examples of competencies as defined by Woodruffe are given in Table 5.3. As Fletcher (1993) notes, Woodruffe's definition is very reminiscent of terminology that we have long associated with assessment centre practice: 'By *dimensions* we mean a cluster of behaviours that are specific, observable, and verifiable, and that can be reliably and logically classified together' (Thornton and Byham 1982: 117) – Table 5.4 gives some illustrations. Though this definition doesn't make any explicit reference to such ideas as job-relatedness, performance or effectiveness, all these are features of the job analysis procedure that Thornton and Byham advocate for identifying dimensions. For example, within their 'model job analysis procedure' they include the use of the critical incidents method (Flanagan 1954) for identifying behaviours 'associated with job success and failure' (Thornton and Byham 1982: 132). Thus, it is clear that dimensions are behaviours used in task accomplishment.

Hence, we could take the view that this behavioural interpretation of the term **competencies** is simply a replacement (or synonym) for **dimensions**. Indeed, it is hard to see how a strictly behavioural view of a competency differs to any significant extent from Campbell's definition of performance as behaviour! On the face of it, it looks as though there is at least one redundant concept in here somewhere. There is, however, another interpretation of

*Table 5.3* Examples of Woodruffian competencies (source: Woodruffe 1992: 18)

*Drive to achieve results*
Prepared to compromize to achieve a result; installs solutions within time frame; innovates or adapts existing procedures to ensure a result; takes on problems; suffers personal inconvenience to ensure problems are solved; comes forward with new ideas; sets challenging targets; sets out to win new business; sets own objectives; recognizes areas for self-development; acquires new skills and capabilities; accepts new challenges.

*Incisiveness to have a clear understanding*
Gets a clear overview of an issue; grasps information accurately; relates pieces of information; identifies causal relationships; gets to the heart of a problem; identifies the most productive lines of enquiry; appreciates all the variables affecting an issue; identifies limitations to information; adapts thinking in light of new information; tolerates and handles conflicting/ambiguous information and ideas.

*Sensitivity to others' viewpoints*
Listens to others' viewpoints; adapts to other person; takes account of others' needs; shows empathy in oral and written communications; aware of others' expectations.

---

*Table 5.4* Behavioural dimensions (source: Thornton and Byham 1982: 139–40)

| | |
|---|---|
| *Sensitivity* | Actions that indicate a consideration for the feelings and needs of others. |
| *Initiative* | Active attempts to influence events to achieve goals; self-starting rather than passive acceptance. Taking action to achieve goals beyond those called for; originating action. |
| *Analysis* | Identifying problems, securing relevant information, relating data from different sources, and identifying possible causes of problems. |

what a competency is. To explore this we need to go back to the earlier literature which first brought the term to prominence.

## Competencies as underlying characteristics of the person

What brought the term competency into popular use, particularly in the management development world, was *The Competent Manager*, the book authored by Richard Boyatzis (1982), although the term was in use for some years previously. This is the conceptualization that we associate with the McBer consultancy and, as the definition in Box 5.2 makes clear, we are very much in the realm

Box 5.2    **Definition of a competency as an underlying characteristic of the person**

A competency is an *underlying characteristic* of an individual that is *causally related* to *criterion-referenced effective and/or superior performance* in a job or situation.

- *Underlying characteristic* means the competency is a fairly deep and enduring part of a person's personality and can predict behaviour in a wide variety of situations and job tasks.
- *Causally related* means that a competency *causes* or *predicts* behaviour and performance.
- *Criterion-referenced* means that the competency actually predicts who does something well or poorly, as measured on a *specific criterion* or standard. Examples of criteria are the dollar volume of sales for salespeople or the number of clients who stay 'dry' for alcohol-abuse counsellors. [Note the results/outputs view of performance that is taken here]

(source: Spencer and Spencer 1993: 9)

Competencies can be motives, traits, self-concepts, attitudes or values, content knowledge, or cognitive or behavioural skills – any individual characteristic that can be measured or counted reliably and that can be shown to differentiate significantly between superior and average performers, or between effective and ineffective performers. The following definitions of the above characteristics may be given:

- *Motive:* the underlying need or thought pattern that drives, directs and selects an individual's behaviour; e.g. the need for achievement.
- *Trait:* a general disposition to behave or respond in a certain way; for instance with self-confidence, self-control, stress resistance or 'hardiness'.
- *Self-concept:* (attitudes or values) measured by respondent tests that ask people what they value, what they think they do or are interested in doing.

- *Content knowledge:* of facts or procedures, either technical (how to trouble-shoot a defective computer) or interpersonal (techniques for effective feedback), as measured by respondent tests.
- *Cognitive and behavioural skills:* either covert (e.g. deductive or inductive reasoning) or observable (e.g. active listening skills).

(source: Hooghiemstra 1992: 28)

---

Box 5.3    **An example of a McBer competency**

**Information seeking**
An underlying curiosity, a desire to know more about things, people or issues drives Information Seeking. Information Seeking implies making an effort to get more information, not accepting situations 'at face value'.

**Information-seeking scale**
Level Behavioural Description

0    *None.* Does not seek additional information about a situation, other than what has been given.

1    *Asks questions.* Asks direct questions of immediately available people (or people who are directly involved in the situation even if not physically present), consults available resources. . . .

6    *Uses own ongoing systems.* Has personally established ongoing systems or habits for various kinds of information gathering (may include 'management by walking around', regular information meetings, etc., if these are specifically to gather information).

7    *Involves others.* Involves others who would not normally be involved and gets them to seek out information.

(Intermediate points 2 to 5 also are similarly defined.)

(source: Spencer and Spencer 1993: 34–5)

of fundamental properties of the person – traits, motives and the like – in other words, what people *are*, not simply what they do. Moreover, it is not just any underlying characteristics that we are concerned with – rather, ones that are **causally related** to superior job performance (this being defined in terms of results/outputs). (Box 5.3 gives an illustration of how this sort of a competency is expressed in terms of 'a narrative definition plus three to six *behavioural indicators*, or specific behavioural ways of demonstrating the competency in the job' (Spencer and Spencer 1993: 19).) In other words, competencies, according to this conception, are a determinant or cause of performance, not performance (that is, results/outputs) itself.

The **criterion-referenced causality** element of the definition lends this conceptualization of competencies some distinctiveness. We should note, however, that at least two levels of criteria are applied: this is illustrated by the distinction drawn by the McBer group between **threshold competencies** and **differentiating competencies**. The latter distinguish between average and superior performers, whereas the former are competencies that everyone needs to do the job to a minimally adequate standard; they don't differentiate, in other words. A similar distinction is drawn by Schroder (1989) between **basic** and **high-performance** competencies. Some (Warr and Conner 1992) also identify a third, more **elementary**, level of criterion-referencing and this leads them on to an elaborated definition of a job competency as: 'A set of behaviours, knowledge, thought processes, and/or attitudes, which are likely to be reflected in job performance that reaches a defined elementary, basic or high-performance standard' (1992: 99).

The Warr and Conner and McBer definitions share a number of features in common. First, both are criterion-referenced: whereas Warr and Conner are more explicit about different criterion levels, the McBer approach specifies the definition of performance as outputs/results. This has implications for practice – if we adopt this model we need to distinguish different levels of performance (output) when we carry out our studies to determine what competencies are required to perform a job or, more probably, a family of jobs. Second, both include the idea of causality, although this is expressed in a stronger way in the McBer definition. Third, both refer to underlying characteristics of the person as well as to behaviours.

It is this last point which sets this definition apart from the seemingly behavioural approach taken by Woodruffe. Woodruffe objects to the McBer definition on the grounds that it 'seems to cover pretty well anything' (1991: 30). Indeed so, and mixing up traits, attitudes, thought processes and behaviours would seem to be unhelpful, particularly from a theoretical point of view. Thus, Woodruffe sees behaviourally defined competencies as offering 'a chance to get away from the muddle of traits and motives' (1991: 30). However, if we look at some of Woodruffe's competencies (Table 5.3) we see that the more basic characteristics of the person are implied: 'preparedness to compromise' – true enough we recognize this in behaviour that is displayed, but surely this implies a dispositional characteristic. 'Takes on problems', 'suffers personal inconvenience', 'shows empathy', 'gets to the heart of a problem', 'identifies limitations to information' – here again, these all imply dispositional, attitudinal and similar underlying characteristics of the person. Thus, when we look at examples of Woodruffe's competencies it is clear that they include more than is conveyed by his definition: they are not so exclusively behavioural after all.

Cooper and Robertson develop this as a general point by drawing attention to the non-behavioural nature of many competencies: 'Behaviour needs to be defined unambiguously and it must be observable. Most of the commonly used competencies are not sufficiently specific or observable to be classed as behaviours' (1995: 26). Of course, we might see this as a criticism of the short narrative definitions of competencies that are typically used – and many of the examples throughout this chapter indicate that the criticism is well founded. However, we should note that there are instances of more specific behavioural scales being used, as we saw in Box 5.3, and later in the chapter I will give examples of positive and negative behavioural indicators. That said, it is clear that many competency definitions mix up behaviours and personal attributes as well as referring to desired results.

In Chapter 4 I drew attention to the danger of an undue focus on outputs/results, for example detracting from the means by which results are accomplished – the behaviours that may contribute to a sale. Similarly, undue focus on behaviours runs the risk of denying the importance of what the person is. On these grounds the broader view of competencies, whether that of the McBer group or that of Warr and Conner, might be preferred. It recognizes that aspects of the person, such as personality, are important for job performance, whether one defines this as behaviour or results.

One of the advantages of this broader conception of job competencies has to do with what Warr and Conner refer to as 'syndromes' or 'important combinations' of characteristics. Thus, competencies more broadly defined may be seen as such 'syndromes'. In other words, though we might recognize a competency such as 'drive to achieve results' through its behavioural manifestations, those behaviours are a reflection of some important combination of personal attributes which we would run the risk of ignoring if we were to concentrate solely on behaviours. Moreover, the broader definition of a competency gives added meaning which may help to distinguish the term competencies from the term behaviours. The elements of **causality** and **criterion-relatedness** may also give the term some distinctiveness.

However, it is far from clear that the term is used at all consistently: it has 'a variety of meanings and no accepted consensus on its definition has emerged' (Cockerill 1995: 86). Cockerill's own definition, therefore, muddies the waters even more: 'the relatively stable behaviours which create continuously the processes that enable the organization to learn, adapt to new environmental demands, and change the environment so that it is better suited to the needs of stakeholders' (1995: 86). This brings us back to an organizational perspective – the idea of a distinctive capability possessed by the organization.

## EXPRESSING PERFORMANCE REQUIREMENTS AS BEHAVIOURS

If we were to trace the history of appraisal practice we would see that a behavioural interpretation of performance has long been evident. Though this is true of the UK it is even more so for North America, as evidenced, for example, by the decades of research and practitioner interest in behavioural forms of performance rating – behaviourally anchored rating scales (BARS), behavioural observation scales (BOS), behavioural expectation scales (BES). (For descriptions of these see any one of Bailey 1983; Fletcher 1993; Fletcher and Williams 1992; Cardy and Dobbins

1994; Murphy and Cleveland 1995; Latham and Wexley 1994). These sorts of scales seem not to have been especially popular in British appraisal practice, although examples of behaviourally anchored scales are to be found in assessment/development centres.

Indeed, given the results emphasis in performance management practice in the UK today we might expect there to be relatively little interest in the behavioural aspects of performance. Some evidence suggests that this might be so, although the position isn't completely clear. For example, the IMS survey of performance management practice (Institute of Personnel Management 1992) revealed that relatively few organizations use lists of behavioural competences for expressing performance requirements. And the Industrial Society (1994) found that fewer than 10 per cent of the thousand or so respondents to their survey claimed to use competencies. On the other hand, research by the CBI/Hay (quoted by Sparrow 1996) indicates that some 45 per cent of UK firms are at least thinking about linking rewards to competencies, suggesting perhaps some increase in this means of expressing performance requirements.

But, if these figures truly reflect the extent of interest in behavioural aspects of performance, then performance management practice surely is seriously deficient in ignoring the essence of what people contribute to their jobs. To illustrate the point, here are some examples of research that has highlighted the importance of job behaviours.

## Identifying behavioural dimensions of performance

First, let's consider the now substantial body of work carried out by the McBer group. This work is important, if only because of its extent, although, as I will show below, it is open to challenge on methodological grounds. Much of it is summarized by Spencer and Spencer (1993), who present the McBer Competency Dictionary – essentially a catalogue of twenty-one generic competencies common to the several hundred jobs/professions/occupations studied by McBer consultants over the years. Also included are competency models for a range of jobs, e.g. salespeople, helping and human service workers, managers. Taken as a whole, then, what we have here is a statement of the competencies (and their behavioural manifestations) linked with effective/superior performance (output/results) in a wide range of jobs. By way of illustration,

Table 5.5 summarizes the generic competency model for helping and human service professionals. As we saw in Box 5.3, each of these competencies has a narrative definition with one or more scaled behavioural indicators.

One of the important features of the McBer model is the criterion-relatedness of the competencies. But this cannot go unquestioned. Remember that the McBer conception of performance uses measures of outputs/results as criteria of effectiveness. The identification of these is crucial:

> The first and most important step in a competency study is to identify the criteria or measures that define superior or effective performance in the job to be studied. Ideal criteria are 'hard' outcome measures, such as sales or profit data for business managers, or patents and publications for research scientists. For military officers, good criteria would be unit performance outcomes, such as combat inspection scores or reenlistment

*Table 5.5* The McBer generic competency model for helping and human service workers (abbreviated from Spencer and Spencer 1993: 186–7)

| Weight | Competency |
| --- | --- |
| XXXXX | Impact and influence |
| XXXXX | Developing others |
| XXXX | Interpersonal understanding |
| XXX | Self-confidence |
| XXX | Self-control |
| XXX | Other personal effectiveness competencies (e.g. accurate self-assessment, affiliative interest – genuinely likes people) |
| XXX | Professional expertise |
| XXX | Customer service orientation |
| XXX | Teamwork and cooperation |
| XXX | Analytical thinking |
| XX | Conceptual thinking |
| XX | Initiative |
| XX | Flexibility |
| XX | Directiveness/assertiveness |

'Weight' refers to the relative frequency with which each competency distinguishes superior from average performers.

rates. For human service workers, the best criteria are *client* outcomes. For example, for alcoholism counselors the best measure of performance is percentage of clients who are still 'dry', regularly employed, and have had no arrests for drunkenness in the year following counseling.

(Spencer and Spencer 1993: 94)

These criteria are then used to identify:

a clear group of superstars and a comparison group of average performers. A third group of poor (ineffective or incompetent) performers can also be identified if the purpose of the study is to establish competency levels that predict minimal success in a job.

(Spencer and Spencer 1993: 96)

The other steps in the McBer method are summarized in Figure 5.1.

But are the sorts of examples given by Spencer and Spencer really 'ideal' or 'good' criteria? Such criteria attribute to individual performers outputs or results which may not be wholly within their control. So, in the case of counselling it is of course possible that the behaviour of the counsellor has some impact on the result of the counselling process – but so do characteristics of the person being counselled, as well as the circumstances in which they find themselves. This is a general point about results and, as we saw earlier, it is used as part of the argument against regarding output as performance. Is it proper, therefore, to use such criteria as indicators of individual effectiveness? On the other hand, can we *not* use them? We might take the view that we have no choice in the matter. Schmidt (1993) draws attention to this difficulty in his critique of Campbell's behavioural model. The essence of Schmidt's argument is that it is often difficult to interpret the significance or meaning of behaviour in itself – there are times when we need results in order to do this:

Campbell, McCloy and Oppler correctly state that consequences and results are often not fully under the control of the individual. That is true. But we may have to use results and consequences anyway; we may have no choice. In many cases, the best we can do is try to make intelligent judgements about the extent to which specific individuals are responsible for observed outcomes.

(Schmidt 1993: 504–5)

*Figure 5.1* The McBer job competency assessment process (source: Spencer and Spencer 1993)

So, from a conceptual point of view we might reasonably choose to define performance in terms of behaviour, and doing so helps to distinguish the relationship between behaviour and results. But it is obvious that we can't dispense with outputs and results. As is evident from the behavioural models, results provide the context – they make clear what behaviour should be directed towards. And in so doing they help to avoid the **activity trap** that I referred to in the previous chapter.

But as we saw earlier, it is equally clear that an excessive focus on outputs is undesirable. So, in managing performance we need *both* results *and* behaviour.

However, in using results/outputs as criteria we must be sure that they satisfy the requirements of 'good' criteria (Table 5.6): this is partly an issue of measurement accuracy and partly an issue of fairness. The determination of output-based criteria for jobs is far from problem-free; not only does this present a difficulty in using outputs for performance management purposes but it also

*Table 5.6* Requirements for good performance criteria (source: Altink *et al.* 1997: 293)

| | |
|---|---|
| *Reliable measurable* | Should measure behaviours and outcomes in an objective manner |
| *Content valid* | Rationally related to the job performance activities |
| *Defined specific* | Cover identifiable behaviours and outcomes |
| *Independent* | Important behaviours and outcomes should be included in a comprehensive criterion |
| *Non-overlapping* | Criteria should not overlap |
| *Comprehensive* | No important behaviours or outcomes should be omitted |
| *Accessible* | Criteria should be phrased and named in a way that is comprehensible |
| *Compatible* | Criteria should fit in with an organization's goals and culture |
| *Up to date* | Criteria should be regularly reviewed in reponse to organizational change |

represents a threat to the methodological adequacy of competency research. Competencies identified via the McBer method will only be as good as the criteria that are used: if these are deficient, then the competencies will be deficient too.

As another illustration of research showing the importance of a behavioural perspective on performance let me give an example from a high-involvement work organization using advanced manufacturing technology (Parker *et al.* 1994). I have included this example because it is methodologically rigorous, and, though it uses methods different from the McBer approach, the end result is a set of dimensions which are very similar in kind to McBer competencies. Box 5.4 describes the company briefly, explains how the dimensions of performance effectiveness were identified and illustrates their nature.

---

**Box 5.4   Dimensions of performance effectiveness in a high-involvement work organization**

**The company**
An electronics company 'which designs, manufactures and installs equipment to measure, regulate, and control operations in such process industries as chemicals, nuclear power, and oil'.

**How the dimensions of performance effectiveness were identified**
The study was carried out in the assembly department and sought to identify dimensions of performance effectiveness for shop-floor staff.

The researchers used the repertory grid method with shop-floor operators as elements. The grids were administered to seven staff in managerial and supervisory roles. The usual method of triads was used to elicit constructs. After elicitation participants were asked to rate their elements (operators) on each construct (on a five-point scale ranging from high to low performer) and on an overall performance scale. The grids generated 129 constructs.

---

Grids were subjected to principal components analysis to identify 'those constructs which were most closely associated with elements of performance effectiveness'. A 'grounded theory' approach then was used to classify into dimensions the eighty constructs deriving from the principal components analysis. Finally, the dimensions identified were validated by feeding back to and discussing with production management staff. This led to certain of the dimensions being merged.

### Dimensions of performance effectiveness
The process described above led to four higher-order dimensions being identified, certain of which contained several dimensions of performance effectivenes. These are summarized below:

*Process ownership*
1   Ownership of the production process
2   Goal/task-oriented
3   Multi-skilled/broad knowledge of the process

*Social skills*
1   Social confidence
2   Effectiveness of communication with and across group boundaries
3   Team-working and co-operation

*Personal style*
1   Flexibility/adaptability
2   Systematic/planful

*Loss prevention*
1   Loss prevention: characterizes an individual who is organized; keeps a tidy work area and knows where everything is; shows good attention to detail; is consistent in quality and output; and exhibits good housekeeping skills.

Each of the dimensions of effectiveness is defined in the manner shown above for 'loss prevention'.

(source: summarized from Parker *et al.* 1994: 5, 8, 11)

In this approach we have no independent criterion or criteria of effectiveness – the dimensions themselves are what is meant by effective performance. More precisely we might see the dimensions as 'mental models', that is, constructions of operator characteristics which are perceived to be effective. We should also note that in this case the perceptions are those of managers and supervisors. Shop-floor operators may or may not share these perceptions. A fuller picture would be obtained by including operators as study participants, as Parker *et al.* (1994) themselves recognize. This is important from a practical point of view in the context of 360° appraisal, for example – though it may be helpful to involve others in measuring performance, the value of doing so may be reduced if those others have not had a hand in defining what performance is to be measured in the first place.

### Forward-looking requirements

Let me give one more example which adopts different methods from the previous two but which shares the feature of methodological rigour. Though the context in this example was selection, the approach taken is no less relevant for performance management. Box 5.5 summarizes what was done. At heart, the approach exemplifies the traditional approach to job analysis – study the job and deduce required person characteristics. But a major difficulty with this is that is backward-looking – at best it takes jobs as they are today. Schneider and his co-workers attempt to anticipate what might be required for the future.

---

**Box 5.5  A future-orientated approach to identifying behavioural dimensions of performance**

*Task analysis*
Based on interviews/group discussions with incumbents and supervisors and through observation. This ascertains '(1) the goals of the job and (2) the tasks that need to be accomplished for the goals to be met'. These tasks are adminstered in a survey to gather quantitative information on the criticality/importance of each task and the relatve amount of time spent on each. The tasks are the basis of line manager ratings of employee effectiveness.

---

*Personal attributes analysis*
What attributes of the person are required to carry out the tasks that have been identified? Again, interviews/group discussions (with incumbents/supervisors) are used to identify required knowledge, skills and abilities, which are used to compile a questionnaire. The administration of this requires each attribute to be rated, amongst other things, on its importance for effective job performance.

*Anticipating the future*
The foregoing steps are typical of much job analysis practice as advocated in North American literature. But a distinctive feature of the approach adopted by Schneider and his co-workers is the attempt to anticipate future strategic demands and incorporate these in the specification of person attributes:

> To incorporate strategic issues into a 'present' job analysis we first gather information about the kinds of issues in the job, the company, and/or the larger environment that may affect the job in the future. This is accomplished in a workshop composed of subject matter experts (e.g., job incumbents, supervisors, managers, human resource staff, strategic planners) and job analysts. The participants might also include experts in a relevant technical field, economists, demographers, and so forth, depending on the specific job of interest.

In the light of this information the tasks identified earlier are re-rated in terms of importance and time spent. Also, new tasks may be added. The personal attributes similarly are re-rated, again with the possibility of new ones being added.

Comparative analysis of the present and future profiles is likely to reveal points of similarity and points of difference. This may necessitate changes to personnel procedures, such as selection or training.

(source: summarized from Schneider and Konz 1989: 53 and Schneider and Schechter 1991: 221)

From the point of view of performance management the comparative analysis of present-day and future job tasks may reveal differences which will require a range of responses. For example, changes to job design or work organization, or perhaps even more substantial structural reorganization, may be required. Where new skills are indicated there may be implications for selection or training; it also is possible that a developmental approach to performance management will allow at least some needed personal attributes to be developed through the job itself.

The account by Schneider and Konz (1989) is one of the few descriptions that we have of a future-oriented approach. Sparrow and Boam (1992) and Shackleton (1992) discuss forward-looking competency profiles and refer to various tools, such as visioning workshops and business scenarios, which may play a part in identifying such profiles. These sorts of activities involve substantial effort – the equivalent of two person years went into the development of scenarios used by British Airways to inform their business planning (Moyer 1996) – so they are unlikely to be used simply to identify skills etc. required for the future.

Though anticipating the future is highly speculative, the application of structured tools may help to bring some rigour to the process. Even so, there must be some threat to the validity of forward-looking profiles. But we need to balance against this the threat to validity that comes from an over-reliance on traditional backward-looking approaches to job analysis – the risk I mentioned above, that of ending up with a picture of jobs (and associated behavioural requirements) as they are today or, worse, as they were.

A number of important practical points arise from the three examples that I have given. One is that they all illustrate rigorous, systematic methods to identify the behaviours that are relevant to the job(s) in question. For any performance management system which seeks to incorporate behaviours this is essential. Second, the examples show that many methods are available for use – indeed it is essential to adopt multiple methods. Third, it is no less essential to draw on multiple sources – at the very least, job incumbents and supervisors, and others (e.g. customers, co-workers) may have a part to play too. Such involvement is important on two grounds. One is that it is consistent with the participative philosophy advocated for performance management. The other is that a participative approach generally is seen as having many process benefits (e.g. Sparrow 1994), such as generating ownership of the behaviours that are identified. Fourth, the examples have not illustrated the analysis of single jobs but, rather, categories or families of jobs.

*Table 5.7* Competencies for job families in changing environments I: new managerial roles (source: Pearn 1992)

---

**Competencies for new managerial roles**
I *Achieving results*
- Planning and organizing
- Focus on outcomes
- Continuous improvement
- Monitoring and evaluating

II *Analysing and deciding*
- Broad-based thinking
- Analytical thinking
- Understanding business
- Objective decision-making

III *Working with people*
- Rational persuasion
- Team-oriented working
- Interpersonal effectiveness
- Flexible management style

As well as a brief definition of each competency there are more specific positive and negative behavioural indicators, for example:

**Continuous improvement**: constantly seeks and brings about better/improved ways of working in both short and longer term.

*Positive indicators*
- Seeks advice from others, e.g. team, customers, suppliers, service departments
- Proposals aimed at permanent solution not just quick fix
- Involves team at all stages
- Sees potential for reaching and maintaining higher standards

*Contra-indicators*
- Proposes short-term solutions without considering long-term consequences
- Fails to consult others or to build on their contributions
- Focuses on only one or two opportunities for improvement
- Does not recognize alternative ways of tackling problems, e.g. special project team, quality circles

---

Many of the case studies that have been published in recent years have been of models of competencies for job families. For example, in Glaxo Manufacturing Services (Pearn 1992) the interest was in three new managerial roles; Shackleton (1992) describes the development of competencies required for the future by partners in an accountancy organization – these models are shown in Tables 5.7 and 5.8. A feature of both these models is an organizational context of change.

*Table 5.8* Competencies for job families in changing environments II: partners in an accountancy practice (source: Shackleton 1992: 165–6)

1    *Identifying selling opportunities.* Being alert to and acting on indications of opportunities for expansion of existing business into new areas of the client company and/or diversification into new categories of business.
2    *Understanding the client/colleague in their own terms.* Active listening, clarifying, reflecting back the content and feeling behind statements, avoiding jargon and misinterpretation.
3    *Commercial awareness.* Using questions and statements to indicate an understanding of the totality of the business, i.e. strategy, marketing, competition, etc., as well as its financial structure.
4    *Flexibility.* Modifying own approach or style in order to achieve set goals.
5    *Communicating persuasively and effectively.* Clear and fluent oral communication of ideas with persuasive impact on the listener; clear, concise written communication.
6    *Goal-setting.* Setting realistic targets, quantifiable or behavioural, that are well defined, specific and measurable.
7    *Encouraging and building on ideas.* Assessing ideas objectively and building on them; encouraging (verbally and non-verbally) others to contribute; avoiding irrational criticism.
8    *Giving feedback.* Commenting on both the negative and positive aspects of others' behaviour and performance in a clear, balanced and constructive way.
9    *Delegating.* Effective use of colleagues, knowing when, how and to whom to delegate responsibility.
10   *Leadership.* Ability to guide and direct individuals or groups towards the achievement of objectives; taking the initiative.
11   *Helping groups to achieve consensus.* Looking for common ground; mediating between opposing views; being prepared to compromise on own views (after full discussion) for sake of group

# A CONCLUDING COMMENT

This, and the preceding chapter, have illustrated the ambiguity of the term performance: there is far from unanimous agreement about what it means. Competencies only add to the confusion. In everyday parlance the word performance is used in a loose way to embrace both outputs and behaviours. This is unhelpful from a theoretical point of view because it fails to recognize the causal relationship between behaviours and results; it also fails to recognize that it is not just the contribution of the individual that brings about results. Loose use of the term is also unhelpful because outputs and behaviours may require different kinds of performance management interventions.

The term competencies has come to be widely used in recent years but here again there is enormous confusion. Partly this stems from the existence of another term – competences. Often it is far from clear how the one term or the other is being used in everyday organizational parlance. Sometimes the two terms are simply used as synonyms. However, some attempts have been made to distinguish different meanings. Thus we find that 'competences' is used in two senses, denoting distinctive properties of the organization or job requirements. So far as 'competencies' are concerned, one meaning places emphasis on the personal attributes which underlie behaviour – what people are; a second interpretation concentrates on the clusters of related behaviours – that is, what people do. But if we define competencies in behaviour terms, how, then, does this usage differ significantly from the earlier term 'dimensions'? Indeed, does this behavioural interpretation differ all that much from the conception of performance as behaviour? I'll explore this issue a little more in the next chapter in considering the causes of performance.

# 6 *Individual performance*
## *Determinants*

So, we have two interdependent conceptions of individual performance. We need to embrace both if we are to manage what employees do and achieve at work. We also need to understand the causes or determinants of employee performance as these have implications for performance management interventions. This is far from straightforward and in many respects our present understanding remains decidedly rudimentary.

Early models were vague as to the nature of performance but saw it as a function of the individual's ability and motivation, and this idea remains prominent in contemporary theories. However, recent theories have considerably elaborated the basic proposition. One important illustration of this is the theory of performance put forward by Campbell (Campbell 1990; Campbell *et al.* 1993; Campbell *et al.* 1996) and his colleagues.

## A THEORY OF PERFORMANCE AS BEHAVIOUR

We have already seen in Chapter 5 that Campbell defines performance in terms of goal-relevant behaviour and he proposes that this may be categorized into eight main factors or components. But what determines behaviour? In Campbell's view there are three major **determinants**:

1 Declarative knowledge, that is, knowledge about facts and things (knowing *what* to do).
2 Procedural knowledge and skill.

$$PC_i^a = f \begin{bmatrix} Declarative & Procedural\ Knowledge & \\ Knowledge\ (DK) \times & and\ Skill\ (PKS) & \times\ Motivation\ (M) \end{bmatrix}$$

| | | |
|---|---|---|
| Facts | Cognitive skill | Choice to perform |
| Principles | Psychomotor skill | Level of effort |
| Goals | Physical skill | Persistence of effort |
| Self-knowledge | Self-management skill | |
| | Interpersonal skill | |

$i = 1,2, \ldots , k$ performance components

*Predictors of Performance Determinants*[b]

$DK = f$[(ability, personality, interests), (education, training, experience), (aptitude/treatment interactions)]

$PKS = f$[(ability, personality, interests), (education, training, practice, experience), (aptitude/treatment interactions)]

$M = f$(whatever independent variables are stipulated by your favourite motivation theory)

*Note*: This entire scheme can be repeated for educational performance, training performance and laboratory task performance.
[a] Obviously, performance differences can also be produced by situational effects such as the quality of equipment, degree of staff support or nature of the working conditions. For purposes of this model of performance, these conditionals are assumed to be held constant (experimentally, statistically or judgementally).
[b] Individual differences, learning and motivational manipulations can only influence performance by increasing declarative knowledge or procedural skill or by influencing the three choices (that is, influencing motivation).

*Figure 6.1* Determinants of job performance: knowledge, skill and motivation (source: Campbell *et al.* 1993)

3  Motivation – defined as choice behaviour, that is:
  • the choice to perform (expend effort);
  • choice of level of effort to expend;
  • choice to persist over time in the expenditure of that level of effort.

These determinants are portrayed diagrammatically in Figure 6.1.
  So, what is being proposed here is that the *direct* cause of what people do (their performance) is some function of knowledge,

skill and motivation. The precise combination is unknown as the effects of personal factors are difficult to disentangle.

Underlying these three determinants are certain **predictors** or **antecedents**. Campbell does not elaborate on these but it is clear that he is referring to three distinct sets of antecedent – attributes of the individual, their prior learning experience and interactions between the two. In other words, the knowledge and skill that employees have are a function of factors that are internal to the person (their abilities and traits, etc.) and of factors external to them, such as their education, the training they have received, etc. These antecedent factors thus are seen as having an **indirect** influence on performance (behaviour). Aspects of the work context also come into this category of indirect factors, as I shall come on to discuss in a moment.

## Individual differences as antecedents

The role of individual difference variables in relation to performance remains controversial in some respects. Though there is some agreement (Eysenck 1994; Cooper and Robertson 1995) that intelligence and personality are the two main domains of individual difference that are of most interest to psychologists, there is considerable disagreement as to the nature and scope of the two terms.

### Intelligence

What is intelligence? Cognitive ability – such as reasoning – remains at the heart of many theories but some writers have put forward wider-ranging models; Gardner (1983), for example, has proposed a theory of multiple intelligence which includes, as well as more traditional ideas, such notions as musical intelligence and interpersonal intelligence. Moreover, as Sternberg (1990) has shown, the lay person also sees an element of social competence in intelligence. Such broadening is reflected in some of the more modern theories through such ideas as **practical intelligence** (which emphasizes competence; Sternberg and Wagner 1986) and **tacit knowledge** (eg, Sternberg 1994) – in terms of Campbell's model, of course, both of these concepts would be seen as determinants rather than antecedents. Also, in recent years interest has developed in such aspects of intellectual functioning as cognitive style (e.g., Streufert and Nogami 1989; Warr and Conner

1992), thereby blurring the distinction between personality and intelligence. However, for the most part these newer ideas have yet to have much impact in practice. The long-standing **factor theories** of general mental ability and more specific abilities continue to dominate.

We have evidence that ability tests (when properly constructed, chosen and used) do predict job performance (as measured using a range of indicators) across a wide range of jobs (see Cooper and Robertson 1995 for a brief review). What remains a matter of dispute is *why* such tests predict. One explanation (e.g. Anderson 1992, contends that what intelligence tests measure is the speed with which individuals process information. Though theoretically interesting, this notion does not take us very far as, for practical purposes, we don't really have direct measures of information processing. At best, therefore, conventional tests are some proxy measure of underlying processing capability. Indeed, many tests of very specific abilities are in effect measures of declarative or procedural knowledge (skill). If, for example, we consider the sorts of paper and pencil test that may be used in clerical selection then we find tests of spelling, grammar, arithmetic, etc. In other words, with these sorts of tests we measure what people know and their knowledge of how to do things.

## Personality

Still more controversial is the nature of personality. One of the problems here is that there are many conceptions of personality, although, as with intelligence, in work settings it is the factor or **trait** conception which predominates. So, if we go to a test publisher wanting to buy a personality questionnaire the likelihood is that we will be offered something that measures traits. But this concept is itself controversial. What exactly is a trait? How broadly is the concept to be defined? How many traits do we need to be able to describe personality? Are traits simply descriptions or do they have explanatory value as well? These issues continue to rage (for recent reviews, see Hogan 1991; Mount and Barrick 1995; Schneider and Hough 1995; Hough and Schneider 1996).

For example, some (e.g., Digman 1990; Goldberg 1993) claim that there is today a general consensus that the factor structure of personality may be described in terms of five factors:

- neuroticism (emotional stability) – emotional, tense, insecure, nervous, easily upset (at the negative end of the factor);
- extraversion – sociable, talkative, energetic;
- openness to experience – imaginative, curious;
- agreeableness – good-natured, co-operative, caring, courteous;
- conscientiousness (sometimes referred to as **will to achieve** or **dependability**) – hardworking, achievement-oriented, persevering, planful, responsible, careful.

The adequacy of the five-factor model (FFM) is a matter of some dispute and some authorities (e.g., Hough and Schneider 1996) have argued for different classification schemes with a slightly larger number of factors. For present purposes, however, I will use the FFM to illustrate something of the demonstrated relationships between personality and performance. To take just one example, various studies (Mount and Barrick 1995; Schneider and Hough 1995) have shown an association between measures of **conscientiousness** and different indicators of job performance, such as employee reliability, personal discipline and effort. The conscientiousness factor is of particular interest because it is linked with motivational determinants of performance. In the same way that the boundaries between the intelligence and personality domains have become blurred, so too have those between personality and motives. If we take a broad view of personality as comprising dispositional characteristics generally, then motives (such as the need for achievement, goal-orientation, the need for power, etc.) and other attributes such as values, interests, self-efficacy, etc. fall within this domain.

For the most part the interest in personality–performance relationships continues to fall within the selection area; in other words, the interest is in using measures of personality to predict job performance. This has had rather a chequered history. Numerous reviews (e.g., Guion and Gottier 1965; Adler and Weiss 1988) drew somewhat unoptimistic conclusions about personality–performance relationships. In the 1990s, however, several studies have appeared which take a more positive line and today there is considerable advocacy of a construct-oriented approach (e.g., Schneider and Hough 1995; Robertson 1994):

> when investigators carefully conceptualize the role of personality vis-à-vis the criterion domain(s) of interest, when they

select appropriate, construct valid measures based on a job analysis, or when they systematically develop new measures built around a construct model of effectiveness, personality attributes are found to be relevant and potent predictors.

(Klimoski 1993: 112–13)

Examples of new work-related measures that have been developed in recent years include 'integrity' or 'honesty' tests (Ones *et al.* 1993) and 'customer service orientation' (see Schneider and Hough 1995). Such tests measure 'compound personality variables' (Hough and Schneider 1996) – that is, contructs that have been synthesized from some combination of personality traits that are believed to predict the work-related criterion of interest. Courtesy, helpfulness, co-operativeness and pleasantness, for example, all are qualities that we might wish to measure in assessing service orientation.

As well as measures of such trait syndromes, research shows that certain aspects of performance (for example such behaviours as demonstrating effort and contextual performance) may be susceptible to prediction by questionnaire measures of personality traits. But even when a construct-related approach is taken, the magnitude of the association (as indicated by correlation coefficients) between personality measures and performance indicators remains of a modest order (e.g., Robertson and Kinder 1993; Schneider and Hough 1995). In part, this may be because of deficiencies in our measures – both personality questionnaires and the independent criterion measures (such as a line manager's ratings). And, as with intelligence, there is the question of what is actually being measured. Many personality questionnaires use behavioural statements as their items – to this extent, therefore, we are merely using one representation of behaviour to predict actual behaviour in the workplace.

## The problem of competencies

The problem, which stems from the ambiguity of the concept, has to do with where, if at all, competencies fit within a theory of performance. If we take a behavioural view, like Woodruffe's (1992), then the fit is apparently straightforward: competencies are job-relevant behaviours and as such they seem to be no different from Campbell's conception of performance, that is:

performance ≡ behaviour ≡ competencies. Yet, as we saw in the previous chapter, there are reasons for questioning the behavioural view – not least of which is that the definitions of many competencies imply much more than behaviours.

The Spencer and Spencer (1993) and Warr and Conner (1992) definitions, on the other hand, do see a place for personal characteristics. This is illustrated by the flow diagram (from Spencer and Spencer 1993) shown in Figure 6.2. This model doesn't distinguish between antecedents (predictors) and determinants in the way that Campbell does. Rather, personal characteristics generally are seen as direct predictors of behaviour, the one exception to this being skill, which seems to be regarded as synonymous with behaviour in the McBer model. All this reinforces the indistinct nature of competencies. We might take the view that it may be helpful to see competencies as a middle-order variable of some kind – that is, as clusters of behaviours signifying some syndrome of personal characteristics (rather like the compound traits men-

*Figure 6.2* Competency causal flow model (source: Spencer and Spencer 1993)

tioned earlier, but embracing a wider range of attributes) that are required to achieve some defined level of output. But do we really need this extra term, especially when our lexicon of person- and behaviour-related terms is already more than replete?

Irrespective of this issue of where (if at all) competencies fit within a theory of performance, it remains the case that the person-centered explanations are deficient because they pay insufficient attention to factors outside the person, that is **system** or **contextual** factors. These too have an influence on what people accomplish and on how they behave.

## JOB CONTEXT AS A DETERMINANT OF PERFORMANCE

Campbell's model (Figure 6.1) makes just a small reference to contextual factors:

> Obviously, performance differences can also be produced by situational effects such as the quality of equipment, degree of staff support, or nature of the working conditions. For purposes of this model of performance, these conditionals are assumed to be held constant (experimentally, statistically, or judgmentally).
>
> (Campbell *et al.* 1993: 43)

Unfortunately, in practice, this assumption does not hold true. Valuable though it is, Campbell's model is not enough even to fully describe all the factors that determine performance, let alone explain them. This is not to criticize the model for what it is – one which explicitly concentrates on the individual level of analysis and which does not claim to be all-encompassing – but rather to recognize that a more complete theory needs to include other factors.

As one might expect, the early models which sought to incorporate situational/contextual factors were rather rudimentary. Blumberg and Pringle, for example, recognized the importance of ability and motivation (although rather broadened their scope by using the terms **capacity to perform** and **willingness to perform**) but added **opportunity to perform** as a third determinant. They gave as examples of opportunity factors the following: 'tools, equipment, materials, and supplies; working conditions; actions of coworkers; leader behaviour; mentorism; organizational policies, rules, and procedures; information; time; pay' (1982:

562). They saw such factors as either **enabling** or **constraining**. In similar vein, Guzzo and Gannett (1988) write of facilitators (driving performance towards the maximally attainable level) and inhibitors (restricting performance towards the minimally acceptable level).

Two recent models of employee work performance which incorporate person and situational factors are those of Cardy and Dobbins (1994) and Waldman (1994). The Cardy and Dobbins model is of particular interest because it seeks to incorporate both the output view of performance and the behavioural one. However, it does not capture interactions among the various determinants; these are better brought out by Waldman, who takes a behavioural view of performance and draws on total quality management ideas.

Whereas Waldman adopts a behavioural definition of performance, Cardy and Dobbins distinguish between what the worker accomplishes, produces or delivers (referred to as **work outcomes**) and job-relevant behaviours, seeing these as two categories

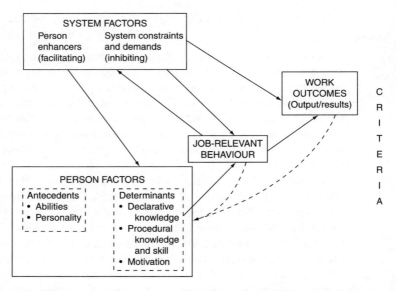

*Figure 6.3* Determinants of job performance: person and system factors (source: adapted from Campbell *et al.* 1993; Cardy and Dobbins 1994; Waldman 1994)

of performance – the distinction drawn in the two previous chapters, in other words. Work outcomes are seen as being *jointly* determined by system factors and job-relevant behaviours – the relationship of person factors to work outcomes is not direct, in other words, but operates via job-relevant behaviours. These relationships are shown diagrammatically in Figure 6.3, which derives from the models presented by Campbell *et al.* (1993, 1996), Cardy and Dobbins (1994) and Waldman (1994).

## Person factors

Though Cardy and Dobbins see person factors as having a direct effect on job-relevant behaviours, Campbell, as indicated above, takes a two-tier approach to the treatment of person factors – knowledge, skill and motivation are seen as the direct determinants of job-relevant behaviour, and other characteristics of the person (such as personality traits) are seen as underlying antecedents of those determinants. The importance of personal factors for performance management lies in the fact that they are what employees bring to the job and they may be capable of being enhanced or inhibited.

## System factors

What are system factors? Contemporary literature (e.g., Waldman 1994) takes a broad view of what is meant by system factors, regarding them as existing at 'multiple levels within an organization' (Waldman 1994: 517) – system-wide, department, work unit, team, etc. But as with the performance construct, mapping the domain or boundaries of system factors remains a difficulty. Schneider and Hough (1995) note this difficulty in offering what they refer to as an 'heuristic catalogue' of situational factors, which they do not claim to be comprehensive, but which clearly illustrates that the domain of system factors is very broad. An abbreviated version of their list (showing only extra-individual factors) is given in Table 6.1.

What influence do system factors have? Though some research (e.g., Peters and O'Connor 1980) has focused on the constraining effect that system factors may have, the prevailing view today (eg, Guzzo and Gannett 1988; Waldman 1994) recognizes that there may be either facilitating/enhancing/enabling effects or inhibiting ones. Thus, following Waldman, the category of system

*Table 6.1* Potential situational (or system) factors (source: abbreviated from Schneider and Hough 1995: 119)

*Task characteristics*
- Consistency of task
- Stage of skill acquisition with respect to task
- Amount of task structure
- Time on task
- Amount of time pressure to complete task
- Skill variety, task identity, task significance, autonomy and feedback

*Goal characteristics*
- Specificity
- Complexity
- Difficulty
- Rewards associated with goal attainment
- Conflict with other goals
- Performance versus mastery goal

*Characteristics of physical environment*
- Ambient conditions (e.g. light, noise, heat)
- Time of day
- Danger of bodily harm
- Workplace layout (e.g. open-plan office versus non-open-plan office; amount of privacy at workstation)
- Work locus (home versus office)

*Characteristics of work role*
- Role ambiguity
- Role overload
- Role conflict

*Characteristics of social environment*
- Personality of co-workers (supervisors, subordinates and peers)
- Management style of immediate supervisor (e.g. autocratic versus democratic)
- Cohesiveness of work group
- Amount of social support from co-workers, friends and family
- Work primarily in groups versus work primarily independently

*Characteristics of organization*
- Organizational values
- Organizational reward systems
- Level of employee ownership in organization
- Amount of organizational instability (e.g. rapid changes in leadership, downsizing, growth)
- Nature of administrative policies and procedures (e.g. level of bureaucracy)
- Organizational structure (e.g. matrix versus hierarchical)

factors includes **person enhancers** and **system constraints and demands**.

### Constraining and inhibiting factors

Under this heading we have 'characteristics of technological and work processes, as well as organizational policies, structure, and culture' (Waldman 1994: 523). More specific examples of factors identified as constraints would include those investigated by Peters and O'Connor (1980) for example, such as tools and equipment, time availability, and the work environment. Evidence pertaining to certain of the last of these has been reviewed recently by Baron (1994). Many of the findings are unsurprising. For example, conditions that are too noisy, too hot or too cold have been shown to have deleterious effects; level of illumination, air quality and crowding are examples of other such environmental factors. Baron sees these factors as having an indirect effect on performance (and other outcomes, such as work attitudes). Environmental factors are presented as having their impact 'on a wide range of mediating mechanisms and processes occurring within individuals' (Baron 1994: 34). Summarizing Kane (1993), Bacharach and Bamberger note that 'constraints may have a negative impact on the performance of particular job functions by making it more difficult for individuals to take maximum advantage of their job-related knowledge, skills and abilities, and by reducing their overall level of task effort' (1995: 80).

The idea that aspects of the situation may have a constraining effect on aspects of the person is far from new. Mischel (1977), for example, argued that 'strong' situations have a constraining effect in that they inhibit the expression of individual differences – in other words, in 'strong' situations people tend to behave in a similar way regardless of their different personalities or a particular individual will behave in a required way because the situation demands it rather than because it is his or her 'natural' predisposition. This, presumably, is the way in which organizational culture (that is values and norms) is intended to operate.

### Facilitating and enhancing factors

Waldman refers to certain system factors as 'person enhancers' which 'affect performance indirectly by first influencing aspects of the individual. . . . Person enhancers are proposed to involve aspects of HR systems, leadership processes, and job design that may develop and motivate individuals' (1994: 519). Campbell *et al.* take a similar view and regard system factors as antecedents which have an indirect effect on performance (behaviour) by first changing the employee's declarative knowledge, procedural knowledge and skill, and/or motivation. In other words, person enhancers may have multiple effects – that is, they simultaneously affect several person factors. For example, goals, goal-setting and feedback have motivational and informational (that is, knowledge-related) effects.

Various narrative (e.g., Kopelman 1986) and meta-analytic reviews are helpful to us in identifying interventions which may have enabling effects. Of particular interest is the work of Guzzo and his colleagues (Katzell and Guzzo 1983; Guzzo *et al.* 1985; Guzzo 1988). This examined the impact of various behavioural science/human resource interventions on performance (variously defined) and identified the following as generally having positive effects: training, socio-technical interventions, goal-setting, work redesign, supervisory methods, and appraisal and feedback. But continuing uncertainty surrounds the effect of some system factors which are commonly regarded as person enhancers: a particular case in point is financial incentives, for which the effects are by no means uniformly positive.

What all of this indicates for performance management is that there are many interventions which may affect people's work behaviour (albeit indirectly). Though it is far from strong, there is at least suggestive evidence that the use of multiple interventions has positive impact over and above those achieved by single interventions (Guzzo and Gannett 1988).

### Direct or indirect effects

Thus far system factors have been presented as having indirect effects on work behaviour, that is, person factors are seen as mediators – constraints and facilitators alike are seen as operating in this way. However, the way in which constraints operate remains a matter of some debate. On the one hand, Campbell *et al.* (1993) take the view that constraints have an indirect effect on work behaviour – they influence motivation first. Against this, Guzzo and Gannett contend that inhibitors may also have direct effects: 'Barriers to performance such as shortages of tools and too little time can make it physically impossible to complete tasks effectively' (1988: 38). So, individuals may have the motivation and the requisite knowledge and skill, but are constrained by some aspect of the work system from doing what is expected of them – as when rain stops play, for example.

When we turn to the work system perspective on performance we also find the argument that system factors may have a more direct effect. Thus, as noted earlier, we find claims (in particular in certain of the early quality management literature) that system factors account for some 85 per cent of the variation in work output. Yet, as Masterson and Taylor (1996) note, there is little hard evidence to support these claims; rather, they are more of an assumption than an established fact (Cardy and Dobbins 1994). Though we might wish to dispute how much of work output is attributable to system factors as compared to employees' behaviour, there is no doubting the direct effect of the former. For example, the quality of output produced by tool-makers will partly be a function of the machines in use, not just the facility with which they are operated by the worker. And in sales jobs the number of units sold will be subject to the influence of buyer behaviour, the price and other attributes of what is being sold. All this, of course, merely echoes the arguments put forward earlier for not regarding output as performance.

### Distinct entities or opposites

Another matter of some dispute is whether facilitators and inhibitors should be regarded as distinct entities or as opposites. If we take the '**opposites**' perspective, a deficit in a system factor would be seen as a constraint, whereas sufficient presence of the same factor would be taken as facilitating. Guzzo and Gannett (1988) prefer the '**distinct entities**' perspective. So, for example, the absence of needed tools is likely to be a constraint, restricting performance towards the minimally acceptable level. But having the required tools doesn't guarantee maximum performance – this is still dependent on the worker's knowledge, skill and motivation. Facilitators, on the other hand, are those situational factors which enhance performance.

But this issue is far from resolved. Surely it is possible for certain system factors, albeit manifested in different ways, to have both facilitating and constraining effects? Job design and supervisory behaviour are two illustrations. As I will discuss in Chapter 7, there are supervisory behaviours which are supportive and performance-enhancing in their effect. But then there are other behaviours which may be damaging in their effect; for example negative feedback. Thus, the distinction betweeen enhancing and constraining factors may not be so clear cut as it is sometimes presented. Moreover, the impact of system factors on person factors (and vice versa) is further complicated by interactions between them.

## Person-system interaction

Earlier I gave examples of how system factors impinge upon aspects of the person and so affect their performance. But, of course, so far as work systems are concerned employees aren't passive recipients who will invariably respond in the way that management wishes. People have different values, motives, etc. and so they do not respond in the same way to a given system. A line manager with half a dozen staff may find that some prefer and respond positively to her participative management style. But others, because of their particular dispositions, find this threatening and would rather have a more directive approach – this is their idea of strong leadership.

However, not only can the system affect the person, but the person can affect the system. This is partly a matter of perception. For example, though system factors sometimes are seen as constraints (whether direct or indirect in their effect) it is possible, suggest Guzzo and Gannett, for them to be seen as 'a challenge', that is as 'an obstacle to be overcome' (1988: 38). This, then, points to the element of choice which may be found within jobs. Stewart draws attention to this in the context of managerial jobs (and certain others) in her identification of demands, constraints and choices: 'there is a core of work, **demands**, that anyone in the job will have to do; these demands are the tasks that cannot be ignored or delegated if the job holder is to survive in the job' (1991: 14). Constraints 'are the factors that limit what the job holder can do: they include resource limitations and people's attitudes' (1991: 15). Choices are the areas of opportunity within a job – what the manager decides she or he will do.

To some extent all three aspects of managerial jobs are partly a matter of perception – managers need to perceive themselves as having choice over what they do. In the same vein, Stewart refers to job holders 'exaggerating the work that they must do' (demands) and 'exaggerating the constraints' (1991: 14), both of which may be forms of impression management (Rosenfeld *et al.* 1995). But the scope for individual performers to influence their job varies also according to its design, in particular according to the extent of autonomy allowed. Waldman (1994) sees this, and hierarchical level, as factors moderating the relationship between person and system factors. Thus, managerial jobs, for example, are likely to offer greater scope for the incumbent to decide how to go about the job and, quite possibly, for deciding what the job is.

Moreover, those at the higher levels are able to influence not only the nature of their own jobs but also the design of other jobs within the work system. Though system factors may have a direct impact on the behaviour and output of those working within the system, the system itself is a product of managerial choices and decisions. It is for this reason that Deming (1986) and others see managers as having the responsibility for improving work systems so as to remove performance problems. This seems to be an implicit recognition of the importance of person factors over system factors, at least for certain jobs.

In view of the reciprocal relationship between system and person factors we might suppose that the 'person factors' and 'system factors' boxes in Figure 6.3 ought to be connected. Though system factors have a direct impact on person factors, the effect of the latter on the former is indirect in that it operates through behaviour.

The idea of reciprocal and interacting influences was mentioned earlier in this chapter and it is a theme which is found throughout the literature (e.g., Schneider 1987; Davis-Blake and Pfeffer 1989; Chatman 1989; Edwards 1991). Over and above the examples already mentioned, Kanfer notes:

> motivation and performance exert reciprocal influences on one another. Not only does motivation affect performance, but performance can affect motivation. Knowledge of how one has performed or is progressing on a task may weaken or strengthen subsequent task motivation depending on performance level, attributions about the cause of performance, and motivational conditions.
>
> (Kanfer 1995: 337)

Kanfer is referring here to the place of feedback in employee performance. Though this is a system factor I've included (in Figure 6.3) feedback loops leading from outcomes and behaviours to person factors so as to make more explicit the importance of this factor.

## Person *and* system

There is no doubt that both person *and* system factors influence work behaviours and outputs. For example, if we consider a counter-productive behaviour such as absence we find research has shown that personal factors (including the individual's circumstances) are one contributory determinant, but organizational culture and policies for managing absence also are important. What is far from clear is how much of the variation in performance (whether defined as outputs or job behaviours) is attributable to one set or the other. If we subscribe to Deming's (1986) thinking our position would be that most workers (certainly those on the shop floor, that is, the direct producers or service deliverers) within an organization function or operate at about the same level and that variation in what they produce is mostly accounted for by system factors that are outside the individual's control. However, this hasn't been confirmed empirically (Cardy and Dobbins 1994). Moreover, some (e.g., Stone and Eddy 1996) have argued that system accounts of performance have underestimated the importance of person factors, almost (others have argued – e.g. Masterson and Taylor 1996) to the point of ignoring the role of the individual. As noted earlier, employees are not passive within the work system – they react (positively or negatively to the ways in which they are treated).

Very often many system factors will be seen as fixed (and may in reality be so) and outside the control of individual performers or their linemanager, and as such they may be regarded as being outside the boundaries of a performance management system. For example, once a work system has been designed it may well be difficult to change, and in consequence it may have to be taken as given. Equipment may be difficult to replace or modify. And there are invariably resource limitations of one sort or another. However, some of the more encompassing models of performance management recognize the constraining and facilitating implications of system factors. For example, Rummler and Brache (1995) refer to **job management**, which they describe as managing the **human performance system**; this is illustrated in Figure 6.4. They use the term human performance system so as to emphasize the context within which the employee performs, arguing that managers have a 'tendency to overmanage individuals and under-manage the environment in which they work' (1995: 24).

Rummler and Brache assert that, in their experience, '*about 80 percent of performance improvement opportunities reside in the environment*' (1995: 73; italics in original). As noted above, such

*Figure 6.4* Factors affecting the human performance system (source: Rummler and Brache 1995)

claims have been challenged given the absence of confirmatory evidence. What seems most likely is that the extent of variation attributable to system/person factors varies from job to job (Cardy and Dobbins 1994). Key factors here would seem to be hierarchical level and the amount of autonomy that is allowed by the job (Waldman 1994). At higher levels and in jobs offering greater autonomy personal factors may actually be more important than aspects of the system.

## Attributing cause

If we accept that job behaviour and output are caused by system and person factors we next must ask whether those different causes are actually recognized by line managers? An answer to this question might be obtained by considering how managers explain the performance of their staff. A common finding is that managers attribute the causes of performance to internal factors, that is, characteristics of the performer: this is particularly so in the case of poor performance. Job holders, on the other hand, are more likely to attribute such performance to external factors – aspects of the system outside themselves and their control. Though such attributions may be correct, it also is possible that they may be in error. Bernardin and Beatty (1984) summarize a number of attributional errors that have been discussed in the literature, as shown in Table 6.2. However, as Cardy and Dobbins

*Table 6.2* Attributional factors in assessing performance

1  Raters may underestimate the importance of situational factors and overestimate ratee factors as causes of behaviour.
2  Raters and ratees may differ in their causal attributions, with ratees emphasizing situational factors and raters using ratee factors.
3  Raters may attribute causes to the most salient features of the environment, including novel or unique ratees.
4  Raters may tend to weight ratee behaviours that have affective consequences for the raters themselves more heavily than other behaviours, especially if these affective consequences are serious.
5  Ratees may be held more responsible for behaviour that leads to reward than for behaviour that prevents losses.
6  Attributions may be related to affective relationships. If raters like ratees, they may attribute good actions to them and bad actions to circumstances. If they dislike ratees, they may follow the reverse pattern.

(1994) note, the attributional research does not answer the question because it focuses on actors' and observers' perceptions rather than reality. In reviewing the limited amount of appraisal research which attempts more directly to grapple with this issue, they go on to conclude that appraisers are not especially good at attributing cause. They further conclude that where there are deficiencies in employee performance it appears that undue weight, to the performer's detriment, is attached to them. This in its own way is an error of attribution and is in line with the conclusion of Mitchell and O'Reilly that *'when errors occur* they occur in the direction of blaming the subordinate' (1983: 168). There are implications here both for the practice of performance management and for performance management training.

## A CONCLUDING COMMENT

If we use the term performance in a loose way it clearly embraces both work outputs and behaviours. Organizations are interested in both. Indeed, organizations also are interested in individual's inputs – the personal attributes that they bring to a job. But it is equally clear that it is unhelpful, both theoretically and practically, to use the single term 'performance' to apply to outputs, behaviours and inputs. From a theoretical point of view, using the term as a catch-all does nothing to help us to understand the nature of performance and its causes. It is also clear that performance, whether defined as outputs or behaviours, is multiply determined.

Why do all of these theoretical issues matter for performance management? Because there are a number of implications for practice. For example, a range of interventions is needed to manage performance. Performance management is far from telling people what they have got to do. Providing direction is important of course, and from this point of view some performance management activity must be employee-focused. But as system factors have an impact on job behaviours and outputs, the context of individuals' jobs must be explicitly recognized and managed. Many of the models (especially the employee-centered ones) are largely silent on the need to manage system factors. One implication of this is that managers are likely to need training so as to focus attention on both system and person factors when work is planned and when performance is measured and reviewed. Also, for any job we would expect to see a range of criteria in use, quite possibly both output and behavioural measures. And this may mean that no single system will suit the whole of an organization. There seems to be some recognition of this in organizational practices, as evidenced by the greater prevalence of performance management systems for managerial staff and the rather different nature of those systems as compared to ones applying to manual staff.

# 7 Reviewing and supporting performance

When we talk about performance it is clear that in a loose way we refer to two very different things – behaviour and output/results. They necessitate different means of expressing requirements, that is, different performance criteria to serve as the basis for reviewing employee performance. Such review, an essential element in performance management, requires some sort of performance measurement, or at least the monitoring of performance, and feedback to the job holder: we commonly associate this with annual appraisal. That such review might happen only once a year under formal appraisal is, of course, one of the main criticisms of typical appraisal schemes. Within performance management, by contrast, it is advocated that review and the provision of feedback should happen much more frequently. Consequently I will pay more attention to these aspects of review and feedback than to formal appraisal, especially as the latter is dealt with in many other texts (e.g., Fletcher 1993; Fletcher and Williams 1992; Murphy and Cleveland 1995).

Though feedback may be self-generated (by the job holder) or come from peers, the line manager is commonly seen as having a key role to play. Likewise, the line manager is seen as an important agent for providing support for the job holder. This may be direct, through such activities as coaching, or indirect, via other resources that may be within the manager's control. Support for this broad view of the role of the line manager in reviewing performance and providing feedback (and providing reward –

see Chapter 8) comes readily from a consideration of the research on management and managerial behaviour.

## THE ROLE OF THE LINE MANAGER

There are many models which tell us about the nature of the manager's job. For example, in the UK we have the MCI National Standards. These see the central purpose of management jobs as being 'To achieve the organization's objectives and to continuously improve its performance' (Management Charter Initiative 1990: 14) – in other words, the function of the manager's job is seen in terms of performance management, albeit at the organizational level. The National Standards define the manager's job in terms of four key roles: managing operations, finance, people and information. For each of the roles a number of units and elements of competence are identified, some illustrations of which are provided in Table 7.1. In turn, for each element there are a number of performance criteria, as shown in Table 7.2. Taken together these two tables show clearly that performance management is a core feature of the MCI model of the manager's role.

A more behavioural than functional view is found in Yukl's

*Table 7.1* Units and elements of management competence (source: abbreviated from Management Charter Initiative 1990: iii)

| Unit | Element |
| --- | --- |
| Maintain and improve service and product operations | Create and maintain the necessary conditions for productive work |
| Plan, allocate and evaluate work carried out by teams, individuals and self | Set and update work objectives for teams and individuals |
| | Provide feedback to teams and individuals on their performance |
| Create, maintain and enhance effective working relationships | Establish and maintain the trust and support of one's subordinates |
| | Counsel staff |

(1994) taxonomy of managerial practices (Table 7.3). Not surprisingly, many of these practices are directly relevant to the management of employee performance, for example 'clarifying roles and objectives', 'monitoring', 'supporting', 'recognizing'

*Table 7.2* Performance criteria for elements of job competence (source: Management Charter Initiative 1990: 10–11)

---

**Key Role**   **Manage People**
**Unit**   **Develop teams, individuals and self to enhance performance**

**Element**   **Identify, review and improve development activities for individuals**

*Performance Criteria*
- Development objectives and activities are based on a balanced assessment of current competence, potential future competence and career aspirations are in line with current and anticipated team/organizational requirements.
- Individuals are encouraged and assisted to evaluate their own learning and development needs and to contribute to the discussion, planning and review of development.
- Plans contain clear, relevant and realistic development objectives and details of supporting development activities.
- Development activities optimize the use of available resources.
- Plans are reviewed, updated and improved at regular intervals after discussion and agreement with the appropriate people.
- Where development activities prove inappropriate and/or the resources used are unsuitable or inadequate, realistic alternatives are discussed, agreed and implemented.

**Element**   **Develop oneself within the job role**
*Performance Criteria*
- Current competence and areas for development are identified against appropriate competence/development models.
- Objectives are achievable, realistic and challenging in terms of current and anticipated competence and updated at regular intervals.
- Where necessary, personal objectives include areas for development which are required for effective team operation.
- Sufficient and realistic amounts of time and resources are allocated to achieve set objectives.
- Progress and performance are reviewed with appropriate people at suitable intervals and results used to inform future development.
- Responsibility is accepted for achieving own development objectives.
- Feedback is compared with own perceptives of performance and used to improve future performance.

---

*Table 7.3* Definitions of Yukl's managerial practices (source: Yukl 1994: 69)

*Planning and Organizing.* Determining long-term objectives and strategies, allocating resources according to priorities, determining how to use personnel and resources to accomplish a task efficiently, and determining how to improve co-ordination, productivity and the effectiveness of the organizational unit.

*Problem-Solving.* Identifying work-related problems, analysing problems in a timely but systematic manner to identify causes and find solutions, and acting decisively to implement solutions to resolve important problems or crises.

*Clarifing Roles and Objectives.* Assigning tasks, providing direction in how to do the work and communicating a clear understanding of job responsibilities, task objectives, deadlines and performance expectations.

*Informing.* Disseminating relevant information about decisions, plans and activities to people who need it to do their work, providing written materials and documents, and answering requests for technical information.

*Monitoring.* Gathering information about work activities and external conditions affecting the work, checking on the progress and quality of the work, evaluating the performance of individuals and the organizational unit, analysing trends, and forecasting external events.

*Motivating and Inspiring.* Using influence techniques that appeal to emotion or logic to generate enthusiasm for work, commitment to task objectives and compliance with requests for cooperation, assistance, support, or resources; setting an example of appropriate behaviour.

*Consulting.* Checking with people before making changes that affect them, encouraging suggestions for improvement, inviting participation in decision-making, incorporating the ideas and suggestions of others in decisions.

*Delegating.* Allowing subordinates to have substantial responsibility and discretion in carrying out work activities, handling problems and making important decisions.

*Supporting.* Acting friendly and considerate, being patient and helpful, showing sympathy and support when someone is upset and anxious, listening to complaints and problems, looking out for someone's interests.

*Developing and Mentoring.* Providing coaching and helpful career advice, and doing things to facilitate a person's skill acquisition, professional development and career advancement.

*Managing Conflict and Team-Building.* Facilitating the constructive resolution of conflict and encouraging co-operation, teamwork and identification with the work unit.

*Networking.* Socializing informally, developing contacts with people who are a source of information and support, and maintaining contact through periodic interaction, including visits, telephone calls, correspondence and attendance at meetings and social events.

*Recognizing.* Providing praise and recognition for effective performance, significant achievements and special contributions; expressing appreciation for someone's contributions and special efforts.

*Rewarding.* Providing or recommending tangible rewards such as a pay increase or promotion for effective performance, significant achievements and demonstrated competence.

*Table 7.4* Specific behaviours for managerial practices (source: summarized from Yukl 1994: 92–5, 131–3, 126–7)

### Specific behaviours for managing the work

*Guidelines for defining job responsibilities*
- Meet with the subordinate to mutually define the job
- Establish priorities for different responsibilities
- Explain the subordinate's scope of authority

*Guidelines for setting perfomance goals*
- Set goals for relevant aspects of performance
- Set goals that are clear and specific
- Set a deadline for the attainment of each goal
- Set goals that are challenging but realistic
- Consult with a subordinate in setting goals
- Formalize agreements in writing

*Guidelines for assigning tasks*
- Clearly explain the assignment
- Explain the reasons for an assignment
- Verify legitimacy, if necessary
- Check for comprehension
- Follow up to check on compliance

### Specific behaviours for managing relationships

*Guidelines for recognizing*
- Recognize a variety of contributions and achievements
- Actively search for contributions to recognize
- Recognize improvements in performance
- Recognize commendable efforts that failed
- Don't limit recognition to high-visibility jobs
- Don't limit recognition to a few best performers
- Provide specific recognition
- Provide timely recognition
- Use an appropriate form of recognition

*Guidelines for coaching and training*
- Identify training needs
- Explain why additional training is needed
- Build the person's self-confidence
- Make explanations meaningful
- Sequence training content to facilitate learning
- Provide opportunity for practice with feedback
- Allow ample time for learning complex tasks
- Verify that training has been successful
- Encourage application of skills on the job

*Table 7.5* The McBer general managerial competency model (source: Spencer and Spencer 1993)

| Weight | Competency |
| --- | --- |
| XXXXXX | Impact and influence |
| XXXXXX | Achievement orientation |
| XXXX | Teamwork and co-operation |
| XXXX | Analytical thinking |
| XXXX | Initiative |
| XXX | Developing others |
| XX | Self-confidence |
| XX | Directiveness/assertiveness |
| XX | Information seeking |
| XX | Team leadership |
| XX | Conceptual thinking |

(Weight refers to the relative frequency with which each competency distinguishes superior from average performers).

and 'rewarding'. Associated with each of these is a large number of 'specific component behaviours' (Yukl 1994) – that is, prescriptive guidelines as to what managers should do: some examples are given in Table 7.4.

Research on competencies also tells us about performance-management-related activites in which managers should engage. Table 7.5 shows the McBer generic managerial competency model, that is, characteristics of individuals that are related to effective performance (i.e., results). Again, we can identify a number that would seem to have especial relevance for the management of employee performance, such as 'achievement orientation', 'developing others', 'interpersonal understanding' and 'directiveness/assertiveness'. An illustration of how one of these is defined is given in Table 7.6.

All the models described so far derive, to varying extents, from empirical research on managerial behaviour and effectiveness. Such research also points to the highly interactive nature of managerial work, much of that interaction being with subordinates. Moreover, the models together clearly point to the important role of the line manager and the tables provide several specific examples of the sorts of activities in which managers need to engage in the management of employee performance.

*Table 7.6* A managerial competency defined (source: abbreviated from Spencer and Spencer 1993: 54–6)

---

**Developing others**
Expresses the genuine intent to teach or to foster the learning or development of one or several other people.

**Level  Behavioural Description**

−1  *Discourages.* Expresses stereotypical or personal negative expectations, resents subordinates, students, clients. Has a 'pacesetter' management style.

0  *Not applicable, or makes no explicit efforts to develop others.*

1  *Expresses positive expectations of others.* Makes positive comments regarding others' abilities or potential even in 'difficult' cases. Believes others want to and can learn.

3  *Gives reasons or other support.* Gives directions or demonstrations with reasons or rationale included as a training strategy; or gives practical support or assistance, to make job easier.

5  *Reassures and encourages.* Reassures others after a setback. Gives negative feedback in behavioural rather than personal terms, and expresses positive expectations for future performance or gives individualized suggestions for improvement; or breaks difficult tasks into smaller components, or uses other strategies.

7  *Creates new teaching/training.* Identifies a training or development need and designs or establishes new programmes or materials to meet it; designs significantly new approaches to teaching traditional materials; or arranges successful experiences for others to build up their skills and confidence.

9  *Rewards good development.* Promotes or arranges promotions for especially competent subordinates as a reward or a development experience; or gives other rewards for good performance.

(All of the scale points are defined as illustrated above.)

---

# PERFORMANCE REVIEW

Let me begin this section with a brief reminder of certain of the key points about contemporary practice in the UK. At one extreme there are organizations where no review takes place; this is not uncommon amongst those which do not have policies for managing performance. By contrast, a healthier picture is found amongst those organizations which do have performance management policies of some sort, the core activity being a joint discussion between manager and employee. The IMS survey (Institute of Personnel Management 1992) also tells us that performance review is more frequent than annual review in about 60 per cent of organizations with formal performance management systems: the Industrial Society (1994) survey indicates that six-monthly or quarterly reviews are most likely.

## Performance measures

The starting point for performance reviews, particularly the more formal ones, will be the performance contract or agreement (Chapter 4). For example, in Standard Life there is a performance plan which comprises a 'job mission' statement (specifying the single main purpose of the job) and a 'performance description' – the outputs, indicators and activities to be completed in fulfilling the mission. Mercury Communications use a performance contract which includes statements of the job purpose and agreed account-abilities (outputs to be achieved), and specifies the review process. These, then, are examples of the preference, noted in Chapter 4, for organizations to use seemingly more objective means of expressing performance measures. One of the advantages of such measures is that they do lend themselves fairly readily to the collection of relevant supporting data. This is one part of performance review, namely **monitoring**.

## Performance monitoring

As we saw from Yukl's definition in Table 7.3, this includes gathering information about work activities and checking on the progress and quality of work, amongst other things. Such information might be generated naturally, as it were, as part of the way in which the work system operates. But as Box 7.1 illustrates, there are in fact many ways in which monitoring may be carried out, whether by the line manager or by others – indeed, by the job holder. Quite apart from gathering information which may be used for keeping track of progress with tasks/goals or providing feedback, such monitoring behaviour in itself may carry an important message for the employee: 'the frequency with which a manager monitors a subordinate's performance may help shape that subordinate's beliefs about the relative importance of his or her various work activities' (Larson and Callahan 1990: 531).

---

Box 7.1    **Performance monitoring activities**

The behaviour involved in monitoring can take many forms, including the following: (1) observation of work operations (e.g. visiting work facilities, walking around the office or plant, watching subordinates do a task), (2) reading written reports (e.g. performance summaries, progress reports, computer printouts), (3) watching computer screen displays of performance data, (4) inspecting the quality of samples of the work, (5) holding progress review meetings with an individual or group, (6) surveying clients or customers to assess their satisfaction with organization products and services, (7) conducting market surveys to assess customer needs and preferences, and (8) holding meetings after an activity or project is completed to determine what went well and what can be improved next time.

(source: Yuks 1994: 103)

---

## Progress reviews

Though the very act of monitoring may have a direct impact on employee performance, as indicated above, it is more usually thought of as being linked with some other managerial behaviour, such as revising work objectives or providing feedback (Larson and Callahan 1990). Thus, there may be a review meeting of some kind between the employee and manager; such discussions are widely advocated in the performance management literature – Costello (1994), for example, describes several purposes of **progress reviews** and Whetten *et al.* (1994) describe **personal management interviews**, as shown in Box 7.2. Such reviews might take place on some regular periodic basis – in Hewlett-Packard, for example, they are monthly; quarterly formal reviews (and informal discussions as needed) are expected in Zeneca Pharmaceuticals; at least two a year are required in Legal & General (Life and Pensions) and Standard Chartered Bank; and informal reviews take place every three to six months in Standard Life with continuous feedback throughout the year. There is thus a case for saying that they should happen as and when required – to coincide with completion of a task or when a particular problem arises, for example. From this point of view, in other words, it is sensible for the review cycle to coincide with the work cycle.

Box 7.2   **Purposes of progress reviews and personal management interviews**

*Progress reviews*
Provide a *formal* opportunity to discuss overall performance results. Progress review meetings allow the manager to summarize informal feedback and are vital to managing performance. . . .
The overall purpose of a progress review is to:

- Progress toward goals and objectives established in performance and development plans.
- Review objectives and plans in light of business changes.
- Discuss needed changes, revisions or additions to the performance and development plan.
- Make plans for improvement, if necessary. If progress is insufficent, the manager must determine what the problems are, solicit the employee's perspective and suggested solutions, and utilize appropriate coaching skills. In some cases a formal improvement plan will need to be developed.

(source: Costello 1994: 93)

*Personal management interviews*
Regular and private meetings which provide managers with the opportunity to coach and counsel subordinates and to help them improve their own skills and job performance. Meetings should focus on such items as the following: (1) managerial and organizational problems, (2) information sharing, (3) interpersonal issues, (4) obstacles to improvement, (5) training in management skills, (6) individual needs, (7) feedback on job performance and (8) personal concerns or problems.

(source: Whetten *et al.* 1994: 219)

# FEEDBACK

So far as the provision of feedback is concerned, one important characteristic is that it should be timely. So, for example, good performance should be recognized when it occurs. Farr contends that 'informal or day-to-day feedback is more important than feedback that occurs during the annual or semi-annual performance appraisal session in terms of its impacts on work performance and attitudes' (1993: 177). This makes sense as we should have rather modest expectations of what can be achieved during the once-a-year event that is the appraisal interview (especially if this is the only feedback-giving activity that takes place). But positive outcomes (e.g., in terms of performance and work attitudes) may arise from the annual event where there has been more frequent review and feedback during the year. In this regard, Taylor *et al.* (1984) propose that regular feedback should bring about closer agreement over performance standards between employees and the organization (that is, the manager). Also, Ashford (1989) suggests that where there is regular feedback it may be easier to convey negative feedback when this is necessary.

A common form of providing recognition is to give credit or praise (social reward) or some more tangible reward for something that has been done well. Praise may have motivational and reinforcing consequences, although, as Lockett points out:

> Giving praise is more than a vague 'well done' or a pat on the back. An effective credit provides specific information to people about their behaviour and why it is creditworthy. This specific information gives credibility to the praise and encourages the element of performance to be repeated.
>
> (Lockett 1992: 86)

Thus, feedback also serves an informational purpose (Farr 1993). But in order to be effective, feedback should possess characteristics other than timeliness, as the model depicted in Figure 7.1 illustrates.

These characteristics apply whether the feedback is positive or negative. Thus, instances of poor performance should be tackled at the time rather than being stored up for the annual appraisal or not dealt with at all. Yet we know that managers are reluctant to get to grips with performance problems. Indeed, do they provide

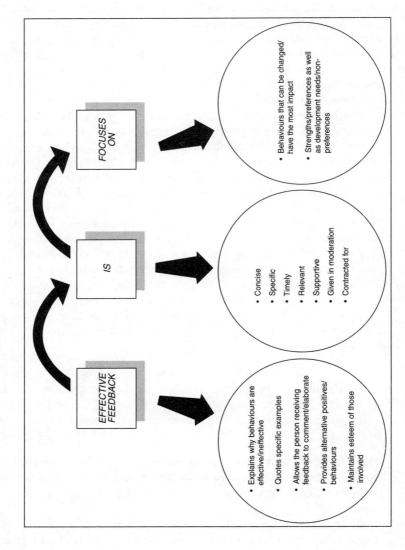

*Figure 7.1* Feedback (source: Latham and Marchbank 1994)

*Table 7.7*: Sources of feedback on performance (source: Nicholson and West 1988: 167)

| Have you had any feedback from the following sources on how well your superiors think you are doing in your present job? | Yes (%) | No (%) |
|---|---|---|
| Formal appraisal system | 38 | 62 |
| Informal communications from boss | 79 | 21 |
| Other sources | 60 | 40 |
| | $N = 2,061$ | |

*Table 7.8*: Extent of feedback from different sources (source: Nicholson and West 1988: 168)

| How much feedback do you get in your job from . . . ? | A great deal/quite a lot (%) | Moderate (%) | Little or none (%) |
|---|---|---|---|
| Superiors | 23 | 44 | 32 |
| Colleagues | 24 | 54 | 22 |
| Clients, customers, contacts | 33 | 45 | 23 |
| Job indicators (i.e. visible results/output) | 50 | 36 | 14 |
| | $N = 1,031$ | | |

enough feedback at all? Illustrative evidence of deficiencies in the incidence of feedback provision comes from two large-scale surveys of British Institute of Management members carried out some years ago by Nicholson and West (1988). Tables 7.7 and 7.8 show the relevant data.

## Sources of feedback

Nicholson and West conclude from these data that the extent of the feedback being provided by managers is less than might be desired. In their view, providing feedback 'is primarily a boss's job, and on this evidence most of our manager's bosses aren't doing this part of their jobs' (1988: 165). But although feedback from supervisors is valued by job holders, as is that from co-workers, it is feedback from the task and the self, Farr (1993) reports, that is regarded as the most useful. Indeed, the individual is generally seen as more credible and trustworthy as a source of feedback than are external sources. Credibility, trustworthiness and sincerity of intent are important characteristics which influence the recipient's processing of the feedback that is delivered (Fedor 1991).

The Nicholson and West findings confirm the importance of the job itself as a source of feedback about performance. Indeed, there is the argument that job performance is actually the fundamental source of 'objective job-related feedback' (Fedor 1991: 82) and that feedback from all other sources (the manager, the self or others) is the result of some internal process of interpretation and evaluation. Certainly, the important role of feedback from the job itself has been recognized in various models of job design. For example, feedback is one of the core job characteristics in the Hackman and Oldham (1980) model, and Warr has identified the importance of feedback as 'a minimum requirement for the establishment and maintenance of personal control and for the development and utilization of skills' (1987: 261), with consequent implications for employee mental health.

However, for feedback to be accepted it first needs to be perceived as such by the recipient. Perception is very much a selective process, as we cannot possibly attend to all of the stimuli that bombard us. This is particularly important as feedback that is given informally will not necessarily be signalled as such by the sender. The sender may be trying to give a hint, but whether the recipient takes it depends on it being perceived. It then will be processed, interpreted and evaluated by the individual (Fedor 1991). This process is likely to be influenced by our mood at the time, our past experience, our expectations, our internal standards about performance and many other factors (Ashford 1989). Thus, senders of feedback should not assume that the message they believe they have sent will be interpreted by the recipient in the way intended. As part of their processing of the feedback recipients will decide whether the behaviour/incident/etc. that is the subject of the feedback is their responsibility. If the feedback is positive we are more likely to attribute that success to ourselves, whereas if it is unfavourable we are more likely to adopt a situational explanation.

The point being made here is that the recipient of feedback is far from passive. That we selectively attend to feedback messages implies that the sender needs to signal clearly that feedback is being provided. The sender also needs to be clear about the message that is being sent and it needs to be delivered in a supportive way, as in the model in Figure 7.1, for example.

Another implication of the idea that feedback recipients are active rather than passive is that we might actively seek out feedback from others about our performance, although as Ashford (1986) points out that this may sometimes go against prevailing norms. But even if we do not solicit feedback from others we are likely, from time to time, to reflect on our performance, and in this sense feedback may be self-generated.

## Self-assessment

The self-generation of feedback necessarily involves **self-appraisal**. This might be encouraged on a formal basis within the context of performance appraisal or performance management. Survey evidence suggests the incidence of use is, however, on the low side. For example, Long's (1986) survey of appraisal practice reported that 28 per cent of responding organizations claimed to use self-appraisal. The IMS performance management survey (Institute of Personnel Management, 1992) reported a similar figure of 25 per cent for organizations with formal systems (and less for others). The surprising, and scarcely believable, figure is that of 71 per cent reported by the Industrial Society (1994). Unfortunately, the form of the question asked in this last survey is not reported and so we do not know if like is being compared with like, but it is hard to believe that there has been such an enormous shift in practice in the space of two years (the interval between the IMS and Industrial Society surveys), particularly as a 1995 survey by Saville and Holdsworth (quoted by Thatcher 1996) reports an incidence of use of 31 per cent amongst large organizations.

However, whatever the incidence or nature of self-appraisal on a formal basis, it nonetheless is something that we all engage in, and we may be more reliant on self-generated feedback when feedback isn't provided by others (Ashford 1989). Accurate self-assessments may also have functional value: for example, Ashford notes that 'they allow employees to correct errors and better tailor their performances to the current situation and the demands of the larger control system' (1989: 143). Furthermore, Campbell and Lee (1988) have identified the potential developmental value of self-assessments, such as helping to identify areas of disagreement. Though it might be feared that the voicing of disagreement may lead to dispute and disharmony, there is the possibility that discussion of differences will lead to benefits – at the very least, difficulties that aren't brought out into the open are likely to remain unresolved.

That self-assessment is naturally occurring needs to be recognized by managers as there will not necessarily be agreement between the feedback that they wish to provide and the perceptions that job holders have of their own performance. Figure 7.2 shows this diagrammatically. As the figure illustrates, some job holders may overestimate their performance (relative to the assessments made by others, such as the linemanager – this is cell 2) whereas some may underestimate their performance (cell 4). And as Campbell and Lee (1988) indicate, there may be several reasons for discrepancies between self-assessments and those made by managers. For example, there may be differing expectations as to what performance is expected, although this ought to be less of a problem where there has been discussion and there is a clear performance contract, of course. Managers might have insufficient information about what the job holder has done. The two parties may agree on what was done (or not done) but have different explanations. But whatever the reasons, cells 2 and 4 may present performance management problems. Consider employees in cell 4, for example. Their perceptions of underperformance may suggest low self-efficacy. As we saw in Chapter 3, self-efficacy is associated with goal-acceptance, and so the performance management task here may be one of persuading the employee to believe in a higher level of competence. This, of course, assumes that the more accurate view of performance is the one held by the line manager. This may not be the case; the job holder's view may be the more accurate. There may, in fact, be a performance problem, although this is not to say that it lies within the employee – it may rest within the work system.

The issue of accuracy in performance assessment is a proble-

| | Self-evaluation | |
|---|---|---|
| | Behaviour is on track re.goal attainment (positive self-assessment) | Behaviour is off track re.goal attainment (negative self-assessment) |
| **Behaviour is on track re.goal attainment (positive self-assessment)** | 1 | 4 |
| **Behaviour is off track re.goal attainment (negative self-assessment)** | 2 | 3 |

*Other-evaluation*

*Figure 7.2* Possible relationships between other- and self-evaluations of goal progress (source: Ashford 1989)

matical one (Ashford 1989). One problem is deciding what accuracy is. In practical terms this ought to be reduced if care is taken to define performance and how it will be measured, but there can be no guarantees that there will be no ambiguity about this, especially as there may be parties other than the manager in the employee's role set who have a view about what the performers should be doing and how well they should be doing it. Where there is a performance contract it will typically be agreed between the job holder and their manager – the expectations of other interested parties most probably will not be taken into account, certainly not in a formal way. A second problem concerns the accuracy of different assessment sources. It is generally assumed that the manager will be the more accurate source (Bernardin 1986), but this assumption is very much open to question. As I shall come on to discuss in considering multiple appraisal, different sources each have their advantages and disadvantages.

Of the four cells in Figure 7.2, possibly more serious, and perhaps more difficult for the manager to deal with, would be an employee in cell 2, that is, where the employee sees him- or herself as being on track but where this view is not shared by the manager. Again, this assumes that the manager is in the right, as it were, and that the poor performance is attributable to the employee rather than (or more than) the situation. Managers' reluctance to deal with poor performance is understandable. It is likely to be time-consuming and may involve disciplinary procedures. It may also be confrontational, especially if the individual is held to be at fault. And confrontation becomes more likely the longer the problem is put off; what should be constructive feedback could all too easily become destructive (London 1995). Moreover, employees generally do not want to hear bad news, especially about themselves, as this may be ego- threatening (Ashford 1989) and this may lead to such defensive impression management behaviours as disclaimers (Eder and Fedor 1989) and excuse-making (Higgins and Snyder 1989), all of which has implications for the way in which poor performance is dealt with.

## Dealing with poor performance

Much of the practical advice for dealing with poor performance advocates a problem-solving approach which recognizes that the causes of poor performance may lie within the work system (e.g., Lockett 1992). One well-established example of such advocacy is found in *Analyzing Performance Problems*, by Mager and Pipe (1990). They set out a flow diagram which serves as a model for diagnosing performance problems. Table 7.9 illustrates some of the sorts of question which need to be asked as part of the diagnostic process.

One of the clear implications of the discussion in Chapters 4, 5 and 6 of the nature and causes of performance is that performance is multi-faceted and multiply determined. In dealing with poor performance it is especially important to identify its causes. To misdiagnose a performance problem and attribute the cause to the performer does little, if anything, to solve the problem and may

*Table 7.9* Diagnosing performance problems (source: summarized from mager and Pipe 1990)

*What is the performance discrepancy?*
- What is the difference between what is being done and what is supposed to be done?
- What is the event that causes me to say that things aren't right?

*Is it a skill deficiency?*
- Are the person's present skills adequate for the desired performance?

*Is the skill used often?*
- How often is the skill or performance used?
- Is there regular feedback on performance?
- Exactly how does the person find out how well he or she is doing?

*Are there obstacles to performing?*
- Does the person know what is expected?
- Are there restrictive policies, or a 'right way of doing it', or a 'way we've always done it' that ought to be changed?
- Can I reduce interference by
  – improving lighting?
  – changing colours?
  – increasing comfort?
  – modifying the work position?
  – reducing visual or auditory distractions?

*Which solution is best?*
- Have all potential solutions been identified?
- Does each solution address itself to one or more problems identified during the analysis (such as skill deficiency, absence of potential, incorrect rewards, punishing consequences, distracting obstacles)?

even make matters worse, as the manager's response may be punishing rather than performance-improving (Bell and Tetlock 1989). Campion and Wong, for example, argue that 'There is a common tendency to blame the worker rather than the job when performance is poor' (1991: 602) and note that a performance problem is one of the situations in which the design of the job should be considered. Correct diagnosis is important, therefore, for better performance management and it is in the interests of fairness to the employee. A problem-solving approach which focuses on performance is also one of the means by which the manager demonstrates supportiveness (Whetten *et al.* 1994) and is consistent with a coaching approach, that is, 'a joint process in which manager and employee work together to find solutions to present work problems' (Anderson 1993: 141).

Answers to the sorts of questions posed by Mager and Pipe (Table 7.9) help to diagnose the cause(s) of the performance problem and possible solutions are identified. Adopting such a participative, problem-solving approach may help to reduce employee defensiveness and, in terms of procedural justice, may promote a sense of fairness about the assessment by enabling employees to put their point of view and challenge that of the manager (Greenberg 1986). After all, no single source observes so much of our behaviour at work as we do ourselves. And though our own explanations for the causes of our behaviour are sometimes suspect, allowing self-appraisal may reveal motivational or situational factors affecting performance. This kind of participation may also signal that the job holder's contribution is valued and regarded as important.

## Multiple appraisal

Earlier I referred to the problem of accuracy in performance assessment. This is well documented in relation to self-appraisals, as numerous studies (summarized in Williams 1989) have shown that we tend to rate our performance more highly than do our coworkers or our managers. Very often it is assumed that the assessments made by others, particularly line managers, are more accurate. This, of course, is very much open to challenge. Though line managers have a legitimate role in assessing performance this is not to say that they are necessarily the 'best' people to make those judgements. First, the manager cannot observe all that the job holder does or accomplishes – the manager, in other words, has only a partial view of performance. And this may have become a greater problem in those organizations which have experienced downsizing, delayering and the like as spans of control may have become wider. This leads to the possibility that job holders will have relatively little contact with their managers. Second, it is possible that the manager values results more highly than behaviours – that this is a possibility is suggested by the prevalence of results-based systems of performance management. This may be one explanation for discrepancies between self-ratings and supervisor ratings. Third, in some forms of work organization, such as matrix organizations and team-working, it isn't always clear who

*Table 7.10* Objections to subordinate (upward) appraisal (source: summarized from Bernardin 1986)

1 Subordinates lack the information or skills needed to make valid ratings.
2 Subordinates are inexperienced as raters.
3 Subordinates have not been trained to make accurate ratings.
4 Subordinates will inflate ratings to avoid retaliation from managers.
5 Managers will focus too hard on pleasing subordinates.
6 The authority of managers will be undermined.
7 Managers will avoid organizations that use subordinate ratings, causing difficulties recruiting and retaining managers.
8 Subordinates will rate harshly managers who are demanding.
9 Subordinate ratings are nothing more than a popularity contest.

the manager is. So, though managers may be a necessary source of information for performance management activities they are by no means a sufficient source.

We might, therefore, want to draw on others as sources of feedback. As was shown above, there are various advantages and disadvantages with self-generated feedback, but where the purpose of performance management is developmental the advantages probably outweigh the disadvantages. In the case of managers we might also want to draw on those they manage as a source of feedback – this is sometimes referred to as **upward appraisal**. Naturally, objections to this idea have been voiced – Table 7.10 gives a list. Though we can't dismiss these objections out of hand it is clear that at least some of them may be tackled. Training may be provided, for example. Subordinates may be inexperienced at assessment, but so is a novice supervisor. We also need to set against these objections the potential advantages. In particular, subordinates are especially well placed to assess certain aspects of managerial behaviour: Table 7.11 lists those dimensions of behaviour which managers believe can and cannot be assessed by subordinates. These, of course, are the opinons of managers and it may be that subordinates feel that they are in a position to give legitimate feedback on such matters as planning and organizing, for example. This is partly a matter of opinion; also, it is partly a matter of the opportunity to observe, and this is a general point about multi-source feedback. The different sources should be regarded as complementary to one another as each

*Table 7.11* Dimensions of managerial behaviour that managers believe can and cannot be assessed by subordinates (source: Cardy and Dobbins 1994: 161)

| Dimensions that can be assessed | Dimensions that cannot be assessed |
|---|---|
| Leadership | Planning and organizing |
| Oral communication | Budgeting |
| Delegation | Goal-setting |
| Co-ordination | Decision-making |
| Interest in subordinates | Creativity |
| Performance feedback | Quantity of work |
| Providing work guidance | Quality of work |
| Composure and self-control | Analytical ability |
| Interpersonal relationships | Technical ability |

*Table 7.12* Access to information about task and interpersonal behaviours and results (source: Murphy and Cleveland 1995: 134)

| | Subordinates | Self | Source Peers | Next level (supervisor) | Higher level (upper management) |
|---|---|---|---|---|---|
| *Task* | | | | | |
| Behaviours | Rare | Always | Frequent | Occasional | Rare |
| Results | Occasional | Frequent | Frequent | Frequent | Occasional |
| *Interpersonal* | | | | | |
| Behaviours | Frequent | Always | Frequent | Occasional | Rare |
| Results | Frequent | Frequent | Frequent | Occasional | Rare |

views different aspects of performance – tasks and behaviours – from his or her own distinctive perspectives. This is illustrated in Table 7.12.

Table 7.12 is intended to be only a general guide. For example, there may be circumstances where a subordinate works very closely with his or her manager such that there is frequent opportunity to observe task behaviours or results. However, what Table 7.12 does indicate clearly is that to obtain a more fully rounded picture of an individual's performance we should draw on multiple sources of feedback. In particular, the table suggests that some non-traditional sources ought to be drawn on much more than is common – co-workers are a case in point, especially as there is evidence attesting to the accuracy of peer ratings. Moreover, incorporating multiple sources offers the prospect of being able to gather more extensive behavioural data, thereby doing something to redress the overemphasis on results that characterizes much of performance management practice. One further point which arises from Table 7.12 is the implication that greater weight may be attached to the more frequently encountered types of information, and this in itself may affect the judgements that are made.

In addition, there may be others over and above those shown in the Table, such as suppliers or customers/clients, who could be brought in as further sources. The involvement of the latter is, of course, highly consistent with a customer orientation and some (e.g., Cardy and Dobbins 1994) have suggested that this helps to reinforce in employees' minds the ultimate reason for their job. On the other hand, the use of such external sources has been subject to little research and so remains poorly understood. But potential difficulties should be noted. Research by Parasuraman *et al.* (1991), for example, has identified ten dimensions used by consumers in evaluating service quality (Table 7.13) – it is possible that customers may not readily separate the system and person influences on an employee's performance.

What is explained above, in other words, is the core rationale for 360° appraisal. Though there is little doubt that this has become more popular in recent years, it is not clear how widespread the practice is, if only because it is a practice to which many organizations are giving consideration but without yet having a system actually in operation. For example, an Industrial Society survey in 1995 showed that only 8 per cent of those responding had a system of 360° appraisal; a further 13 per cent were thinking about introducing it (cited in France 1997).

Though it is becoming more popular today, multiple appraisal is far from a new idea. One example from some years ago is the experimental programme that was introduced in the Gulf Oil Corporation (Stinson and Stokes 1980). This was designed as a supplement to the normal annual appraisal, and the main steps are described in Box 7.3. The example is of more than historical interest for it serves to illustrate many of the features of present-day practice.

*Table 7.13* Dimensions of service quality (source: Parasuraman *et al.* 1991: 255)

- *Tangibles* include the physical evidence of the service such as the appearance of the service facilities and personnel.
- *Reliability* involves consistency of performance and dependability. It means that the firm performs the service right the first time. It also means that the firm, honours its promises.
- *Responsiveness* concerns the willingness or readiness of employees to provide service. It involves timeliness of service.
- *Competence* means possession of the required skills and knowledge to perform the service.
- *Courtesy* involves politeness, respect, consideration and friendliness of contact personnel (including receptionists, telephone operators and so forth).
- *Credibility* involves trustworthiness, believability, honesty. It involves having the customer's best interests at heart.
- *Security* is the freedom from danger, risk or doubt.
- *Access* involves approachability and ease of contact.
- *Communication* means keeping customers informed in language they can understand. It also means listening to customers.
- *Understanding the consumer* involves making the effort to understand the customer's needs.

---

Box 7.3    **An early experiment in multiple appraisal**

1   The participants (thirty senior executives from eight European countries) each selected between five and eight raters whom believed to be in a position to make a useful assessment of their performance. Self-selection of the raters was regarded as important so as to increase acceptace of the feedback. The participant sent each rater a Rating Form (described below) with a covering letter requesting completion of the form and its return, anonymously, to the HR [Human Resources] Department. The rater also was told how the participant would receive feedback.

2   The completed Rating Forms were analysed by the HR Department to produce a Summary Feedback for each participant.

3   A copy of the Summary Feedback Form was sent to each participant and his or her immediate bosses (who had been briefed previously on what was to happen). Either

party could go to the HR Department for clarification of any of the information on the form.

4   Each participant also completed a self-appraisal, having regard to the content of the Summary Feedback Form. The usual Corporate Appraisal Form was used for this. This was sent on to the immediate boss.

5   Based on the Summary Feedback Form, the self-appraisal and their own views, the bosses next completed a Corporate Performance Appraisal Form and then carried out an interview with the participant.

The Rating Form for the experiment had three main elements: an overall assessment of job performance; an analysis of managerial effectiveness against a seven-factor model of managerial behaviour; and a narrative assessment citing specific incidents to elaborate on the seven-factor analysis. The model of managerial behaviour was largely developed intuitively, although it drew on relevant published research and the outcome of an internal job evaluation exercise. In completing the narrative part of the form the raters had to select the two roles which they felt the participant had performed most effectively, and the two performed least effectively, so as to identify areas in which development was needed.

An evaluation of the experiment showed a high degree of acceptance, by both participants and bosses, although it was recognized that the approach could be threatening for some. The information communicated was found to be highly specific, which is clearly necessary if developmental action is to take place. Furthermore, there was no evidence that overrating had taken place as a result of multiple appraisal. It is believed that the anonymity built into the procedure was essential in encouraging greater honesty.

(source: Stinson and Stokes 1980)

First, the multiple sources were used to supplement the normal annual appraisal. In this instance the link was quite close but an examination of systems by Ashridge Management College shows that the extent of the linkage does vary. There are systems which have a very close tie – including playing a part in salary determination (highly controversial and risky, and seen by some as counter-productive), whereas in other organizations multiple appraisal may be used in more of a supporting way. For example, in both Hewlett-Packard and Mercury Communications 360° appraisal is offered as an option. Of course, 360° appraisal doesn't have to be used in conjunction with appraisal/performance management at all – the purpose may be primarily developmental, with the linkage being to some kind of training/development programme. For example, the Local Government Management Board's Top Managers Programme uses a 360° assessment questionnaire as one of a series of tools for diagnosing development needs. BT and Meridien Hotels both link 360° appraisal to training and development. Even in such cases as these, however, we might expect that performance improvement is ultimately an expected outcome.

Second, the multiple appraisal has both quantitative (ratings) and qualitative aspects. The use of questionnaires is probably the most common approach, but there is quite wide variation in application. For example, an organization might choose to buy an off-the-peg instrument. Or it might prefer a proprietary questionnaire that can be tailored to what it sees as its needs. Or the organization might go its own way and develop something in-house. The different approaches have different advantages and disadvantages, but whatever approach is taken the reliability and validity (that is, job and organizational relevance) of the instrument used need to be established.

One general disadvantage of questionnaires based solely on ratings is that they may lack **specific** examples of performance – this is true of questionnaires which require ratings of behavioural items as the items will be of a more generic kind. Some questionnaires, therefore, may include open-ended questions to allow specific examples to be written in. Standard Chartered Bank uses this approach in its Management Style Questionnaire for providing upward feedback.

Third, the source data are subjected to some analysis, perhaps in the Personnel/HR Department or perhaps independently, so as to maintain the anonymity of raters' assessments. Clearly, the raters themselves are not anonymous as they will have been chosen by the person being assessed – again, this is quite common practice today. Given that ratings are typically used, the analysis that is done will be of a statistical kind. But it is important not simply to feed back average ratings. Part of the rationale for using 360° assessment is that it captures *different* perceptions of performance; it is important, therefore, that the variations be fed back as well as the areas of commonality.

Fourth, who owns the data? There is a strongly argued view that the data fed back are the sole property of the manager being assessed, are for their developmental benefit, and that there should be no obligation on the individual to share the data with anyone else. However, disadvantages (summarized in Box 7.4) may arise from rigidly maintaining this stance, and it is common to find means of enabling recipients to discuss their data with someone else.

---

Box 7.4    **Potential drawbacks of 360° feedback confidentiality**

Regarding multisource feedback as the property of the individual for developmental purposes alone may result in underutilization of the full potential of the process, argues Bracken.

Leaving feedback information solely in the hands of the ratee creates potentially serious implications for sustaining the process and realizing true behavioural change, due to the following factors:

- Ratees are not held accountable for follow-through and may lack motivation to change.
- Ratees see the feedback as supplemental information that is 'nice to have' but tangential to their real work.
- Ratees see the feedback as an 'event', happening only once or only at long intervals and lacking ongoing feedback or support.
- Raters may not see any evidence that their input is being used, and this may eventually reduce their motivation to participate and/or provide honest feedback.

(source: Bracken 1996: 123)

In the Gulf Oil example, where the 360° feedback is linked with the annual appraisal, the data are shared with the line manager and the participant does not have any choice about this. But in other applications, conveying the feedback may fall to an independent facilitator (that is, independent of the line, not necessarily of the organization), whether on a one-to-one basis or within the context of a workshop. Simply providing a narrative report to the recipient is unlikely to be helpful as the recipient may not know how to interpret and act on the feedback. For example, if the recipient is seen differently by different parties, is this because of different **observations** of performance or different **expectations** (Moses *et al.* 1993)? At the very least, then, some training will be required to sensitize the recipient to such issues; the same point applies if a narrative report is to be provided separately to an appraising manager. The issues of voluntariness, feedback ownership and confidentiality are clearly important and complex, and need to be resolved before a scheme is launched.

## A CONCLUDING COMMENT

That managers seem reluctant to give feedback, positive or negative, suggests that simply providing training in the skills of how to give feedback will not be a sufficient intervention. Providing feedback is not just a matter of ability; if we think back to the models of performance discussed earlier, it is clear that there is a motivational element also – in other words, there has to be a willingness to give feedback. In the broader context of performance appraisal Murphy and Cleveland (1995) discuss the need to take into account appraiser motivation (that is, goals) in designing appraisal systems, and this is true in relation to performance management also.

Similarly, training for employees might be considered. Thus, Farr notes that 'Attention also needs to be given to the topic of training work performers to receive feedback in a nondefensive constructive manner' (1993: 177). And, again, Murphy and Cleveland point to the necessity of taking into account employee goals in assessing performance, a point to which I shall return in the final chapter.

The issues involved in giving and receiving feedback become all the more complex when we consider multi-source appraisal as a tool within performance management. The use of multiple appraisal is highly consistent with a participative, developmental approach to performance management. Drawing on several sources is likely to give a more rounded picture of employee performance: different sources bring different perspectives to bear (if they do not, there is not much point in having them) but this in itself is no panacea as all the sources are flawed, again in different ways. The relatively weak evidence we have so far about multiple appraisal is generally positive, but it is clear that there are many pitfalls: 360° feedback brings with it ethical, logistical, political and cost difficulties, and every potential to do more harm than good if not well implemented.

# 8 Rewarding performance

As the review of practice in Chapter 1 illustrated, reward within the context of performance management typically means performance-related pay (PRP; also referred to as merit pay or appraisal-related pay). This is a very narrow view which is flawed in many respects, as I shall go on to show. Reward may be derived from the job itself and, as the examination of management practices in Chapter 6 showed, the line manager has a key role to play here also.

In this chapter I will begin with a critical review of PRP before going on to consider some broader perspectives on reward. There are a number of difficulties surrounding PRP. First, there is very little evidence which confirms the positive effects desired; indeed, there is research which points clearly to possible negative consequences. Second, there is evidence which illustrates the considerable operational difficulties involved in implementing and operating PRP. Third, there is a failure to meet principles which stem from relevant psychological theory. This will lead me on to a consideration of fairness issues, not just in relation to reward but in performance management generally.

## PERFORMANCE-RELATED PAY

As numerous reviews (see Kessler 1994 and 1995 for summaries) have indicated, there are many different forms of PRP and in the early 1990s they have become more commonplace. In the context of performance management the most prevalent form of PRP seems to be 'individual merit and performance-related systems based on some form of appraisal or assessment of the individual using various input (traits, skills, competences) or output (objectives) indicators. They often involve a payment which is integrated into the basic salary' (Kessler 1994: 466–7). The findings from the IMS survey (Institute of Personnel Management 1992) reported in Chapter 1 bear out this interpretation, and the Price Waterhouse Cranfield survey confirms the prevalence of merit pay, especially for managerial (and professional) jobs (Filella and Hegewisch 1994). Indeed, this survey indicates that merit pay is quite common in other European countries.

Research shows that PRP has been introduced for several reasons. Cannell and Wood (1992), for example, found six main reasons amongst UK organizations, as shown in Table 8.1. The Price Waterhouse Cranfield survey tells us that in many European countries which have introduced merit pay the reasons for doing so were often to do with responding to labour market trends and the like – although the claimed reasons may be to bring about motivational or performance improvements. Though the word performance does not specifically appear in the list in Table 8.1 it is implicit in several of the reasons, such as reward and motivation. But (as with performance appraisal) where an organization implements PRP for multiple reasons there is always the risk that none of them will be satisfactorily achieved. Based on their examination of twenty-six organizations for the IPM, Fletcher and Williams, for example, concluded that:

> it is not hard to draw the conclusion that [PRP schemes] are more concerned with managing the pay bill than with managing employee motivation or performance. The former is, of course,

*Table 8.1* Reasons for introducing performance-related pay (source: Cannell and Wood 1992)

- Problems with incremental systems
- Reward and motivation
- Promotion of cultural and organizational change
- Improving communication
- Improving recruitment and retention
- Individualizing industrial relations

a legitimate purpose but schemes typically were not presented with this as their ostensible function.

(Fletcher and Williams 1992: 93)

Hence, conflicting messages may be conveyed to staff and there is a danger that the performance message will get lost, assuming that there is a performance message to be conveyed at all, that is.

## Research on PRP

### Evidence supporting PRP

Heneman reports that 'a number of studies have shown a relationship between performance ratings and changes in pay' (1992: 47), that is, higher performance ratings are associated with higher increases in merit pay. In other words, there is some evidence to suggest that organizations are able to relate PRP to past performance, and to this extent it is possible that the reward function of PRP is being satisfied (assuming, that is, that those affected do perceive a relationship between their performance and any extra pay that they receive). However, Heneman notes that 'The magnitude of the relationship between pay and performance in these studies is *not* large' (1992: 47) – the association is not strong, in other words, pointing to the possible impact of other factors (besides performance) which may affect merit pay decisions. For example, PRP guidelines (to do, say, with the size of increase available) may serve as a constraint, thus reinforcing the impression (which may be reality) that the name of the game is control of the wage bill (see Gerhart and Milkovich 1992).

Furthermore, these studies say nothing about the motivational/incentive effect of pay. On this aspect of PRP much of the evidence seems to be negative rather than positive, as I shall come on to show. As Heneman concludes, 'The results to date on the relationship between merit pay and subsequent motivation and performance are not encouraging' (1992: 258). Indeed, there is negligible evidence of a rigorous kind which supports the positive benefits commonly claimed for merit pay.

### Evidence against PRP

But can we expect PRP to work as a motivator? Can we expect it to improve performance? These questions are extremely difficult to answer, for a number of reasons. Both motivation and performance are affected by many factors, indeed they affect each other (Kanfer 1995). We should not expect to find, therefore, an association between any one intervention (in this case PRP) and a particular outcome. And even if we were to find an association, that in itself would not necessarily mean causation. Despite the difficulties, though, the questions are worth asking and at the very least we should be gathering attitudinal and perceptual data to try to answer them. In other words, what do employees and their managers believe about the effects of PRP?

*Managers' opinions*
We need to consider the opinions of two main sets of managers – those in central functions, such as personnel/HR, and line managers at the sharp end.

As shown in Chapter 1, there is a belief on the part of personnel/HR managers that PRP is more effective in improving organizational performance when used as part of some broader performance management policy. However, given the lack of systematic evaluation carried out by organizations we have to recognize that this is very much a belief which is unsupported by firm evidence.

Fletcher and Williams in their part of the IPM (1992) survey also gathered opinions about PRP, both from HR/personnel and line managers. Doing so revealed discrepant views about PRP:

> in the interviews with the HR and line representatives of the organizations visited, there was little consistency of viewpoint on the motivating power of money. The majority felt that the real motivators at management levels were professional and personal pride in the standards achieved, or loyalty to the organization and its aims, or peer pressure. On the other hand, there were those who believed that money was the prime factor in motivating improved performance. An example of the latter view came from the Personnel department of a large retail organization; however, when line managers in the company were interviewed, they saw matters differently. As one of them said, he was self-motivated – the money came as a result of that, not as the cause of it.
>
> (Institute of Personnel Management 1992: 117)

One of the points that this illustrates is that those at the top or centre of the organization may be proceeding on the basis of a false assumption about the motivating power of money. Thus, Murlis and Wright concluded, 'in retrospect top management, be they ministers or directors of major companies, sought to translate a simplistic motivational view into the way employees were paid and managed' (1993: 9). Yet those affected by PRP – whether recipients or the executors of a policy that someone else has determined – clearly have views about it, and about rewards and incentives more broadly. It would seem sensible for these opinions to be discovered; Thompson, for example, reports that 'employees who have been involved in the design and implementation of a PRP scheme are more likely to perceive it to be fair and more likely to be motivated' (1993: ix).

Some evidence of line managers' views comes from a major survey carried out by Marsden and Richardson (1994) in the Inland Revenue. As well as gathering data from employees affected by PRP (shown below), they also asked those employees' line managers for their views: Table 8.2 shows what was found. Marsden and Richardson conclude thus: 'These results certainly give no comfort to those who feel that staff might understate the extent of positive motivational change. . . . Indeed, the reporting officers were, if anything, even more sceptical of the system's success in this respect' (1994: 251).

*Table 8.2* The views of Inland Revenue appraisers on the impact of performance pay on their staff (source: Marsden and Richardson 1994: 252)

| Performance pay has | Yes (%) | No (%) |
| --- | --- | --- |
| caused many staff to work beyond the requirements of their job | 15 | 79 |
| led many staff to give sustained high performance at work | 14 | 77 |
| helped to increase the quality of the work of many staff | 10 | 82 |
| led to an increase in the quantity of the work of many staff | 22 | 71 |
| made many staff more committed to their work | 12 | 79 |

*Employees' opinions*

We also need to consider the views of employees affected by PRP, who may or may not be recipients of merit increases. Over the past few years some survey evidence has appeared and it paints anything but a positive picture of the impact of PRP. For example, a large-scale survey by the Society of Telecom Executives (1992) showed that only 8.3 per cent of respondents ($N = 1,625$) believed that their performance had been improved by PRP. The survey of Inland Revenue employees by Marsden and Richardson (1994) tells much the same story, as Table 8.3 indicates.

As we saw above, managers were similarly unenthusiastic. Marsden and Richardson thus concluded from their findings that in this case PRP was 'very unlikely to have significantly raised employee motivation – indeed may, on balance, have been demotivating. If it did not improve employee motivation, it is hard to see how the scheme could have enhanced employee performance' (1994: 244). Similar conclusions are drawn by Thompson, based on his employee surveys in three organizations:

> the benefits most often claimed for performance related pay are not met in practice. Firstly, PRP does not serve to motivate (even those with high ratings) and may do more to demotivate employees. Secondly, there was little evidence to suggest that PRP could help to retain high performers and no evidence to point to poor performers seeking to leave the organizations.

*Table 8.3* Inland Revenue employees' assessment of their own motivational responses to performance pay (source: Marsden and Richardson 1994: 251)

| Performance pay has led you to | Yes (%) | No (%) |
| --- | --- | --- |
| improve the quality of your work | 12 | 80 |
| increase the quantity of your work | 14 | 78 |
| work harder | 9 | 71 |
| work beyond the job requirements | 21 | 70 |
| give sustained high performance | 27 | 63 |
| improve your priorities at work | 22 | 64 |
| show more initiative | 27 | 61 |
| be more effective with the public | 9 | 68 |
| improve your sensitivity towards colleagues | 14 | 63 |

Thirdly, employees are negative or broadly neutral on its impact on organizational culture even in schemes that had been in operation for three or more years. Lastly, employees are unclear as to whether PRP rewards fairly (neither agreeing or disagreeing). However, high performers are likely to perceive it to be more fair than low rated performers. There is the risk that PRP may contribute to a downward spiral of demotivation for the bulk of employees and this draws into question the real costs and benefits of such schemes.

(Thompson 1993: ix)

All this British evidence supports Heneman's unenthusiastic conclusion (mentioned earlier), drawn from his examination of North American studies. However, proponents of PRP may be tempted to dismiss the sorts of finding reported above on the grounds that in these particular cases PRP had been poorly implemented and operated. This idea may have some force, if only because there are many factors to be managed in implementing and operating PRP. However, that there are so many factors suggests that failure in implementation and operation is much

*Table 8.4* Operational difficulties associated with performance-related pay (source: derived from Cannell and Wood 1992; Geary 1992; Incomes Data Services 1985; Kessler and Purcell 1992; Kessler 1994; Pearce 1987)

- Does PRP encourage short-termism?
- Does a focus on individual performance lead employees to place their interests ahead of those of the organization more generally?
- What effect does PRP have on team and co-operative working?
- Is PRP appropriate to all organizational cultures?
- Can performance be defined comprehensively?
- How much of performance is within the individual's control?
- What criteria should be used for measuring performance? Outputs? Inputs? Both?
- Can individual performance be measured objectively and fairly?
- What amount of pay constitutes a significant increase in the eyes of employees?
- Can PRP give rise to sex (or other unlawful) discrimination?
- Do line managers have the willingness and ability required to operate PRP?
- Does PRP create divisiveness?
- How should average performers be treated?
- Is there a climate of trust (particularly in line managers–subordinate relations)?
- Will PRP diminish the value of intrinsic rewards?

more likely than success. This leads neatly to operational problems.

## Operational difficulties

A substantial body of research (e.g., Cannell and Wood 1992; Geary 1992; Incomes Data Services 1985; Institute of Personnel Management 1992; Kessler and Purcell 1992; Marsden and Richardson 1994; Thompson 1992, 1993) points to the *many* potential problems which may arise in implementing and operating PRP. An illustrative list of several of these is given in Table 8.4. These all are issues which organizations will inevitably face in seeking to introduce PRP. Resolving them successfully is hazardous to say the least; but avoiding them seems certain to lead to failure.

Another perspective on implementation and operational difficulties may be gained from considering Heneman's framework for merit pay (Figure 8.1). This illustrates the many factors – environmental, organizational and individual – that bear on the operation of PRP (indeed, reward more generally) and shows all too clearly the complexity of the task.

## Psychological theory

Contributing to all this complexity are the implications of a number of psychological theories. Gerhart and Milkovich (1992), Heneman (1992) and Hume (1995) have presented helpful overviews of the several theories which may help to offer a rationale for PRP. Expectancy theory is the one that is perhaps most commonly discussed in relation to PRP (e.g., Lawler 1987; Mabey and Salaman 1995) but there are others, such as equity theory and reinforcement theory; Heneman also identifies a number of economic theories which have implications for PRP.

The implications of expectancy theory for PRP are quite clear. If PRP is to serve a motivational function a number of conditions must be met, as set out in Table 8.5. Certain of these conditions are supported by other theories. For example, reinforcement theory tells us that provision of the reward must be timely – a basic principle of giving feedback, as shown in the previous chapter. Reinforcement theory also supports the expectancy theory performance–reward process link as pay increases must be contingent upon delivery of the desired performance, with greater increases being given for higher levels of performance. All these principles depend on performance being clearly defined – in particular, performance that is desired must be distinguished from that which is not – and clarity of definition would seem to be a precondition for accuracy of measurement. Yet, as shown in earlier chapters, coming up with a clear statement of performance requirements is no easy task – we can try to express performance requirements in terms of products or behaviours, using a range of 'objective' or subjective indicators. Moreover, we might also try to base merit rewards on skills or competencies (Sparrow 1996). And we try to do this within a context of organizational uncertainty and complexity. Indeed, Pearce (1987) contends that under such conditions merit pay may be counter-productive as it is likely to work against the fostering of collaboration and co-operation amongst employees.

*Figure 8.1* Merit pay framework (source: Heneman 1990)

*Table 8.5* Expectancy theory and performance-related pay (source: Heneman 1992: 27)

---

Heneman sets out the following conditions which need to be met if PRP is to serve as a motivator:

- *Performance must be accurately measured.* If it is not, then employees cannot make the perceived link between effort and performance (expectancy) and performance and rewards (instrumentality).
- *Increased pay must be a valued outcome.* For employees to pursue high levels of performance, the end result of such performance must be attractive or have positive valence. Hence, pay increases must have greater valence than alternative outcomes such as leisure. If a pay increase is less attractive than leisure, then an employee will feel less motivated to perform than when promised a pay increase rather than additional time off the job.
- *The relationship between pay and performance must be clearly defined.* The relationship between performance on the job and pay associated with performance must be clearly spelled out by the organization to ensure that performance is perceived by employees as instrumental in attaining a pay increase.
- *Opportunities to improve performance must exist.* If an employee does not have the opportunity to increase or improve performance, then it is futile for that employee to expand effort at a task. If opportunity is not present, both expectancy and resultant motivation will not be present. Employees must have the time, equipment, ability and supervision required to perform a task – which translates into opportunity – before there can be expectations for performance.

---

But meeting these conditions requires considerable sophistication and this is lacking in PRP schemes, which commonly seem to be applied in a universalistic way. Moreover, there is no shortage of research (see Lawler and Jenkins 1992, for one summary) which points to failure in meeting the requirements indicated by psychological theory. For example, it is assumed erroneously that the prospect of increased pay is valued by all employees as a reward. Not so; and for those who do value it, it is unlikely that they look at the prospect of a merit raise in abstract terms. This raises the question of how much of an increase will be seen as significant in the eyes of employees such that they will be motivated to improve their performance. There is no simple answer to this question, either theoretically or practically. Findings reported by Fletcher and Williams indicate organizational confusion on this matter: 'One local authority had a maximum of 15 per cent to be awarded on the basis of performance, and felt that this was insufficient. . . . Yet another local authority, in a not dissimilar position, had a maximum of 10 per cent of merit pay, and thought that this was too large.'

Empirical research indicates that there is no single figure – individual differences are a major factor here. This, of course, adds to the complexity of managing PRP. Furthermore, if the amount on offer is seen as too small it may be taken as insulting – hardly rewarding or motivating! This implies that where there is PRP the performance element may need to be more than organizations are currently paying. This in turn suggests that the cost may come to be too high for organizations.

Moreover, the essential process links are often not made; that is, employees may fail to see a link between their effort and their performance as measured by, say, the appraisal scheme. Likewise, they may fail to see the link between their performance (as measured, that is) and reward through pay. Such failures stem from deficiencies both in the measurement of performance and in the operation of PRP. For example, the performance–reward link may not be perceived because the performance element of pay is wrapped up with, say, a cost of living increase.

Faced with the accumulating evidence which indicates the operational difficulties in introducing and running PRP and suggests that the effects are likely to be negative rather than positive, it seems clear that what is seen as one of the foundation stones of performance management simply is not working as intended. Indeed, faced with the evidence, it is scarcely credible that any sensible organization would want to have a system of PRP, certainly if the aims are to provide reward and to motivate. But, of course, these may not be the real aims. As noted earlier, the true aims may be rather different – such as managing the wage bill or individualizing the employment relationship. Both of these may be legitimate aims in themselves (if presented as such), but neither has much, if anything, to do with motivation or performance. The true reasons, then, would seem to be ideological (Storey and Sisson 1993) rather than anything else. Under such circumstances it would not be surprising if employees were to see the PRP system as downright unfair. This leads on to consideration of the issue of fairness in performance management.

# FAIRNESS IN PERFORMANCE MANAGEMENT

## The fairness of performance management outcomes

It is appropriate to consider fairness in this chapter because employees'. perceptions of fairness very commonly relate to the rewards or other benefits that they receive. All sorts of decisions are made about employees at work. For example, people are promoted, they are awarded merit increases or bonuses (or not, as the case may be), they receive favourable or unfavourable appraisals, they are required to achieve particular targets, etc., etc. And they have views about the fairness or otherwise of those decisions – this is what is referred to as **outcome fairness** or **distributive justice**. Some research on this that is relevant to performance management was carried out by Greenberg (1986). He discovered that there were two distributive factors that contributed to managers perceiving performance evaluations as fair:

- the performance evaluation was based on the performance achieved;
- salary/promotion recommendations were based on the evaluation given.

As we might expect, when employees see these sorts of decisions (e.g., about rewards) as being unfair they tend to be less satisfied with them than when they see them as fair. We might suppose that these perceptions do not matter all that much – life is unfair and that is all there is to it. But perceptions of outcome fairness do have important consequences for aspects of organizational performance – poor employee performance and higher rates or turnover and absenteeism, for example, where outcomes are seen as unfair (Cropanzano and Greenberg 1997).

## The fairness of performance management procedures

Reward (and other performance-management-related decisions) are, of course, the result of some sort of process. In other words, we cannot consider the perceived fairness of the decisions themselves separately from the means by which those decisions are arrived at – this is **procedural justice**. Again, Greenberg's research on performance evaluation is relevant here. He identified five procedural factors which contribute to the perceived fairness of the evaluation process:

- employee input is solicited before the evaluation and is used;
- there is two-way communication during the evaluation interview;
- employees have the ability to challenge or rebut the evaluation;
- the rater is familiar with the employee's work;
- standards are applied consistently.

Several of these factors support the principle that employees should have a **voice** in performance evaluation if they are to have a fair hearing. Indeed, we might want to argue that the principle applies much more widely in performance management, applying not just to appraisal but also to the agreement of the performance requirements, the means by which they will be measured, and such like.

Greenberg's findings endorse other research (e.g., that performance evaluations be based on accurate and unbiased evidence) which has also identified additional procedural factors particularly relevant to performance management. For example, Landy *et al.* (1978) showed that the existence of action plans to improve identified performance weaknesses contributed to perceptions of fairness. Also, Leventhal (1976, 1980) has suggested that one rule of procedural justice is that the concerns of all interested parties be taken into account. We might see this as a principle supporting the use of multiple appraisal; it also supports the case for involving all relevant parties in the design and implementation of performance management systems. Thompson's research, quoted earlier, lends still further support to this position.

As much as we might want to see these as ethical principles which are sufficient in themselves to guide practice, there are likely to be many who will fail to be persuaded on these grounds. However, in the same way that outcome fairness has positive outcomes for organizational performance, so too does procedural justice. For example, research has shown that when procedures are fair employees tend to be more accepting of the decisions made (even if personally unfavourable) than when the procedures are unfair.

For the most part, the procedural factors summarized above fall into two main groups – there are **structural aspects** and **social aspects** (Greenberg 1990). Examples of the former include consistency of application, freedom from bias, and the like. Social aspects are more concerned with the nature and quality of the interpersonal interaction that takes place – do people feel that they have had their say, that they have been treated with dignity and respect in the decision-making process and in the way in which the decision is conveyed to them, that they have enough information about what the procedures are and the way they work?

That there is this interpersonal aspect to fairness reminds us that there is a social basis to the exchange relationship between employer and employee and we might expect this to be part of the psychological contract. But employees do have formal legal contracts and these underlie the economic aspect of the exchange relationship. This brings me back to merit pay.

In the eyes of many employees the principle of merit pay is a 'good thing'; but support for that principle is by no means universal. Marsden and Richardson (1994), for example, showed that 40 per cent of their respondents disagreed with the principle. Though this is a minority (a large one), their opinion none the less points to one reason why organizations should not assume automatically that performance and pay should be related – Lawler (1987) regards this assumption as a serious error. Another erroneous assumption is the managerial belief that pay is sufficiently valued as a reward by all employees to act as a motivator. Brown and Walsh make the point in these terms:

> There is no necessity for pay to play a central role in motivating employees. Although haphazard pay administration can have a potent effect as a demotivator, the importance of pay as a positive incentive is greatly exaggerated. . . . The need for money may be the central motive for being employed at all, but it is rarely enough to ensure that work is done well.
>
> (Brown and Walsh 1994: 450)

Hence, we need to consider rewards, and their incentive value, much more broadly. This includes accepting that individual contribution need not be a basis for determining merit increases. It is clear that there has been some reaction against individual-PRP and increasing interest is being paid to team pay. Drawing on Institute of Personnel Development (IPD) research, Armstrong (1996) identifies a number of requirements for team pay to work well, as shown in Table 8.6. But team pay is no less problematical than individual merit pay, and to adopt it in a reactive way (as happened

*Table 8.6* Requirements for team-based pay (source: Armstrong 1996: 23)

Team pay appears to work best if teams:
● stand alone as performing units for which clear targets and standards can be agreed;
● have a considerable degree of autonomy – team pay is likely to be most effective in teams that are, to a large degree, self-managed operations;
● are composed of people whose work is interdependent and where it is acknowledged by members that the team will only deliver if the members work well together and share the responsibility for success;
● are stable, where members are used to working with one another, know what is expected of them by fellow team members and know where they stand in the regard of their colleagues;
● are mature, where teams are well established, used to working flexibly to meet targets and capable of making good use of the complementary skills of their members;
● are composed of individuals who are flexible, multi-skilled and good team players, while still being capable of expressing a different point of view and carrying that point if it is for the good of the team.

with appraisal-related pay) is hardly a basis for a lasting system. All of this points to the need for a coherent policy framework for financial reward (see Armstrong 1993, for example). But we need also to recognize the potential contribution of rewards other than pay.

## REWARDS OTHER THAN PAY

One of the ways in which rewards may be categorized is to divide them into two main groups – intrinsic and extrinsic. The latter includes pay and many other rewards which may have remunerative consequences, such as promotion, which also brings with it other rewards like enhanced status. Some extrinsic rewards may not be financial in the way that pay is but nonetheless they incur a cost in money terms for the organization. Still other extrinsic rewards, such as recognition or praise from the boss, are wholly non-financial. And there may be other rewards that the line manager may be able to manage. For example, one of the organizations visited by Fletcher and Williams in the IPM research suggested nearly forty non-financial rewards their managers could use; importantly, this organization also trained managers in how to manage reward.

The role of the manager in rewarding and recognizing performance was noted in the previous chapter, these being two of the
key managerial practices identified by Yukl (1994). He offers a
number of guidelines for engaging in these activities, such as
finding out what rewards people value, explaining how rewards
are determined, recognizing improvements in performance, not
limiting recognition to just the best performers, and providing
specific and timely reward and recognition (Table 7.4 gave
more examples). Wright (1996) reviews research which indicates
that positive reward behaviours on the part of line managers/
supervisors are associated with job holder performance – this, of
course, is consistent with what we know about the importance of
feedback. Other advice about giving reward comes from Dickson
*et al.* (1993); though some of this derives from educational settings, it seems no less relevant to the workplace (see Box 8.1).

---

Box 8.1    **Giving rewards**

Rewards seem to work best to motivate and direct when the
recipient appreciates why they are being offered. If the
intention is to enhance learning and performance at a certain
task, then the rewarder should:

- specify the particulars of the accomplishment being praised;
- decide upon criteria for praising and preferably agree
  these with the recipient in advance, so reducing the
  chances of what is happening being constructed as the
  mere exercise of reward power;
- draw attainment criteria from that individual's previous
  levels of performance rather than those of peers;
- focus the recipient's attention on the task and his or her
  accomplishment at it rather than on the reward and the
  rewarder;
- ensure that the attribution of the cause of the positive
  reaction encompasses effort invested in the task and does
  not undermine self-beliefs in ability.

Rewards from others must be seen to be genuine and authen-
tic, rather than manipulative, to be effective.

(source: Dickson *et al.* 1993: 178–9)

---

Then there are intrinsic rewards – 'those that the individual provides himself or herself (e.g. feeling of accomplishment) as a result of performing some task' (Steers and Porter 1991: 478). Though the research evidence on this point is far from clear cut, one of the possible dangers of an undue concentration on extrinsic rewards, particularly those such as PRP, is that intrinsic reward and motivation may come to be diminished.

All this, then, points up the importance of the design of the job so as to make sure that intrinsic factors are present. These include, for example, opportunity for personal control (such as employee discretion, absence of close supervision, participation in decision-making), opportunity for skill use, and task variety (variation in job content, skill variety) (Warr 1996). These are features of jobs in many contemporary 'high-performance' forms of organization (Buchanan 1994). Such factors as these have been shown to promote employee well-being and job satisfaction; a positive, although less consistent, relationship with performance also has been established (Parker and Wall 1996).

## Identifying valued rewards

Though lists of non-financial rewards may be found, either in popular articles and texts or in more academic literature, there is the view that organizations should try to find out the sorts of things that their particular employees will experience as rewarding. Kerr (1988), for example, advocates a data-based diagnosis of an organization's reward system and he sets out an audit tool for discovering what employees find rewarding, discovering how they believe rewards are obtained, and such like. Table 8.7 illustrates some of the rewards that he has identified.

## Rewarding the 'right' thing

Though knowing what employees find personally rewarding is important, those rewards need to be used to reinforce the 'right' thing. Problems in this area have long been recognized and they found expression many years ago in Kerr's (1975) article 'On the folly of rewarding A, while hoping for B'. This has recently (1995) been updated by Kerr and supplemented by a survey of members of the US Academy of Management's Executive Advisory Panel.

The thrust of his article is that there exist numerous examples of

*Table 8.7* Examples of non-financial rewards (source: Kerr 1988: 68)

- titles
- formal commendationas and awards
- favourable mention in company publications
- freedom concerning job duties
- freedom concerning working hours
- private, informal recognition for jobs well done
- challenging duties
- varied, interesting work
- important, meaningful duties and responsibilities
- having influence in setting goals and making decisions

*Table 8.8* Common management reward follies (source: Kerr 1995: 12; *Academy of Management Executive*, **9(1)**, p. 15)

| We hope for . . . | But we often reward . . . |
|---|---|
| • long-term growth; environmental responsibility | • quarterly earnings |
| • teamwork | • individual effort |
| • setting challenging 'stretch' objectives | • achieving goals; 'making the numbers' |
| • downsizing; rightsizing; delayering; restructuring | • adding staff; adding budget; adding Hay points |
| • commitment to total quality | • shipping on schedule, even with defects |
| • candour; surfacing bad news early | • reporting good news, whether it's true or not; agreeing with the boss, whether or not he or she is right |
| • teamwork and collaboration | • the best team members |
| • innovative thinking and risk-taking | • proven methods and not making mistakes |
| • development of people skills | • technical achievements and accomplishments |
| • employee involvement and empowerment | • tight control over operations and resources |
| • high achievement | • another year's effort |

*Table 8.9*  Obstacles standing in the way of dealing with the reward folly (source: *Academy of Management Executive*, **9(1)**, pp. 15–16)

1  *The inability to break out of the old ways of thinking about reward and recognition practices.* In particular, there appears to be need for a new goal and target behaviour definition, including non-quantifiable behaviour and that which is system focused rather than job- or functionally dependent. Among the deterrents to change are the entitlement mentality of workers and the reluctance of managment to commit to revamping or revitalizing performance management processes and systems.

2  *Lack of a holistic or overall system view of performance factors and results.* To a great extent, this is still caused by organizational structures that promote optimization of sub-unit results at the expense of the total organization.

3  *Continuing focus on short-term results by management and shareholders.*

'reward systems that are fouled up in that behaviours which are rewarded are those which the rewarder is trying to *discourage*, while the behaviour he desires is not being rewarded at all' (Kerr 1995: 7). Table 8.8 shows some examples that Kerr (1995) provides, along with a number of others generated by the US Academy of Management's survey. Kerr's view is that these examples point to the need to change reward systems. But this is easier said than done. For example, the US Academy of Management's Executive Advisory Panel was asked to state what it saw as the barriers to change. Three main themes emerged, as shown in Table 8.9. However, the first step in bringing about change is recognizing the need for it, and in this regard the sort of diagnostic activity advocated by Kerr would seem to be especially helpful.

## A CONCLUDING COMMENT

The survey evidence suggests that for many organizations reward is construed narrowly to mean PRP. Of course, it is possible that there is a deficiency in the evidence that we have as the surveys have not asked about other aspects of reward. That said, however, studies of managerial behaviour suggest that reward-related behaviours are not displayed by managers and supervisors to the extent that their subordinates would wish (for example, the under-provision of feedback). Not only this, the emphasis on PRP may be misconceived, in that the evidence does not strongly suggest that the positive benefits expected will be realized. Indeed, given the operational and other difficulties the more likely outcome would seem to be a negative impact – lowered morale, perceptions of injustice. The risks associated with team-based pay are no lower than those already well established for individual-PRP.

Though we might see justice as something that is valuable and proper in its own right, fairness in performance management procedures is important for other reasons as well. So, to take an instrumental view, it makes good business sense – there are positive outcomes for the organization in terms of employee commitment, performance of altruistic behaviours, positive job attitudes, and acceptance of decisions and procedures. But these benefits have to be earned – not just through the procedures themselves but also through the way in which they are designed, developed and implemented.

# 9 *Developing and designing performance management*

The development and design of a performance management system naturally depends heavily on how performance is defined and on the state and nature of the organization's existing sytems, structures, etc. In the broadest sense performance management is concerned with organizational performance but, as was shown earlier, this is a problematic concept. As Dawson points out:

> When people talk of improving organizational performance they can be referring to any one of a number of aspects, including effectiveness (goal attainment), efficiency (amount of resources used to produce a unit of output), productivity in terms of quantity or quality or timing, indicators of morale, and capacity to adapt and change to cope with the unexpected and unpredictable.
>
> (Dawson 1996: 235)

That organizational performance can be defined in so many terms means, of course, that the task of forging a link between individual and organizational performance is far from simple.

Indeed, defining performance at the individual level is no less complex. As we saw, there are two main conceptions – outputs/results and behaviours. But it is probable that employee inputs – their effort, for example – also fall within a loose everyday understanding of the term performance. Herein lies one of the problems of performance management, that of achieving some understanding of what is meant by performance, whether at the individual or organizational level (or anywhere in between). In this chapter I will outline a diagnostic, 'involving' approach as a means of trying to bring about the sort of understanding that is required.

Though it has several meanings, the most common interpretation of the term performance management is that it is a set of activities directed at the individual so as to channel his or her performance in support of organizational performance. That said, these activities exist within a broader framework of some kind. The integrative, holistic approach to performance management that is advocated in much of the literature sees this framework as involving the communication of the organization's mission statement, goals, etc. to all employees. The intent here is to bring individual goals into line with those expressed for the organization as a whole or, in other words, to align individual performance with organizational performance. This, of course, is a very unitarist view which very often is at odds with organizational reality and which may be one of the reasons why performance management systems do not succeed as intended. It may be preferable to try to accommodate the plurality of interests that we are likely to find, at least to the extent of having different systems to suit the needs and requirements of different groups, whether they be departments, type of job or whatever.

Some accounts of employee performance management assume that the organizational framework already exists. For example, earlier I quoted Ainsworth and Smith (1993):

> This assumes that the important corporate issues of 'mission' and the setting of corporate goals have been addressed and resolved. It assumes that objectives for the sub-sections of the organization (the departments, divisions or business units) have been set within the key results areas, and that the senior management group has identified just where the competitive advantage and value added dimensions of the business lie. It further assumes that all of this has been communicated to and understood by those involved.
>
> (Ainsworth and Smith 1993: 5–6)

In many organizations it is likely that all of this does exist and that it operates in the way advocated. But this should not be assumed; for example, the IMS survey of performance management practices (Institute of Personnel Management 1992) revealed that communication was one aspect of their policies which organizations found to be problematical. Furthermore, the survey evidence also revealed that the organizational framework is often deficient in various respects. So, not all organizations have mission statements and even if they do there may be a failure to communicate those statements, and other relevant information, to all employees. Hence, for many organizations the starting point for performance management will have to be at the corporate/organizational level – for example, with its systems for planning, manufacturing/service delivery, employee communication, etc.

But as can be seen from earlier chapters, the predominant nature of performance management systems in UK organizations is that they are in essence evolutionary developments of performance appraisal, or as Lundy and Cowling put it, 'a logical progression' (1996: 307). Being mindful of this I will outline an approach to the development and implementation of performance management which is consistent with the evolutionary stance but which allows for more radical and fundamental change. The basis of the approach comes from Mohrman *et al.* (1989). Though presented as an approach to the design of appraisal systems, it applies readily to performance management as conventionally practised in the UK and I will therefore describe it in performance-management-related terms. I shall use the Mohrman *et al.* model as a general framework within which I shall incorporate other models, including those from the broader literature on the management of change. A characteristic feature of many of the recent models of performance management system design is the strong emphasis they place on diagnosis and analysis.

## INTRODUCING PERFORMANCE MANAGEMENT: EVOLUTION AND ITERATION

One of the attractions of the approach advocated by Mohrman *et al.* (1989) is that it recognizes the organizational context of performance management – mission, strategy, structure, etc. It also recognizes that forms and procedures are commonly associated with performance management and that the core events are 'personal and interpersonal behaviours and processes' (1989: 15). In other words, the approach accommodates both the formal, procedural aspects of performance management and the informal, day-to-day aspects. All this is shown in Figure 9.1.

Figure 9.1 also depicts the design process as political, rational and participative, aspects that will become clear as this chapter proceeds. As a rational process we might view it as a more or less step-by-step sequence of activities, as in Figure 9.2.

## The critical players

### Employees and their managers

Mohrman *et al.* write of the need to 'get the right people involved': 'A cardinal rule in any type of design effort is to get the people who will be using the system involved in its design' (1989: 28). Who, then, is involved in using an organization's performance management system? Most obviously, of course, the organization's line managers and the employees who are on the receiving end of performance management. How might managers (and others) be involved? Armstrong (1994) suggests project teams, Bernardin and Beatty (1984) propose a task force comprising of representatives of the groups that will be affected, and Fletcher (1993) and Yeates (1990) suggest consultative/advisory groups: 'These groups are beneficial in that they help solve real problems, investment of time in them helps demonstrate top management commitment and ensures that conflicts are aired and resolved. They also demonstrate management ownership of the scheme' (Yeates 1990: 132). Examples are to be found, however, and not just in the context of employee performance management: Standard Chartered Bank set up a committee including representatives drawn from all levels of staff; Rolls-Royce Motors set up a team comprising members from all levels (senior management to the shop floor) to investigate total quality issues; Royal Mail conducted workshops with over a thousand staff to help identify current business strengths and weaknesses.

Yet it is the groups most directly affected that are frequently conspicuous by their absence when it comes to the development and implementation of performance management, even though the sorts of consultative processes involved will be familiar to many organizations as they use them as part of their market research activities, for example as a means of keeping in touch with the customer. However, in their IPM research (1992) Fletcher and

Within the figure:

Business strategy goals and objectives

Organization, model, style systems, model, style

Performance appraisal system

Performance appraisal events and behaviours

Political design

Rational design

Participative design

Process of designing

Completed design

Strategy

Organization

Performance appraisal system

Performance appraisal events and behaviours

*Figure 9.1* Designing performance appraisal: a framework for performance management (source: Mohrman *et al.* 1989)

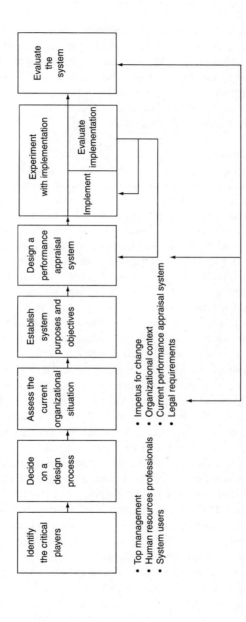

*Figure 9.2* A realistic model for performance appraisal system design: a step-by-step approach for performance management (source: Mohrman *et al.* 1989)

Williams found a high level of involvement in only a couple of organizations; in most it was of a low order, commonly non-existent. The development and design process more usually takes place at the centre of the organization, and where we find such a non-participatory style we would not be surprised to see it reflected in the performance management system itself – e.g. the relative absence of self-appraisal.

**Top management**
Though the groups at the sharp end are important, the design process also has to bring in the organization's senior management and the personnel/HR function. As Mohrman *et al.* point out, the former 'set strategic and philosophical directions for the organization' (1989: 30) and these must be captured by the performance management system. The involvement of managers at the very top or in central functions such as personnel/HR was central to the changes that took place in several of the organizations investigated by Fletcher and Williams. In particular, the CEO (new in ten of the organizations visited by Fletcher and Williams) or the HR Director were key influences. Such top-level commitment needs to be broad-based. In ICI Pharmaceuticals (as it was), Sheard described the establishment of a 'group of senior, experienced business managers from across the organization' (1992: 40). Their task was to serve as a 'personnel steering group' to oversee the implementation of a company-wide initiative called the 'development of people, work and reward' (1992: 40). Such commitment and involvement is important for a number of reasons. For example, Bertsch and Williams (1994), studying the implementation of TQM, showed that the involvement of top management helped to promote the legitimacy of the planned change. And Rodgers and Hunter (1991) have shown that the positive effects of management by objectives (MbO) are greater under conditions of high top management commitment – that is, a high level of support during implementation and active participation in operating MbO. In other words, it is not enough for top management to be involved and supportive during system development; this must continue once the new system is in operation.

Necessary though it is, the commitment of an organization's topmost management doesn't guarantee that the performance management system will be accepted by those to whom it will apply. The danger is that schemes initiated at the top and developed by the centre will simply come to be seen as having been imposed. But if performance management is to stand any chance of succeeding, the commitment of those on the receiving end is essential – involving them in the design and development process may help to bring this about.

### Personnel/HR management

Personnel/HR may be users of information generated by the performance management system (depending upon its purposes and nature), but aside from this, personnel specialists may have a facilitative role to play in the development process. Fletcher and Williams encountered this in their research for the IPM:

> It is important on the one hand to be able to offer support and to give guidance where necessary, but not at the cost of taking control and ownership out of line managers' hands. . . .
> The role of the HR department is likely to remain very significant in effective performance management. . . . It has a strong facilitating and support role to play that is essential if the policies are to be developed and to function in an effective and equitable way. . . . In all this, the most important factor will be the ability of the HR department to balance the conflict between the need to devolve ownership and control, with the need to guide, inform and support. Without that support, it may be that the additional demands performance management places on line managers would be too great.
>
> (Institute of Personnel Management 1992: 116)

The apparent desire to place responsibility for performance management in the hands of line managers may be seen as part of a broader trend to devolve human resource management activities. Some research (Brewster and Söderström 1994), however, suggests that in the UK such broader devolvement is less widely practised than it is in other countries in Europe. Indeed, out of twelve countries, the UK showed the third-lowest level of devolvement.

## Design process

The above remarks about the key players clearly imply a preferred approach to the design process, namely one that is participative and involving. In large organizations the direct involvement of *everyone* who will be affected by performance management is clearly unrealistic, but this need not then become an argument for involving no one! Some suggestions were made above and occasional case accounts of how particular systems have been developed provide some illustrations.

Accounts of managing change (e.g. Dawson 1996) indicate that a participative approach is only one of several which might be adopted. However, a major reason for arguing that a participative, involving approach has special appropriateness with respect to performance management is that performance management is presented as something that should be owned and driven by the line. This implies that the development process should also be driven by the line. Moreover, a number of writers associate performance management with a particular set of values – including trust, openness, free communication and involvement. To advocate such values but then not act in accordance with them when developing a new system will surely mean that the system will be received with scepticism.

This immediately brings to the surface one of the main tensions that will arise in designing a performance management system. We have already identified that there are several key groups affected by or involved in performance management on a day-to-day basis. Some of the interests of these different groups may be shared; but other interests may be in sharp conflict. This is an issue that has been taken up by Murphy and Cleveland (1995). Though they write about appraisal, what they have to say applies no less to performance management. They identify two general strategies that may be adopted in designing a new system: '(a) change participants' goals to fit the needs of the system, or (b) change the system to fit participants' goals' (Murphy and Cleveland 1995: 381).

The former is the traditional approach and most probably is the one which remains dominant today. Thus, performance management systems are developed centrally to meet goals that have been determined centrally. The new system then is 'rolled out', perhaps supported by some training for those expected to work it. But very often the new system is not accepted, with line managers and employees failing to see it as meeting their needs.

Murphy and Cleveland therefore argue for the second approach: 'An alternative to changing the people to fit the system is to change the system to fit the people. This strategy involves assessing the goals pursued by participants in appraisal, then tailoring the system to best fit those goals' (1995: 382). The risk here, of course, is that of developing a system that will fail to meet the needs and requirements as seen by top management. As noted above, it is just as important to maintain their acceptance and commitment. Thus, as Mohrman *et al.* (1989) make clear, the design process is in part political, and it is in assessing the current situation that the interests of the different groups begin to become apparent.

## Assessing the current situation

An organization which routinely carries out monitoring and maintenance of its performance management system will readily have evidence about how well it is working and in consequence will be well placed to fine tune its operation or to make more substantial changes should these be required. However, systematic data often will not be available – as we have seen, organizations commonly do little by way of monitoring and evaluation – and change is likely to come about as a result of the perception of some kind of problem. To this extent the introduction of performance management is often reactive; for example, Fletcher and Williams concluded:

Adopting performance management has not been an entirely reactive process, forced on organizations by external circumstances. There is no doubt that some have developed policies of this kind as a result of deep thought about their values, their attitude to their employees, and their future mission, and without any significant external pressures on them at the time. But the impression obtained from this research is that they probably are in the minority.

(Institute of Personnel Management 1992: 85)

However, in this respect the impetus for introducing performance management may be no different from that for many other changes that arise within organizations. Undoubtedly, there has to be a perception of some need for change; this point is widely recognized in the literature on organizational and cultural change (e.g. Brown 1995; Dawson 1996). Recognizing what the trigger is is an important early step in the diagnostic process. We can see this in the framework put forward by the Strategic Remuneration Research Centre (SRRC) (Table 9.1).

*Table 9.1* Strategic Remuneration Research Centre performance management diagnostic (source: Hendry *et al.* 1997: 21)

---

**1   Reasons**
- What has triggered a reappraisal of the performance management system or rewards at this time?

**2   Objectives**
- What are our strategic business goals?
- Who or what delivers critical performance with respect to business goals?
- What kind of performance contract do we want with employees?
- What is the performance system designed to do (e.g. attract, retain, motivate, control)?

**3   Environment**
*External contingencies*
- What stage of the business cycle are we in?
- What are the effects of the national/societal culture we operate in on attitudes to performance and differentials?
*Internal contingencies*
- What are the motivational assumptions of the relevant group(s) of employees?
- What are the relevant internal employee reference groups and how do they affect attitudes to differentials?

**4   Systems**
- What is the range of things we have to do to support the performance/business goals that affect employees' knowledge, capability and motivation?

**5   Design**
*Content*
- How do we define rewards?
- How do we define incentives?
- What measures are appropriate (e.g. in terms of the short, medium, and long term, financial versus non-financial measures, individual versus group)?
- Can we measure performance in the ways we want to and design rewards appropriately?
- Can people see this connection?
*Process*
- Are there links or disconnections through the whole reward structure?
- Do other managers involved in the design and management of the performance system buy into it?
- Is the process manageable?
- How do we communicate about performance and rewards, including feedback?

**6   Outcomes**
- What is the impact on behaviour (e.g. does the system reinforce the old or motivate new behaviours)?
- Retrospectively, what is the pay-off or success criterion?
- Is it possible to define or develop return on investment criteria, taking into account the costs of designing and administering the scheme, and of paying for rewards?

**7   Monitoring**
- What review process is in place or needs to be created?

---

**Factors to be analysed**

One of the advantages of this framework is that it is specifically oriented towards employee-centered performance management. But there are other diagnostics which may be more or less appropriate depending on how widely the organization wishes to analyse the current situation. For example, Swanson (1994) poses questions which may be asked about performance at three levels – organization, process and individual, as shown in Table 9.2. What these frameworks illustrate is that there are many factors to be analysed in assessing the current situation; for example:

- the organization's mission etc.;
- what the organization's objectives are, whether they are generally known throughout the organization, what is generally understood by organizational performance;
- the organization's prevailing climate and culture;
- organizational structure, including decision-making processes and job design;
- the fit of performance management activities with other personnel/ HR policies and practices;
- communication systems;
- reward systems.

Also, following on from what was said earlier about involving the key players, many of the questions are ones which are best answered by systematically gathering relevant data and evidence from those who are in a position to give an informed view. This reinforces the participative and rational nature of the design process. However, certain of the factors identified above will

*Table 9.2* Performance diagnosis: enabling questions (source: Swanson 1994: 52)

| PERFORMANCE VARIABLES | PERFORMANCE LEVELS | | |
|---|---|---|---|
| | *Organization level* | *Process level* | *Individual level* |
| *Mission/goal* | Does the organizational mission/goal fit the reality of the economic, political and cultural forces? | Do the process goals enable the organization to meet organizational and individual missions/goals? | Are the professional and personal mission/goals of individuals congruent with the organization's? |
| *Systems design* | Does the organizational system provide structure and policies supporting the desired performance? | Are processes designed in such a way as to work as a system? | Does the individual design support performance? |
| *Capacity* | Does the organization have the leadership, capital and infrastructure to achieve its mission/goals? | Does the process have the capacity to perform (quantity, quality and timeliness)? | Does the individual have the mental, physical and emotional capacity to perform? |
| *Motivation* | Do the policies, culture and reward systems support the desired performance? | Does the process provide the information and human factors required to maintain it? | Does the individual want to perform no matter what? |
| *Expertise* | Does the organization establish and maintain selection and training policies and resources? | Does the process of developing expertise meet the changing demands of changing processes? | Does the individual have the knowledge, skills and experience to perform? |

themselves have a key influence on the nature of the design process that comes to be adopted. For example, Mohrman *et al.* argue:

> The critical variables to measure with respect to organizational climate are trust, support, openness, and amount of participation in work tasks. Without a high degree of trust and openness, it is difficult to design a performance appraisal system that meets subordinates' developmental needs. Likewise, the introduction of a participative appraisal system in an organization that is generally managed by top-down mandates will also meet with resistance. . . .
>
> Issues about the influence style of an organization are concerned with how decisions are generally made. Are they generally made quickly, from higher up, or are they made after long deliberations and consensus building from below? If the organization has a top-down mentality and expects decisions to be made quickly, then long drawn-out employee involvement in developing the appraisal system will meet with considerable resistance.
>
> (Mohrman *et al.* 1989: 36–7)

In short, the participative philosophy being advocated here (and throughout much of the performance management literature) is likely to be a non-starter if such values are not held at the topmost levels. The issue of values leads me on to organizational culture.

**Organizational culture**
There are two views about culture and performance management – one is that the latter must fit with the former and the other is that performance management is a means of culture change. Whichever view is taken it is necessary first to know what the existing culture is, if indeed there is a prevailing culture for the organization as a whole – as noted earlier, the idea that an organization necessarily has a single, identifiable culture is very much open to question. Culture may exist at the surface level – 'the way we do things around here' – but the underlying values and basic assumptions may not be generally shared, nor indeed readily identifiable. So, when managers/consultants talk about performance management fitting organizational culture what most probably is meant is that performance management needs to fit the espoused culture –

for example, the values that may be found in the mission statement or are otherwise articulated by the organization's top management (Legge 1995).

From this point of view we might see performance management as a mechanism for inculcating a particular culture, that is, a 'performance culture'. But what exactly is meant by a performance culture is far from clear. Armstrong, for example, associates performance management with a particular set of values – trust, openness, participation and the like. But equally we see a very strong emphasis on results, indicating that a performance culture also has to do with production and output. This is understandable but there is some risk that an overemphasis on results and the bottom line may be at the expense of employee health and well-being. A good illustration of this was provided by one of the organizations visited by Fletcher and Williams (Institute of Personnel Management 1992) – the existing performance culture over emphasized 'bottom-line' results and fear was felt to be the driving force.

Given the considerable difficulty of altering basic values it seems likely that when we talk about using performance management to change culture what probably happens is that we change the 'artifacts', and this, at best, may do no more than modify culture on the surface. In other words, systems and structure change and employee behaviour may follow suit.

The development of 'new' behaviours may be a valuable (and possibly sufficient) outcome in itself. Indeed, changing behaviour seems to be central to many culture change programmes (Williams *et al.* (1993) provide some examples). But there presumably is the intention also to change values. And underlying this may be the intention to change deeper-seated basic assumptions. But does behaviour change lead to internalization of new values? Not necessarily; Legge takes up this issue:

> in theory this internalization is only likely to occur if the individuals involved feel they have some choice and discretion over their new behaviours and that the consequences of engaging in them are positive. . . . If the individual has no choice (other than redundancy), or is heavily 'bribed' to participate, the required behaviour may result, but even espoused values of all but senior management may remain unchanged. As for the

taken-for-granted assumptions, it is debatable whether many of the work groups involved in culture change programmes have had sufficient time to test and be reinforced in the new espoused values for these to be absorbed into unconscious assumptions.
(Legge 1995: 197)

Three points are being made here. The first is that deep-seated change, if it is to come about at all, will only do so in the long term. Second, there is the possibility of simply ending up with compliance rather than commitment (Ogbonna 1992). And this might not be culture change at all. Third, there is the ethical issue of the legitimacy of one group seeking to impose its set of values on another. It would seem naive to suppose that top management's values will simply be accepted. Hendry *et al.* recognize this: 'anyone designing and implementing a system must talk through their assumptions and values, plus those of the people it targets. This is the only way to persuade people to buy into it' (1997: 23).

Note that what is being suggested here is not just the analysis of the current situation but also the determination of what is desired in the future – in other words, identifying whether there is a 'performance gap' (e.g. Csoka 1994). Various tools and techniques are available, from the organizational development (OD) repertoire and elsewhere, to assist in this process, e.g. interviews/discussions with workers and managers, leaders, union officials, survey questionnaires, observation, analysis of company documentation, visioning workshops, scenario planning, business modelling (Brown 1995; Moyer 1996; Prytz 1995; Sparrow and Boam 1992).

### Analysing participant goals for performance management
The widespread advocacy of initial diagnostic/analytical activity is wholly consistent with Murphy and Cleveland's (1995) argument that the goals that line managers and employees have for performance management should be identified. They draw on the ideas of Balzer and Sulsky (1990), who write about performance appraisal effectiveness in terms of satisfying the goals of the different constituencies who may be involved. That they are concerned with **effectiveness** is especially significant as the goals for performance management systems are often expressed in a rather general way, for example to motivate employees, to identify

training and development needs. But what exactly do these things mean? How would we judge if a performance management scheme has been successful in identifying training and development needs? Being more specific about the criteria that we would use not only helps to assess effectiveness but also offers a basis for designing a system that is fit for its purpose. Balzer and Sulsky set out a four-step model to help determine more specific criteria, as shown in Box 9.1.

---

**Box 9.1  Developing criteria of performance management effectiveness**

**Identification of constituent group(s).** There will be at least three: the organization (as exemplified by top management, which may not necessarily be a homogeneous group), line managers and the employees who are subject to performance management.

**Identification of constituent goal(s).** Each group will have a set of goals, for example:

- **The organization**: increasing employee performance (and productivity); encouraging employee motivation; clarifying and communicating what is expected of employees (avoiding role ambiguity); planning work; identifying training and development needs; determining/contributing to administrative decisions – salary, promotion, etc.; justifying personnel decisions, e.g. in case of alleged unfair dismissal.

- **Line managers**: an easy to use system; encouraging employee motivation; clarifying and communicating what is expected of employees (avoiding role ambiguity); increasing employee performance (and productivity); avoiding interpersonal conflict; building and maintaining good interpersonal and working relationships; enhancing one's own status within the organization; managing impressions; developing employees' competence; enhancing employees' self-esteem and other aspects of well-being.

- *Employees*: feedback (especially if it is positive); avoiding interpersonal conflict; building and maintaining good interpersonal and working relationships; enhancing one's status within the organization; managing impressions; identifying and meeting development needs; knowing where one stands for the future – discussing advancement opportunities; developing personal competence; enhancing self-esteem and other aspects of well-being; defending against critiscism; conveying upward feedback; having interesting and satisfying work; seeking improvements to working conditions.

**Identification of specific objective(s).** 'Given the distal nature and vagueness of many goals, specific objectives associated with the constituent groups' goal(s) should be clearly identified' (Balzer and Sulsky 1990: 152). Murphy and Cleveland also make the point that 'it is necessary to move from a general idea of what types of goals [the constituent groups] *might be* pursuing to an assessment of the goals they *actually are* pursuing' (1995: 389). They suggest using direct and indirect means for doing so.

**Selection of criteria.** Criteria are not preordained and hence need to be developed as part of the design process.

(source: adapted from Balzer and Sulsky 1990; Dulewicz and Fletcher 1989; Murphy and Cleveland 1995)

As well as the methods of analysis suggested above, another example particularly relevant to performance management is Kerr's (1988) reward-system questionnaire, discussed in Chapter 8. As part of their 'strategic human resource management (SHRM) profiling', Beer *et al.* (1995: 117) use employee task forces, interviews and feedback within their diagnostic approach, which seeks to accommodate the needs of different stakeholder groups and bring about alignment of human resource management policies and practices with organizational strategy.

As is clear from Box 9.1 each group may have several goals for performance management. Some of these goals may be shared amongst different constituencies, but others may be in conflict. I shall take up these points in the next section.

## Purposes and objectives of the performance management system

As we saw in Chapter 1, performance management may be introduced to serve any one or more of several purposes – for example employee motivation, improving training and development, linking pay to performance, providing feedback on performance, improving employee performance, etc.

What we see here are tensions which have long existed in relation to performance appraisal practice. First, performance management systems are commonly multipurpose, and those purposes are predominantly to serve organizational ends. For example, it is often claimed that some purposes, such as those to do with training and development, are for the benefit of the employee. Yet it is probable that in providing training and development opportunities the organization is intending, first and foremost, to meet organizational needs. This is very reasonable, of course, but if there is also the intention that employees should benefit shouldn't they have some say in the process? Second, a given system may have too many purposes, with the consequent risk that none of them comes to be well served. Third, there may be conflicts between the purposes. The likelihood of conflict becomes more apparent when we recognize that line managers and employees have their own goals for performance management even if they are not an explicit feature of an organization's system. A simplified model of possible conflicts is illustrated in Figure 9.3.

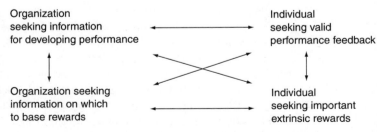

*Figure 9.3* Conflicting interests in performance management (source: Anderson 1993; adapted from Mohrman *et al.* 1989)

### Development or reward?

In their analysis of UK practice Bevan and Thompson (Institute of Personnel Management 1992: 52) concluded that the main purpose of performance management was 'to facilitate the integration of the various components of human resource management (HRM) and mesh them more closely with the business objectives of the organization' (Institute of Personnel Management 1992: 52). They identified two routes to integration, **reward-driven** and **development-driven**:

> Reward driven integration processes concentrate on the role of performance payment systems to change organizational behaviour and tend to place less emphasis on the role of the myriad of human resource policies that can also be used to pursue these objectives. In these organizations changing the remuneration philosophy and practices was seen as the main means of delivering improvements in overall organizational effectiveness. This is emerging as the dominant mode of integration among UK employers.
>
> The second approach to integration – development driven – stresses the importance of ensuring that the range of human resource activities (including training and career development) is right for the organization and that there is a sufficient co-ordination between them. The remuneration dimension is seen as complementary [to] but not dominating this process and, as a result, is not given undue weight within the organization. This approach would appear to be only undertaken by a minority of employers.
>
> (Institute of Personnel Management 1992: 53)

Writ large here are McGregor's Theory X and Theory Y, set out by him over forty years ago and shown here in Box 9.2. The dominant approach to performance management (a results-orientated conception of performance linked to financial reward) is a clear reflection of Theory X. An ever-increasing body of evidence points to the drawbacks of this set of values for performance management practice. For example, the evidence about PRP reviewed in Chapter 8 shows that the motivational benefits claimed for it are difficult to realize in practice, and there is every likelihood that an organization will end up with lowered morale.

## Box 9.2   McGregor's Theory X and Theory Y

### Theory X

1 Management is responsible for organizing the elements of productive enterprise – money, materials, equipment, people – in the interest of economic ends.
2 With respect to people, this is a process of directing their efforts, motivating them, controlling their actions, modifying their behaviour to fit the needs of the organization.
3 Without this active intervention by management, people would be passive – even resistant – to organizational needs. They must therefore be persuaded, rewarded, punished, controlled – their activities must be directed. This is management's task – in managing subordinate managers or workers. . . .

Behind this conventional theory there are several additional beliefs – less explicit, but widespread:

4 The average man is by nature indolent – he works as little as possible.
5 He lacks ambition, dislikes responsibility, prefers to be led.
6 He is inherently self-centered, indifferent to organizational needs.
7 He is by nature resistant to change.
8 He is gullible, not very bright, the ready dupe of the charlatan and the demagogue.

The human side of economic enterprise today is fashioned from propositions and beliefs such as these. Conventional organization structures, managerial policies, practices and programmes reflect these assumptions.

### Theory Y

1 Management is responsible for organizing the elements of productive enterprise – money, materials, equipment, people – in the interest of economic ends.

2  People are *not* by nature passive or resistant to organizational needs. They have become so as a result of experience in organizations.

3  The motivation, the potential for development, the capacity for assuming responsibility, the readiness to direct behaviour towards organizational goals are all present in people. Management does not put them there. It is a responsibility of management to make it possible for people to recognize and develop these human characterisitcs for themselves.

4  The essential task of management is to arrange organizational conditions and methods of operation so that people can achieve their own goals *best* by directing *their own* efforts towards organizational objectives.

This is a process of primarily creating opportunities, releasing potential, removing obstacles, encouraging growth, providing guidance.

(source: McGregor 1957: 23–30)

Though the development–reward dilemma can't be avoided altogether, some of the difficulties may be alleviated by adopting a broader view of reward. If we do this we find that many reward-related practices and behaviours are consistent with a development perspective, e.g. jobs which allow the exercise of autonomy and which provide opportunities for skill use and enhancement, praise, providing feedback/coaching.

## Designing the performance management system

Deciding what the purpose of the performance management system is to be is perhaps the most important part of the whole development process as the design of the system will follow in large part from the decisions that are taken about purpose. The diagnostic frameworks suggested earlier will help decision-makers focus their attention on what they want the system to accomplish, how it will fit with other systems and how those systems might need to be changed.

As noted earlier, the design and development process is as much political as rational (Mohrman *et al.* 1989). Indeed, there is widespread recognition today that it is not just the design process that is political – appraisal (and, by extension, performance management) itself is as well (e.g. Cardy and Dobbins 1994; Murphy and Cleveland 1995; Tziner *et al.* 1996). One of the advantages of the analytical approach is that the potential conflicts of interest can be brought to the surface at an early stage. Resolving them, however, may be problematic and it may be necessary to assess the relative priorities of the different goals of the several interested parties (Murphy and Cleveland 1995). This may necessarily mean, as Fletcher and Williams (1992) have indicated, that the resulting system(s) will involve compromises. Though this may be seen as disadvantageous, the reverse perhaps is more likely to be the case in that organizational reality – the plurality of interests – is better reflected.

This particular step in the overall development process involves answering a whole series of questions about the nature, scope, content and mode of operation of performance management. The two diagnostic frameworks suggested earlier illustrate some of what needs to be asked. A fuller list of questions is offered by Armstrong (1994). Armstrong poses sixty-four questions, some examples of which are shown in Table 9.3. This list offers a very helpful and practical checklist for any organization developing a performance management system. The questions need to be answered in the context of the analysis of the organization's current and desired future state.

This more detailed design step is thus concerned with analysing the requirements and constraints (Roe 1989) associated with the proposed purpose/function. Many of the questions, in other words, focus on what the sytem specifically will be *required* to do, how it will operate. For example, if the purpose of performance management will be a developmental one – the route to improving performance is to be by developing people's capabilities – then we might expect to see behaviours or competencies feature prominently within the system. Following from this will be certain requirements concerning the validity etc. of the performance dimensions that are identified – that is, we would expect to see efforts to identify performance criteria that will meet the requirements set out in Table 5.6. This also means that in practice we would expect to see behavioural dimensions of performance being

*Table 9.3* Designing a performance management system: a checklist (source: Armstrong 1994: 154–7)

1   *General*. What are our objectives in introducing performance management?
2   *Performance agreement*. Should the approach be based on a formal performance agreement, plan or contract?
3   *Objectives*. What do we mean by objectives? Do we, for example, differentiate between short-term and standing objectives?
4   *Performance measures or indicators*. Do we include inputs as well as outputs as factors to be considered in assessing performance?
5   *Attributes and competences*. To what extent is it possible or desirable to develop generic competences?
6   *Performance and development plans*. How should we incorporate development and training plans?
7   *Managing performance throughout the year*. How do we ensure that managers are aware of their responsibilities for managing performance throughout the year and carry them out?
8   *Performance reviews*. To what extent do we incorporate self, upward or peer assessment in the review process?
9   *Performance rating*. Do we need performance rating?
10  *Documentation*. What written guidelines do we need for managers and individuals?
11  *Existing arrangememts*. What account do we take of existing arrangements for performance appraisal?
12  *Performance management for teams*. Do we want to emphasize the importance of incorporating teams into the performance management process?
13  *Performance-related pay*. If we have performance-related pay, how do we prevent this from prejudicing the motivational and developmental aspects of performance management?
14  *Reaction and behaviour of managers/reactions of other employees*. How can we generate ownership of performance management by line managers? How do we get employees to accept and understand performance management?
15  *Training and briefing*. Do we train both managers *and* their staff? What sort of briefing is required?
16  *Pilot testing and implementation*.
17  *Evaluation and quality*.

identified in the sorts of participative, research-based manners described in Chapter 5.

And then when we come to consider constraints we would need to face up to issues such as cost. For example, if an organization were to opt for a reward-driven approach would it be able to afford it? Would it be able to meet the costs of performance-related pay? As Milkovich and Wigdor (1991) have pointed out, if the organization does not allocate sufficient funds to award merit payments that people see as meaningful, then the whole system becomes pointless. But it is not just the direct financial costs that need to be considered – there are also the indirect ones resulting from lowered motivation and morale.

Having reached the point of realizing a prototypical design for the system (or systems), the organization might now be tempted to launch into full scale implementation. However, this may be too hasty: what looks fine on paper may not work in quite the way intended. A phased approach to implementation therefore offers advantages, and I shall come on to this in the next chapter.

## A CONCLUDING COMMENT

As this chapter has shown, the process of designing and developing a performance management system is highly complex and involved. This is true even if we take a very narrow employee-focused approach to performance management.

The design process is partly rational and the diagnostic frameworks that have become more common in recent years present useful questions which help to make the process more systematic and ordered. But the processes of design, as advocated here and by many others, is also a participative one. This is important for several reasons – to help create a system that is fit for its intended purpose, that will be accepted by those who are expected to use it and benefit from it, and that will be perceived as fair. But such an involving approach is likely to bring to the surface potential conflicts of interest stemming from the different goals that different parties have for performance management.

Difficult though they are to deal with, it is important that these differences be identified. Resolving them is less of a rational process than a political one. Consequently, there are no neat answers and no prescriptive solutions when it comes to system design. Inevitably, any performance management system that is developed is going to fall some way short of what might be considered ideal. It is important to accept this because it bears on the expectations that we might have of what performance management will deliver. In their IPM research Fletcher and Williams encountered organizations in which expectations were almost certainly far too high. The danger, of course, is that these expectations will not be realized, leading to disillusionment and, at worst, system decline. This reinforces the need for performance management systems themselves to be managed.

# 10 *Implementing and managing performance management*

As I noted in the previous chapter, once a performance management system has been designed it may be tempting to introduce it across the whole of the organization straight away. This may be a mistake, if only because of the likely magnitude of the task: a phased approach may therefore be more sensible. Moreover, having been introduced it cannot just be left in the hope that it will run smoothly and without any problems. This has been recognized for other approaches to managing performance – for example, TQM. One recent US survey of senior managers in TQM organizations (Longenecker and Scazzero 1996) showed that there were perceived to be various continuing problems, such as individuals not effectively performing their jobs, communication breakdowns, ineffective supervision and several others. Some sort of systematic monitoring or auditing activity is therefore required to identify these difficulties so that they can be overcome. Furthermore, Knights and McCabe (1996) identified the need, in a survey of UK financial services organizations, to manage quality initiatives. This is no less important for performance management – it needs maintenance, monitoring and management. Where possible, such activity should be built in as an integral and routine part of the system itself. All this is often underestimated or even goes unrecognized, as Fletcher and Williams discovered:

> The Chief Personnel Officer of one County Council, when asked what he would do differently if he were starting out to introduce performance management again, said that he would

get across to people that the maintenance costs were high. He was referring to the fact that once it was set up, you could not afford to leave it – it was essential to talk about it and keep it as a live issue.

(Institute of Personnel Mangement 1992: 94)

This is so even if there has been participation by line managers and others in designing the system. The positive effects of such participation may wear off over time if nothing is done to maintain the sense of involvement – for example within the performance management system itself. Monitoring, too, is an involving activity and shows that the opinion of employees and their managers is valued. It has as its central purpose the improvement of the performance management system: this is important as there is little point in carrying out audit and evaluation activities if nothing is done with what is found. The results need to be fed back to those who are able to act on them.

The need for auditing and other tools to improve the operation of organizational systems (of all kinds) has long been advocated. Some specific examples relevant to performance management include the Management Development Audit – a toolkit which, amongst other things, gathered information about various aspects of an organization's appraisal system, such as employee involvement, upward and downward communication. More recently, Fletcher and Williams (1992), Fletcher (1993) and Anderson (1993) provided helpful advice and examples of questionnaires that might be used. And for several decades survey and feedback methods have been part of the repertoire of organizational development tools (French and Bell 1995). The latter methods are of particular interest as they offer the prospect of integrating an audit tool as a core element of the performance management system, as in upward appraisal for example. Later in this chapter I will go on to give examples of some of these tools and techniques.

# EXPERIMENTING WITH IMPLEMENTATION

The implementation of performance management may well be organizational change on a large scale. The more wide-ranging the scope of the system, the greater the scale of the task. Even if the system is relatively circumscribed as an employee-focused intervention, implementation will be a big task. And it should not be assumed that the system (or systems) as designed will run as intended. A phased approach to implementation therefore offers advantages: some experimentation – a pilot test of the prototype – which is monitored systematically may be a sensible first step. Mohrman *et al.* (1989) suggest six questions which should be answered in selecting a suitable site for the piloting, as shown in Table 10.1. It is possible that answers to these questions will reveal that no single site will fit the bill, in which case pilot testing

*Table 10.1* Selecting a pilot site (source: Mohram *et al.* 1989: 43–4)

1  Is the size of the unit appropriate? Is it small enough to be studied carefully but large enough for the variety necessary to generalizability?
2  Is the structure of the unit typical of other units?
3  Is the function of the unit generalizable?
4  Is the unit politically acceptable? Will other units believe that this was a representative pilot site?
5  Does the unit have a stigma? (Is it known as the most productive, loosest, hardest, laziest?)
6  Are top managers supportive? Piloting is often arduous and disruptive. Without top managers' support, you may be asked to leave before you find out what you need to know.

*Table 10.2* Content of performance management briefing (adapted from Anderson 1993; Yeates 1990)

- The aims and objectives of the performance management system.
- How the system has been developed
- How it fits the business strategy.
- The links with other systems.
- Benefits to key parties – employees, managers and the organization.
- Full details of the performance management cycle, its various elements, including methods and documentation – that is, the process of the scheme, how it works, etc.
- Precisely what is expected of each party, at every stage in the performance management cycle.
- Performance management outcomes: how the performance management cycle is completed, what happens to performance management data, including confidentiality of data.
- Training provision.

may have to extend across a number of sites. The piloting provides an opportunity to test out not just the system itself but also the accompanying support systems, such as the briefing/publicity and training that will be required. Briefing/publicity needs to cover what the system is for, why and how it has come about, and various other matters as indicated in Table 10.2.

Though some briefing (Anderson 1993) will be required it is unlikely that this in itself will be enough. The models of performance management discussed at the start of the book all emphasize the importance of communication much more generally, and I will come on shortly to other aspects of organizational communication. But so far as implementation is concerned training will be needed for both parties most actively involved in performance management. The training that should be provided for managers depends on the specific content of the performance management system, but if we draw on what is advocated in the literature it seems likely that the sorts of things listed in Table 10.3 will need to be covered.

Fletcher and Williams found that there were many organizations where the level of training provided was insubstantial, with only occasional examples of more wide-ranging interpersonal skill training (e.g., Wright 1996) which extended beyond the

*Table 10.3* Content of performance managment training for managers

- Goal-setting and work planning, including the establishment of performance measures – not just the 'mechanical' aspects such as characteristics of 'good' goals, but also motivational issues and the relevant interpersonal skills (Hale 1993)
- Managing the job context – helping to find ways of overcoming constraints
- Understanding of competencies/behavioural dimensions – the particular ones in use in the organization
- Gathering performance information and measuring performance – objectives/ goals/results and behaviours/competencies
- Providing feedback and receiving/responding to feedback
- Reviewing/identifying causes of performance – distinguishing between system and person factors
- Coaching
- Discussing employee development
- Conducting informal and formal performance reviews
- Managing reward

narrow confines of appraisal-related activity. Training for the recipients' of performance management – those to whom it is done – is advocated in some models of performance management (e.g., Masterson and Taylor's (1996) *Total Performance Management*) but occurs in practice even less than that provided for line managers. That said, we need to recognize that managers are employees too and so the training provided to them may serve a dual purpose even though this probably is not intended explicitly. But specific employee training would seem to be sensible; Table 10.4 suggests what might be covered.

The piloting may reveal that some changes are required. These may be changes to the system itself or changes to some aspect of the organizational context. In this way the design and implementation process is an iterative one – the feedback loops in Figure 9.2 illustrate this. Once any issues that need to be resolved have been sorted out, the new system may then be progressively introduced over a period of time. Fletcher and Williams (Institute of Personnel Management 1992) discovered that many performance management schemes were implemented rather hastily. But the more extensive the change, the longer the time-scale needs to be – many of the changes associated with performance management are of a long-term nature.

Those involved in the piloting could later become involved in this promulgation. For example, the use of 'line manager coaches' (as in ICI Pharmaceuticals) is one illustration.

The job of introducing and integrating performance management in departments was given to line managers throughout the business. These managers, known as 'performance management

*Table 10.4* Content of performance management training for employees

- Participating in goal-setting – work and developmental goals
- Understanding competencies/behaviours – the particular ones in use in the organization
- Self-review/self-assessment
- Self-management behaviours
- Providing upward feedback
- Receiving feedback

coaches', were selected by their heads of department because they had legitimacy and status with their peers, good interactive skills, and welcomed involvement in the process of changing the culture.

(Sheard 1992: 42)

Mercury Communications adopted a similar approach – 120 staff were trained as occasional trainers to help implement their new system.

But once a new system has been introduced it cannot simply be left in the hope that it will run smoothly – it needs to be managed and maintained. Part of the managing of performance management requires having an infrastructure for organizational communication.

## COMMUNICATION

The importance of vision, mission and strategy as the framework for performance management is strongly emphasized in much of the practitioner-oriented literature (as Table 1.5 showed). Prominence is also given to organizational communication. At the very least we would expect downward communication about matters such as the nature of the corporate/business plan, productivity/ efficiency, products/services, etc. However, as we saw when considering the reality of organizational practice, this is very often deficient, although organizations with formal performance management systems fare rather better than those without. Generally, though, organizations regard communications as a problem area.

### Downward communication

Townley notes that:

Management communication systems are likely to use a number of different methods, although with a preference for oral rather than written presentations. The most common form of communication with employees across all employment sectors is the systematic use of the 'management chain'. . . . The most common combination of communication methods is the use of the management chain allied with newsletters.

(Townley 1994: 597)

Townley notes also that traditional methods such as notice boards continue to be widely used. The use of the management chain is especially important in the context of performance management given the key role that is seen for line managers. However, there are broader aspects to performance management – keeping employees informed about what is going on in the organization – so we might expect to see a wide range of communication media in use.

Also, downward communication is not directed solely at individuals. In particular, there has been a growth in the practice of team briefing. Though such downward communication may serve to convey information, organizations also regard it as a process of influence – persuading/convincing the employee to subscribe to organizational goals and values (a very unitarist perspective, in other words). But if this is an entirely one-way flow there is the risk that it will be seen simply as propaganda.

## Upward communication

The incidence of upward communication remains of a relatively low order, and exists most commonly in the shape of formal means such as suggestion schemes or attitude surveys. Not only that, upward communication is often of a relatively passive kind, as in the case of attitude surveys where the content and any subsequent action are firmly controlled by management. Possibly more active is the upward communication sometimes found in the context of quality management initiatives – joint problem-solving, for example; here the intention is likely to be conceived more broadly as one of employee involvement.

## Two-way communication

One of the problems with means of downward and upward communication is that they are predominantly one-way. Related to this, another problem is that communication is management-controlled. For example, downward communication is typically intended to convey information that management has determined should be passed on. Similarly, when it comes to forms of upward communication such as attitude surveys it will usually be management which determines the content of the survey.

This 'one-sidedness' is evident in many of the purposes of communication programmes. Table 10.5 summarizes many of

*Table 10.5* Reasons for introducing organizational communication programmes (source: adapted from Townly 1994: 610)

*Educative purposes*
● Encourage sense of responsibility
● Improve employees' understanding of company policy and business generally

*Production benefits*
● Motivate employees toward higher productivity
● Make the organization work better
● Gain acceptance of change
● Increase work flexibility

*Participation and involvement*
● Involve employees in company affairs – participation and involvement
● Motivate employees/improve morale

*'Industrial relations purposes'*
● Moderate wage demands/influence negotiations
● Reduce work disruption
● Minimize trade union influence
● Make managers manage

*External pressures*
● Employee pressure
● Trade union pressure
● Legal requirements
● Pre-empt expected leislation

*Broader 'political' considerations*
● General social trend
● Discharge responsibilities of company/'right to know'

the reasons why organizational communication programmes have been introduced. A number of similarities with performance management may be discerned. First, there is a responsive aspect to organizational communication programmes; as with performance management, external pressures are a major stimulus. Second, employee communication is seen as helping to improve organizational and individual performance – this clearly is consistent with the goals of performance management. Third, although a purpose of communication may be to inform there is a broader intention to *involve*. Here again, this last theme is evident in the advocacy about performance management – e.g. not just communicating the mission statement but creating a sense of mission – albeit not in practice.

It seems likely that if these broader purposes are to be served, communication must at least be two-way. As well as receiving information about matters that affect them, employees want to have the opportunity to have some say. As Marchington notes, 'employees like to have the opportunity to find out why (certain) decisions have been made, plus the potential to influence those which are felt to be within their own domain' (1995: 291).

More than this, if such purposes as the involvement of employees are to be achieved organizational action must go beyond communication. So, for example, the literature (e.g., Beaumont 1993; Hyman and Mason 1995; Marchington 1995; Ramsay 1996) shows that employee involvement and participation, which may be seen as a management philosophy or movement in its own right, may comprise direct and indirect means (e.g., task participation and consultation/representative participation) and financial involvement (e.g., Marchington 1995). Clearly, then, employee involvement practices are consistent with performance management.

## DOES PERFORMANCE MANAGEMENT WORK?

The short answer to this question is that we do not really know. And one of the main reasons why we do not know is that organizations do not do much to discover systematically how their performance management systems are operating and what they are accomplishing. To be fair, though, it is difficult to test certain of the outcomes expected. For example, how effective is performance management in improving organizational performance?

### The effectiveness of performance management: organizational performance

According to the IMS survey (Institute of Personnel Management 1992), improving organizational performance is the reason most commonly cited for introducing performance management. However, using a number of financial indicators the IMS researchers distinguished between high-performing and low-performing organizations but were unable to find any association with the presence or absence of formal performance management systems. But perhaps this is too much to expect. As was shown in earlier chapters, organizational performance is a very complex concept and requires multiple measures. Demonstrating an association between performance management and financial indicators may be too much to hope for. We need to use a much wider range of indicators of organizational functioning if we are to identify the contribution being made by performance management.

There is some recognition of this within organizations – the IMS survey showed that a number of indicators are used, including labour turnover, productivity, attitude surveys and salary information. Productivity measures were generally considered to be the most useful across all organizations, with formal performance management organizations attaching particular value to employee attitude surveys and salary information. Moreover, formal performance management organizations were more likely to use the outcome of their monitoring and evaluation activities to make changes to their policies and practices. However, it would seem that these indicators are used in an essentially impressionistic way as organizations commonly do not do much by way of systematic monitoring and evaluation.

## Do organizations monitor and evaluate?

The IMS researchers asked organizations to give their own estimates of the effectiveness of their systems and a majority claimed that they were 'moderately effective'. However, it is far from clear that this judgement is based on any evidence – as noted above, it is very much an impression: of all organizations responding to the IMS survey, 'just over half . . . conducted any monitoring and evaluation at all' (Institute of Personnel Management 1992: 48). In other words, nearly half of organizations do not!

## Benefits claimed for performance management

In the light of the IMS findings about the nature of monitoring methods and the relatively low incidence of systematic monitoring we need to be sceptical about claims made for the benefits of performance management. The Industrial Society survey reports that about two-thirds of their respondents claim benefits with respect to training planning and about 60 per cent for individual motivation. But for other aspects the proportion reporting benefits is relatively low: for example, quality – 22 per cent; customer service – 21 per cent; financial performance – 11 per cent.

Other evidence about benefits comes from the case studies carried out by Fletcher and Williams (Institute of Personnel Management 1992). They found that very few organizations claimed that their performance management activities had improved organizational performance. Rather more common was the view that:

> performance management helped the individual to see his or her part in the wider enterprise with greater clarity. It conveyed a sense of corporate direction and increased identification with the broader aims and goals, with a resulting rise in commitment.
> (Institute of Personnel Management 1992: 98)

Matters such as these are, of course, susceptible to investigation by employee opinion surveys. Fletcher and Williams were able to carry out such surveys in nine of their participating organizations and discovered quite strong associations between the presence of formal performance management policies and such outcomes as goal clarity, high commitment, job satisfaction, etc.

Further evidence about the impact of performance management on staff comes from surveys carried out for the Audit Commission (1995d) in seventeen local authorities. Using a version of the questionnaire developed by Fletcher and Williams the Audit Commission surveyed staff opinion about two sets of issues – 'know-how' and 'feel-good'. These are defined in Box 10.1. Employee opinions on these two factors were associated with a 'performance management index' (Audit Commission 1995d: 5.48). The main findings were that:

- Performance management policies contribute to staff 'know-how'; those authorities with the highest 'know-how' scores tend to have well-established performance management programmes extending to all staff.
- Staff with strong 'know-how' also tend to 'feel-good' about their work.

---

Box 10.1 **Performance management effectiveness: 'know-how', 'feel-good' and the performance index**

'Know-how' measures staff understanding of their role. The survey asked staff about the clarity, priority, difficulty and feedback of goals they were set, and how they thought they had contributed to these goals.

The 'feel-good' factor measures job satisfaction and commitment. The survey asked staff how they felt about the authority, in terms of personal identification, involvement and loyalty. They were also asked to assess their job satisfaction.

The 'performance index' is an indicator of the satisfactoriness of performance management systems. It derives from ratings of six main aspects of performance management: internal communication, external communication, personal appraisal, performance review, financial planning, aims and objectives.

(Source: Audit Commission 1995d)

---

## Effectiveness of organizational communication

As with other aspects of performance management, organizations tend not to evaluate their organizational communication activities. Not surprisingly, therefore, the evidence about effectiveness suggests that management has a more rosy view than do employees at lower levels in the organization. In particular, when an organizational communication programme is newly introduced there may initially be suspicion, although employee responses may become somewhat more positive over time (Townley 1994). A loss of momentum following initial enthusiasm has also been noted (Ramsay 1996) – here again, this endorses the need for continuing management.

The Audit Commission (1995d) evidence (reported earlier) indicates the beneficial effect of good communication on employee attitudes. But the feeling on the part of employees that they do n0t have as much information as they would like about what is going on, the reasons for decisions and such matters persists. This may be one reason why organizational communication fails. Employees may see the communication as too one-sided – as not providing them with information of relevance or interest to them or as not providing an opportunity to have some say.

Second, employees may see themselves as having no voice or a voice that is not heard. This view may be reinforced if there is excessive management control over the means and content of communication. For example, as Hyman and Mason comment in relation to attitude surveys:

> First, the organization must encourage this method to ascertain information and views on a broad range of company activities and policies, and not just wish to hear 'what it wants to hear', no matter how negative the opinions and attitudes appear to be. And second, the organization should respond positively to generalized feelings and views, rather than just collecting and collating data to be filed away in the personnel department.
>
> (Hyman and Mason 1995: 82)

Third, the organization's senior management may fail to see the psychological (e.g., Williams 1991) and political (e.g., Townley 1994) nature of communication. In the latter regard the senior and other managers who design and implement organizational communication programmes may take insufficient account of the perspectives of those expected to deliver the communications. For example, the management chain is regarded as a key communication channel and particular importance attaches to it because it offers the potential for two-way communication.

As in performance management generally, therefore, the role of the line manager is highlighted (possibly with the intention of strengthening the role), with particular emphasis being placed on their interpersonal skills for conveying and gathering information (Wright 1996). Yet line managers and supervisors may not be committed to organizational communication in the way that their senior managers would wish (Marchington 1995). For example, formal communication activities, like team briefing, may be seen as burdensome, as something extra to be done on top of an already heavy workload (even though in some instances the amount of time taken up is actually very short). Moreover, some line managers and supervisors may feel threatened, particularly if the communication truly is intended to be of an involving kind. And many commentators (e.g., Hyman and Mason 1995; Marchington 1995; Townley 1994) have commented on the lack of skill on the part of managers and supervisors, and on the insufficiency of the support (such as training) provided for them.

For all these reasons, organizational communication may achieve less than organizations would hope for. As with performance management, it is important for organizations to have realistic expectations of the benefits that will be realized. Though firm evidence that organizations are getting what they want is, for the most part, lacking, the data that are available do suggest that worthwhile benefits (for organizations and employees) can be obtained. Thus, monitoring is important as a means of finding out what is being achieved as well as for helping to improve the operation of the system.

# MONITORING PERFORMANCE MANAGEMENT SYSTEMS

## Fitness for purpose

There are a number of levels of monitoring that might be attempted. At the most basic, certain procedural aspects of the performance management system might be monitored. For example, if it is expected that completed forms be returned to the personnel/HR department, does this in fact happen? Non-return clearly is an indicator of some kind of problem – for some reason(s) the system hasn't been accepted – which needs to be investigated.

A more sophisticated level of evaluation would be to carry out some analysis of what gets written on the forms. For example, training and development-related recommendations might be analysed and followed up to ensure that action is taken. This is important, as the failure to take action may lead to the system becoming discredited. If the performance management system is used for pay purposes, merit awards might be monitored by sex and ethnic groupings to ensure that there is no unlawful discrimination.

Completed forms might also be content-analysed to confirm that work objectives conform to the requirements of 'good' (SMART) objectives. Where they do not, this might reveal a training need or, indeed, a more fundamental weakness in the operation of the system. For example, if this sort of analysis was to be done by taking a vertical slice through the organization some assessment could be made of whether the goal-setting process is operating in the cascading fashion that is typically advocated. Are objectives related to key result areas? Are they related to/integrated with organizational and departmental objectives? In other words, is it possible to identify the 'performance logic' (Rummler and Brache 1995) which links the goals? This is tricky, of course, as the idea of the balanced scorecard suggests that the performance logic will not always be as logical and clear cut as we might imagine. But this sort of analytical activity is in itself a tool for diagnosing performance problems – a tool for improving and managing performance in other words. However, all these sorts of evaluative activity seek to establish how fit the system is for its purpose and how well the objectives set for it are being met.

This is problematical as measurable criteria for performance management typically are not established. The series of steps set out by Balzer and Sulsky (1990) offers a way forward here; as noted in Chapter 9, the development of criteria helps to clarify what the system is for as well as setting standards against which the effectiveness of the system will be measured. The criteria used for evaluating a performance management system will necessarily be context-specific and so absolute standards do not really apply. This is understandable given that several parties have an interest in the operation and outcomes of performance management. Hence, any evaluation must capture these several perspectives – senior managers, line managers, employees.

## Senior managers

One illustration of an approach which aims to gather senior managers' (and others') perceptions of performance management activities is the 'good practice review' developed by the Audit Commission (1995d). This is outlined briefly in Box 10.2. Though designed for local government the idea (and many aspects of the questionnaire) may be adapted readily for use elsewhere. Many of the questions shown in Box 10.2 are like those suggested in Chapter 9. I made the point there that organizations which routinely carry out monitoring and maintenance activities will, as a matter of course, be assessing their current situation, an important first step in developing a performance management system. This reinforces the need to see evaluation not as something that gets tacked on at the end but rather as an integral part of managing performance management. Several of the questions in Box 10.2 also highlight the importance of capturing the experience of those most directly affected by performance management – line managers and staff.

---

**Box 10.2 'Good practice' review of performance management**

The objectives of the self-diagnostic good practice review are:

- to provide an assessment by members, chief officers and middle managers of the strengths and weaknesses of the authority's performance management systems
- to identify which elements of the performance managment system should be improved

Good practice review is based on a questionnaire designed to reflect respondents' views on the effectiveness of the authority's policies on managing performance. Councils should seek a separate assessment from three different groups of people:

- members
- chief officers/management team
- middle managers

The self-assessment form asks forty-two questions about six aspects of performance management:

- specification of objectives, e.g:
  - Does the authority have a clear and articulated view of its mission and core values?
  - Is there a clear set of aims (or goals) and objectives (or targets) for the authority as a whole?
- financial/business planning
- performance review, e.g.:
  - Are performance indicators used extensively to monitor inputs, outputs, service efficiency and service effectiveness?

> - Are qualitative indicators (including measures of cus-
> tomer satisfaction) used in situations where quantitative
> measures are neither practical nor relevant?
> - Does the review of performance result in actions to
> remedy poor performance?
> • individual appraisal, e.g.:
> - Is it an effective two-way process (e.g. by including
> self-assessment, upward appraisal and participation in
> goal-setting)?
> • external communication
> • internal communication, e.g.:
> - How effectively have corporate and departmental
> objectives been communicated throughout the authority?
> - Are line managers and more junior staff actively
> involved in the development of goals and objectives?
> - Are all staff given adequate information on how well
> the authority has achieved its objectives?
> (source: Audit Commission 1995d)

## THE IMPACT OF PERFORMANCE MANAGEMENT ON LINE MANAGERS AND EMPLOYEES

Many writers (e.g., Anderson 1993; Armstrong 1994; Balzer and Sulsky 1990; Dickinson 1993; Fletcher 1993; Fletcher and Williams 1992; Murphy and Cleveland 1995) advocate seeking line manager and employee opinion as part of evaluation activity. What sorts of things should be covered? This depends on the specific nature of the system(s) in use but it is likely that information would need to be gathered about how procedural aspects of the system are experienced as well as feelings about what happened and opinions on the impact of the system.

As a formal system performance management commonly comprises many specific procedures and events that may merit particular attention, such as the analysis of forms that I mentioned above. Employee opinion about these events is important also. For example, the communication and review of objectives and other aspects of performance is a central part of performance management systems and some sort of formal meeting continues to be central to this. Hence, there is a place for evaluation of the kind long advocated for appraisal interviews and other aspects of appraisal systems. Such audits might concern themselves with factual matters – what was discussed and what action arose – as well as subjective and attitudinal dimensions like perceptions of accuracy and fairness. This more focused monitoring may have diagnostic value in shedding light on which procedures are working well and which need improvement.

But there is an important place, too, for broader-ranging surveys of reactions to and attitudes towards performance management in all its aspects. A checklist of the sorts of things that might be covered is given in Box 10.3.

---

**Box 10.3   A checklist for evaluation**

- Aspects of goals and goal-setting:
  - How involved staff feel in setting their work goals
  - How clear and specific they feel their goals to be
  - How clear people feel their work group to be about its goals
  - How clear people are about the organization's goals
  - What sense people have of how their work contributes to departmental and organizational goals
  - The perception of an emphasis on short-term goals
  - Perceptions of goal difficulty
- Other aspects of the work, e.g. job demands
- Feedback on individual peformance
- Aspects of organizational communication:
  - Communication of organizational mission
  - Communication of business plan
  - Communication about organizational performance
- Aspects of organizational climate:
  - Perceptions of openness/trust
  - Perceptions of fairness
  - Sense of empowerment
  - Sense of involvement
  - Feeling of team working/sense of co-operation

---

> – Perceptions of management/supervisory style
> – perceptions of climate for learning/development
> - Organizational commitment
> - Job involvement/ownership
> - Job satisfaction
> - Employees' sense of well-being
> - Perceived impact on motivation, e.g. perceived relation-
>   ship between effort and reward
> - Employee's sense of personal competence
> - Perceived impact on performance
> - Perceptions of and attitutes towards reward

## Gathering the data

A range of methods may be used, including interviews, group discussions and questionnaires. Some combination is likely to be useful as each method has its advantages and disadvantages. For example, questionnaires allow the collection of quantitative data on a large scale but the format may be constraining, even if some open-ended write-in questions are included. Interviews, on the other hand, allow participants more freedom of expression. And interviews and group discussions may have a particular part to play in the process of developing a questionnaire. As suggested above, if there is no employee involvement in developing the questionnaire there is the risk that it will not be seen as an instrument of two-way communication.

Though it makes sense for organizations to tailor interview schedules and questionnaires to fit their own particular systems, this does not mean having to reinvent the wheel in every case. There are many examples available which can be adapted and modified to suit. If an organization wants to look specifically at, say, the feedback/performance review discussion, the sorts of questions set out in Table 10.6 might be asked of the job holder.

There also is a substantial body of other research on which an organization may draw in developing opinion questionnaires. For example, Fletcher and Williams (Institute of Personnel Management 1992) drew on scales from the behavioural science literature in developing a questionnaire for the IPM research on performance management. This questionnaire was further developed

*Table 10.6* Evaluating the performance review/feedback discussion (source: drawn from Anderson 1993; Fletcher and Williams 1992)

- How much notice were you given that you were going to be interviewed?
- Was this enough time for you to prepare for the discussion?
- Did the interviewer mention any parts of the job that you had done particularly well?
- Was there any mention or discussion of the weaker aspects of your performance in the job during the interview?
- Were your training/development needs mentioned or discussed in the interview?
- Were you able to agree with the interviewer on what your objectives should be for the next year?
- Were factors outside your control discussed?
- Did the interview make you feel that you *wanted* to improve your performance in the job?
- After the discussion, were you any clearer in your own mind about what you could do to improve your work?
- Were you able to put forward and discuss your ideas and feelings at the interview?
- Was the discussion frank and open?
- Did you receive accurate and useful feedback on how your boss feels you are getting on in your job?
- Were follow-up actions agreed to improve your performance?

by Fletcher for use within local authorities by the Audit Commission (1995d) – the 'know-how' and 'feel-good' indicators described in Box 10.1. Broad-brush indicators like 'know-how' and 'feel-good' might, however, simply be *too* broad and it may be more useful to focus on more specific measures of the sorts of things listed in Box 10.3. Are staff clear about their goals and what is expected of them? Do they feel that they get enough feedback on their performance? Do they feel that they know what is going on in the organization? Do they feel that the performance management system is fair? Do they feel that their efforts are rewarded? Examples of items which might be used to answer such questions as these are given in Box 10.4. These are intended merely to be illustrative so as to make the point that scales do already exist that organizations may wish to use if they have the internal resources to search them out and carry out their own survey.

Advantages of using well-established scales are that the development work has already been carried out and (where relevant)

Box 10.4    **Employee opinions about performance management: some specimen questions**

**Aspects of goals and goal-setting**
*Participation in goal-setting*
- I am allowed a high degree of influence in the determination of my work objectives
- I really have little voice in the formulation of my work objectives (R)
- The setting of my work goals is pretty much under my own control
- My supervisor usually asks for my opinions and thoughts when determining my work objectives

*Goal specificity*
- My work objectives are very clear and specific: I know exactly what my job is
- I think my work objectives are ambiguous and unclear (R)
- I understand fully which of my work objectives are more important than others; I have a clear sense of priorities on these goals

*Goal difficulty*
- I should not have too much difficulty in reaching my work objectives; they appear to be fairly easy (R)
- My work objectives will require a great deal of effort from me to complete them
- It will take a high degree of skill and know-how on my part to attain fully my work objectives
- My work objectives are quite difficult to attain

The above items are scored on a seven-point scale from (1) 'strongly disagree' to (7) 'strongly agree'; items marked (R) are reverse scored.

(source: Steers 1973; in Cook *et al.* 1981)

**Aspects of fairness in discussing and reviewing performance**
*Indicate the extent to which your supervisor did each of the following:*
- Was honest and ethical in dealing with you
- Gave you an opportunity to express your side
- Used consistent standards in evaluating your performance
- Considered your views regarding your performance
- Gave you feedback that helped you learn how well you were doing
- Was completely candid and frank with you
- Showed a real interest in trying to be fair
- Became thoroughly familiar with your performance
- Took into account factors beyond your control
- Got input from you before a recommendation
- Made clear what was expected of you
                    (source: Folger and Konovsky 1989)

**Aspects of supervisory reward behaviour**
- My supervisor always gives me positive feedback when I perform well
- My supervisor gives me special recognition when my performance is especially good
- My supervisor would quickly acknowledge an improvement in the quality of my work
- My supervisor commends me when I do a better than average job
- My supervisor personally pays me a compliment when I do outstanding work
- My supervisor informs his/her boss and others when I do outstanding work
- If I do well, I know my supervisor will reward me
- My supervisor would do all that he/she could to help me go as far as I would like to go in this organization if my work is consistently above average
- My good performance often goes unacknowledged by my supervisor (R)
- I often perform well in my job and still receive no praise from my supervisor (R)

Scored on a seven-point scale from 'strongly agree' to 'strongly disagree'
                    (source: Schriesheim *et al.* 1991)

the psychometric properties of the measures are known. There may also be normative data which would allow an organization to compare itself with others, as in the case of the work by Fletcher and Williams and the Audit Commission. Opinion surveys, using standard measures, thus have a place where organizations wish to benchmark themselves against others. But already-established measures might not capture exactly the language used in an organization and in this sense the questionnaire might not 'fit'. For this reason an organization might prefer to develop a tailor-made questionnaire and use it over a period of years as part of regular monitoring and diagnostic activity. Repeated use also helps to offset the initial development costs – organizations get a better return on their money, in other words.

Many of the items in Box 10.4 are about supervisory behaviours. This is to be expected given the central role that line managers have to play in performance management. But what the examples illustrate is how upward appraisal/feedback can serve a dual purpose. On the one hand it is a tool to assist the personal development of line managers. But when the data are aggregated across a department or the organization as a whole they become a tool for managing the performance management system. But in order for either of these purposes to be served the data do need to be fed back and action taken.

## Taking action

Surveys raise expectations and if organizations embark upon such activity without being prepared to act on what they find this is likely to cause more harm than good. It is essential, therefore, to feed back the data, partly to develop understanding further and partly to assist in solving any problems that are identified and to seek suggestions for improving those aspects of performance management which are not working well.

As noted above, an opinion survey may be used as an individual feedback instrument – as in upward (or multiple) appraisal (discussed in Chapter 7). In the present context, though, we are not so much interested in changing the behaviour of individual managers but rather in improving aspects of the system. Results, therefore, need to be reported back and it often is suggested that this be done in a cascading way, starting at the top of the organization. It is also essential that what is fed back is relevant, that is relevant to the particular department, unit, team, etc. Moreover, it is helpful if the findings are discussed with the recipients – they may be able to help interpret the data and offer explanations for what has been found. They may also be able to suggest remedial actions, should these be needed. It is important that positive, improving action (rather than punishment) happens, otherwise the reaction is going to be defensiveness and lowered trust (Hinrichs 1996). Used in this constructive way, then, surveys are a valuable tool for helping manage the performance management system *and* for managing performance.

## A CONCLUDING COMMENT

Though the term performance management is open to a number of interpretations, in the UK it has come to take on a particular meaning. It denotes a system where the level of intervention is the individual employee and the overall intent is to align individual performance with organizational performance. This, in other words, is a unitarist perspective and as such it may represent one of the threats to performance management as it fails to recognize the plurality of interests that are so much a part of organizational reality. It is also far too simple a view – the idea of the balanced scorecard points to the complexity of organizational performance and we should not expect that it will be an easy task to align individual performance with possibly conflicting and contradictory goals.

Typically, performance management is presented as a cycle of activity in which an especially important role is seen for the line manager. Thus, performance management is commonly presented as something that is (or should be) owned and driven by the line. What is less well established, however, is the extent to which this particular aspect of advocacy is matched by reality. There is little to suggest that much is done to bring about ownership or to support managers in this task.

The core of performance management practice, for many organizations, would seem to be traditional performance appraisal, perhaps with appraisal-related pay tacked on to it. The organizational context and aspects of the work system seem, on the face of it, to be taken for granted. Core practice, then, is narrow, it reflects outmoded (Theory X) ideas about motivation and it may be overly focused on their performance at the expense of other aspects of individuals, such as their well-being. Much contemporary practice may also be too narrow in concentrating so much on the individual whilst under emphasizing the job itself and the immediate job environment. A properly holistic and integrated approach would recognize the many influences on performance and its different facets (both output and behavioural conceptualizations) and reflect this through multiple interventions operating at multiple levels. This is not to say that the management of employee performance should be ignored – quite the contrary. But we should be modest in our expectations of what narrowly focused interventions will achieve, especially if the consequences for those who are affected by them are ignored.

To take account of the needs and interests of those who will be affected requires a more involving approach to the design and development process. This offers the prospect of a performance management system more in keeping with Theory Y than Theory X. In such a system we would expect to see the sorts of things that are advocated in the prescriptive and normative literature, for example:

- effective organizational communication;
- empowering and enriching work organization and job design;
- a broad view of performance – not just goals/outputs but also behaviours/competencies;
- participation in goal-setting;
- frequent feedback;
- a broad view of reward;
- the promotion of employee well-being.

Perhaps this is all too utopian. Certainly, the evidence we have from surveys of practice – performance management, employee involvement and the like – does not offer much comfort. But perhaps we should not be too surprised. Financial constraints in organizations are often real enough and the participative approach that is advocated in so much of the literature is time-consuming and costly. Moreover, the control-related (and other) advantages of Theory X thinking are very appealing. But this theory views people as costs and liabilities. Much-espoused today is the view that employees are assets or resources. But espousal is not enough; Pettigrew and Whipp (1993) demonstrated in their research on competitiveness that staff actually have to be valued as assets and treated as such, and this means policies and practices for information sharing, participation and involvement, skill development and a long-term perspective (Pfeffer 1994). Approached in these broader terms, performance management may have a future.

# References

Adler, S. and Weiss, H. M. (1988) Recent developments in the study of personality and organizational behaviour. In C. L. Cooper and I. T. Robertson (eds) *International Rview of Industrial and Organizational Psychology*, Chichester: Wiley.

Ainsworth, M. and Smith, N. (1993) *Making it Happen: Managing Performance at Work*, Sydney: Prentice Hall.

Altink, W. M. M., Visser, C. F. and Castelijns, M. (1997) Criterion development: the unknown power of criteria as communication tools. In N. Anderson and P. Herriot (eds) *International Handbook of Selection and Assessment*, Chichester: Wiley.

Andersen, B. (1995) The productivity term. In A. Rolstadås (ed.) *Performance Management: A Business Process Benchmarking Approach*, London: Chapman & Hall.

Anderson, G. C. (1993) *Managing Performance Appraisal Systems*, Oxford: Blackwell.

Anderson, M. (1992) Intelligence. In A. P. Smith and D. M. Jones (eds) *Handbook of Human Performance*, vol. 3, London: Academic Press.

Armstrong, M. (1993) *Managing Reward Systems*, Buckingham: Open University Press.

Armstrong, M. (1994) *Performance Management*, London: Kogan Page.

Armstrong, M. (1995) *A Handbook of Personnel Management Practice*, 5th edn, London: Kogan Page.

Armstrong, M. (1996) How group efforts can pay dividends. *People Management*, January, pp. 22–7.

Ashford, S. J. (1986) The role of feedback seeking in individual adaptation: a resource perspective. *Academy of Management Journal*, **29**, pp. 465–87.

Ashford, S. J. (1989) Self-assessments in organizations. *Research in Organizational Behaviour*, **11**, pp. 133–74.

Atkinson, A. A., Waterhouse, J. H. and Wells, R. B. (1997) A stakeholder approach to strategic performance measurement. *Sloan Management Review*, Spring, pp. 25–37.

Audit Commission (1995a) *Calling the Tune: Performance Management in Local Government*, London: Audit Commission.

Audit Commission (1995b) *Paying the Piper . . . Calling the Tune*, London: Audit Commission.

Audit Commission (1995c) *Paying the Piper . . . Calling the Tune. Management Handbook*, London: HMSO.

Audit Commission (1995d) *Paying the Piper . . . Calling the Tune: People, Pay and Performance in Local Government*, London: Audit Commission.

Audit Commission (1995e) *Paying the Piper: People and Pay Management in Local Government*, London: Audit Commission.

Bacharach, S. B. and Bamberger, P. (1995) Beyond situational constraints: job resources inadequacy and individual performance at work. *Human Resource Management Review*, **5(2)**, pp. 79–102.

Bailey, C. T. (1983) *The Measurement of Job Performance*, Aldershot: Gower.

Balzer, W. K. and Sulsky, L. M. (1990) Performance appraisal effectiveness. In K. R. Murphy and F. E. Saal (eds) *Psychology in Organizations*, Hillsdale, NJ: Erlbaum.

Baron, R. A. (1994) The physical environment of work settings. *Research in Organizational Behaviour*, **16**, pp. 1–46.

Bate, P. (1984) The impact of organizational culture on approaches to organizational problem-solving. *Organization Studies*, **5(1)**, pp. 43–66.

Bateman, T. S. and Organ, D. W. (1983) Job satisfaction and the good soldier: the relationship between affect and employee 'citizenship'. *Academy of Management Journal*, **26**, pp. 587–95.

Beaumont, P. B. (1993) *Human Resource Management*, London: Sage.

Beer, M., Eisenstat, R. A. and Biggadike, E. R. (1995) Strategic change: a new dimension of human resource management. In G. R. Ferris, S. D. Rosen and D. T. Barnum (eds) *Handbook of Human Resource Management*, Cambridge, MA: Blackwell.

Bell, N. and Tetlock, P. (1989) The intuitive politician and the assignment of blame in organizations. In R. A. Giacalone and P. Rosenfeld (eds) *Impression Management in the Organization*, Hillsdale, NJ: Erlbaum.

Bernardin, H. J. (1986) Subordinate appraisal: a valuable source of information about managers. *Human Resource Mangement*, **25**, 421–39.

Bernardin, H. J. and Beatty, R. W. (1984) *Performance Appraisal: Assessing Human Behavior at Work*, Boston, MA: Kent.

Bernardin, H. J., Kane, J. S., Ross, S., Spina, J. D. and Johnson, D. L. (1995) Performance appraisal design, development, and implementation. In G. R. Ferris, S. D. Rosen and D. T. Barnum (eds) *Handbook of Human Resource Management*, Cambridge, MA: Blackwell.

Bertsch, B. and Williams, R. (1994) How multinational CEOs make change programmes stick. *Long Range Planning*, **27(5)**, pp. 12–24.

Bevan, S. and Thompson, M. (1991) Performance management at the crossroads. *Personnel Management*, November, pp. 36–39.

Blumberg, M. and Pringle, C. C. (1982) The missing opportunity in organizational research: some implications for a theory of work performance. *Academy of Management Review*, **7**, pp. 560–9.

Borman, W. C. and Motowidlo, S. J. (1993) Expanding the criterion domain to include elements of contextual performance. In N. Schmitt, W. C. Borman and Associates *Personnel Selection in Organizations*, San Francisco, CA: Jossey-Bass.

Bounds, G., Yorks, L., Adams, M. and Ranney, G. (1994) *Beyond Total Quality Management*, New York: McGraw-Hill.

Boyatzis, R. E. (1982) *The Competent Manager*, New York: Wiley.

Brabet, J. and Klemm, M. (1994) Sharing the vision: company mission statements in Britain and France. *Long Range Planning*, **27(1)**, pp. 84–94.

Bracken, D. W. (1996) Multisource (360–degree) feedback: surveys for individual and organizational development. In A. I. Kraut (ed.) *Organizational Surveys*, San Francisco, CA: Jossey-Bass.

Bredrup, H. (1995a) Background for performance management. In A. Rolstadås (ed.) *Performance Management: A Business Process Benchmarking Approach*, London: Chapman & Hall.

Bredrup, H. (1995b) Competitiveness and competitive advantage. In A. Rolstadås (ed.) *Performance Management: A Business Process Benchmarking Approach*, London: Chapman & Hall.

Bredrup, H. (1995c) Performance measurement. In A, Rolstadås (ed.) *Performance Management: A Business Process Benchmarking Approach*, London: Chapman & Hall

Bredrup, H. (1995d) The traditional planning hierarchy. In A. Rolstadås (ed.) *Performance Management: A Business Process Benchmarking Approach*, London: Chapman & Hall.

Bredrup, H. and Bredrup, R. (1995) Performance planning to ensure business achievements. In A. Rolstadås (ed.), *Performance Management: A Business Process Benchmarking Approach*, London: Chapman & Hall.

Brewster, C. and Söderström, M. (1994) Human resources and line management. In C. Brewster and A. Hegewisch (eds) *Policy and Practice in Human Resource Management*, London: Routledge.

Brief, A. P. and Motowidlo, S. J. (1986) Prosocial organizational behaviour. *Academy of Management Review*, **11**, pp. 710–25.

Brinkerhoff, R. O. and Dressler, D. E. (1990) *Productivity Measurement*, Newbury Park, CA: Sage.

Brown, A. (1995) *Organizational Culture*, London: Pitman.

Brown, W. and Walsh, J. (1994) Managing pay in Britain. In K. Sisson (ed.) *Personnel Management*, Oxford: Blackwell.

Buchanan, D. A. (1994) Principles and practice in work design. In K. Sisson (ed.) *Personnel Management*, Oxford: Blackwell.

Cameron, K. S. (1986) Effectiveness as paradox: consensus and conflict in conceptualizations of organizational effectiveness. *Management Science*, **32**, pp. 539–53.

Cameron, K. S. (1995) Organizational effectiveness. In N. Nicholson (ed.) *Blackwell Encyclopedic Dictionary of Organizational Behaviour*, Oxford: Blackwell.

Campbell, A. and Yeung, S. (1991a) Creating a sense of mission. *Long Range Planning*, **24(4)**, pp. 10–20.

Campbell, A. and Yeung, S. (1991b) Brief case: mission, vision and strategic intent. *Long Range Planning*, **24(4)**, pp. 145–7.

Campbell, D. J. and Lee, C. (1988) Self-appraisal in performance evaluation: development versus evaluation. *Academy of Management Review*, **13(2)**, pp. 302–14.

Campbell, J. P. (1977) On the nature of organizational effectiveness. In P. S. Goodman and J. M. Pennings (eds) *New Perspectives on Organizational Effectiveness*, San Francisco, CA: Jossey-Bass.

Campbell, J. P. (1990) Modeling the performance prediction problem in industrial and organizational psychology. In M. D. Dunnette and L. M. Hough (eds) *Handbook of Industrial and Organizational Psychology*, Palo Alto, CA: Consulting Psychologists Press.

Campbell, J. P. and Campbell, R. J. (1988) Industrial-organizational psychology and productivity: the goodness of fit. In J. P. Campbell, R. J. Campbell and Associates *Productivity in Organizations*, San Francisco, CA: Jossey-Bass.

Campbell, J. P., Gasser, M. B. and Oswald, F. L. (1996) The substantive nature of job performance variability. In K. R. Murphy (ed.) *Individual Differences and Behaviour in Organizations*, San Francisco, CA: Jossey-Bass.

Campbell, J. P., McCloy, R. A., Oppler, S. H. and Sager, C. E. (1993) A theory of performance. In N. Schmitt, W. C. Borman and Associates *Personnel Selection in Organizations*, San Francisco, CA: Jossey-Bass.

Campion, M. A. and Wong, C. S. (1991) Improving efficiency and satisfaction through job design. In J. W. Jones, B. D. Steffy and D. W. Bray (eds) *Applying Psychology in Business*, Lexington, MA: Lexington Books.

Cannell, M. and Wood, S. (1992) *Incentive Pay*, London: Institute of Personnel Management.

Cardy, R. L. and Dobbins, G. H. (1994) *Performance Appraisal: Alternative Perspectives*, Cincinnati, OH: South-Western.

Cascio, W. F. (1993) Downsizing: what do we know? What have we learned? *Academy of Management Executive*, **7(1)**, pp. 95–104.

Chakravarthy, B. (1986) Measuring strategic performance. *Strategic Management Journal*, **7**, pp. 437–58.

Chatman, J. A. (1989) Improving interactional organizational research: a model of person-organization fit. *Academy of Management Review*, **14(3)**, PP. 333–49.

Cockerill, A. P. (1995) Competencies. In N. Nicholson (ed.) *Blackwell*

*Encyclopedic Dictionary of Organizational Behaviour*, Oxford: Blackwell.

Collin, A. (1989) Managers' competence: rhetoric, reality and research. *Personnel Review*, **18(6)**, pp. 20–5.

Connock, S. (1991) *HR Vision: Managing a Quality Workforce*, London: Institute of Personnel Management.

Cook, J. D., Hepworth, S. J., Wall, T. D. and Warr, P. B. (1981) *The Experience of Work*, London: Academic Press.

Cooper, D. and Robertson, I. T. (1995) *The Psychology of Personnel Selection: A Quality Approach*, London: Routledge.

Costello, S. J. (1994) *Effective Performance Management*, New York: Irwin.

Cropanzano, R. and Greenberg, J. (1997) Progress in organizational justice. In C. L. Cooper and I. T. Robertson (eds) *International Review of Industrial and Organizational Psychology*, vol. 12, Chichester: Wiley.

Csoka, L. (1994) *Closing the Human Performance Gap*, New York: The Conference Board.

Dale, B. G. (ed.) (1994) *Managing Quality*, Hemel Hempstead: Prentice Hall.

Dale, B. G. and Boaden, R. J. (1994) A generic framework for managing quality improvement. In B. G. Dale (ed.) *Managing Quality*, Hemel Hempstead: Prentice Hall.

Davis-Blake, A. and Pfeffer, J. (1989) Just a mirage: the search for dispositional effects in organizational research. *Academy of Management Review*, **14(3)**, pp. 385–400.

Dawson, S. (1996) *Analysing Organizations*, Basingstoke: Macmillan.

Deming, W. E. (1986) *Out of the Crisis*, Cambridge, Mass: Massachusetts Institute of Technology.

Dickson, D., Saunders, C. and Stringer, M. (1993) *Rewarding People*, London: Routledge.

Dickinson, T. L. (1993) Attitudes about performance appraisal. In H. Schuler, J. L. Farr and M. Smith (eds) *Personnel Selection and Assessment*, Hillsdale, NJ: Erlbaum.

Digman, J. M. (1990) Personality structure: emergence of the five-factor model. *Annual Review of Psychology*, **41**, pp. 417–40.

Dulewicz, V. and Fletcher, C. (1989) The context and dynamics of performance appraisal. In P. Herriot (ed.) *Assessment and Selection in Organizations*, Chichester: Wiley.

Earley, P. C. and Shalley, C. E. (1991) New perspectives on goals and performance. *Research in Personnel and Human Resources Management*, **9**, pp. 121–57.

Eccles, R. G. (1991) The performance measurement manifesto. *Harvard Business Review*, **68(1)**, pp. 131–7.

Eder, R. W. and Fedor, D. B. (1989) Impression management: its interpretive role in the supervisor–employee feedback process. In R. A. Giacalone and P. Rosenfeld (eds) *Impression Management in the Organization*, Hillsdale, NJ: Erlbaum.

Edwards, J. R. (1991) Person-job fit: a conceptual integration, literature review, and methodological critique. In C. L. Cooper and I. T. Robertson (eds) *International Review of Industrial and Organizational Psychology*, vol. 6, Chichester: Wiley.

Eysenck, M. W. (1994) *Individual Differences: Normal and Abnormal*, London: Erlbaum.

Farr, J. L. (1993) Informal performance feedback: seeking and giving. In H. Schuler, J. L. Farr and M. Smith (eds) *Personnel Selection and Assessment*, Hillsdale, NJ: Erlbaum.

Fay, C. (1995) The changing nature of work. In H. Risher and C. Fay (eds) *The Performance Imperative*, San Francisco, CA: Jossey-Bass.

Fedor, D. B. (1991) Recipient responses to performance feedback. *Research in Personnel and Human Resources Management*, **9**, pp. 73–120.

Feldman, D. C. (1995) The impact of downsizing on organizational career development activities and employee career development opportunities. *Human Resource Management Review*, **5(3)**, pp. 189–221.

Filella, J. and Hegewisch, A. (1994) European experiments with pay and benefits policies. In C. Brewster and A. Hegewisch (eds) *Policy and Practice in Human Resource Management*, London: Routledge.

Flanagan, J. C. (1954) The critical incident technique. *Psychological Bulletin*, **51**, pp. 327–58.

Fletcher, C. (1993) *Appraisal: Routes to Improved Performance*, London: Institute of Personnel Management.

Fletcher, C. (1994) Performance appraisal in context: organizational changes and their impact on practice. In N. Anderson and P. Herriot (eds) *Assessment and Selection in Organizations*, Chichester: Wiley.

Fletcher, C and Williams, R. (1992) *Performance Appraisal and Career Development*, 2nd edn, Cheltenham: Stanley Thornes.

Flood, P. C. and Olian, J. D. (1996) Human resource strategies for world-class competitive capability. In P. C. Flood, M. J. Gannon and J. Paauwe (eds) *Managing Without Traditional Methods*, Wokingham: Addison-Wesley.

Folger, R. and Konovsky, M. (1989) Effects of procedural and distributive justice on reactions to pay raise decisions. *Academy of Management Journal*, **32(1)**, pp. 115–30.

France, S. (1997) *360° Appraisal*, London: Industrial Society.

French, W. L. and Bell, C. H. (1995) *Organization Development*, 5th edn, Englewood Cliffs, NJ: Prentice Hall.

Gardner, H. (1983) *Frames of Mind: The Theory of Multiple Intelligences*, New York: Basic Books.

Geary, J. F. (1992) Pay, control and commitment: linking appraisal and reward. *Human Resource Management Journal*, **2(4)**, pp. 36–54.

George, J. M. and Brief, A. P. (1992) Feeling good – doing good: a conceptual analysis of the mood at work/organizational spontaneity relationship. *Psychological Bulletin*, **112**, pp. 310–29.

Gerhart, B. and Milkovich, G. T. (1992) Employee compensation:

research and practice. In M. D. Dunnette and L. M. Hough (eds) *Handbook of Industrial and Organizational Psychology*, Palo Alto, CA: Consulting Psychologists Press.

Gill, D. (1977) *Appraising Performance: Present Trends and the Next Decade*, London: Institute of Personnel Management.

Goldberg, L. R. (1993) The structure of phenotypic personality traits. *American Psychologist*, **48**, pp. 26–34.

Graham, J. W. (1986) Principled organizational dissent: a theoretical essay. *Research in Organizational Behavior*, vol. 8, Greenwich, CT: JAI Press.

Greenberg, J. (1986) Determinants of perceived fairness of performance evaluations. *Journal of Applied Psychology*, **71(2)**, pp. 340–2.

Greenberg, J. (1990) Organizational justice: yesterday, today, and tomorrow. *Journal of Management*, **16(2)**, pp. 399–432.

Guinn, K. (1987) Performance management: not just an annual appraisal. *Personnel*, August, pp. 39–42.

Guion, R. M. and Gottier, G. F. (1965) Validity of personality measures in personnel selection. *Personnel Psychology*, **18**, pp. 135–64.

Guzzo, R. A. (1988) Productivity research: reviewing psychological and economic perspectives. In J. P. Campbell, R. J. Campbell and Associates *Productivity in Organizations*, San Francisco, CA: Jossey-Bass.

Guzzo, R. A. and Gannett, B. A. (1988) The nature of facilitators and inhibitors of effective task performance. In F. D. Schoorman and B. Schneider (eds) *Facilitating Work Effectiveness*, Lexington, MA: Lexington Books.

Guzzo, R. E., Jette, R. D. and Katzell, R. A. (1985) The effects of psychologically based intervention programmes on worker productivity: a meta-analysis. *Personnel Psychology*, **38**, pp. 275–91.

Hackman, J. R. and Oldham, G. R. (1980) *Work Redesign*, Reading, MA: Addison-Wesley.

Hale, R. (1993) *How to Introduce Target Setting*, London: Kogan Page.

Hall, R. H. (1996) *Organizations: Structures, Processes and Outcomes*, 6th edn,. Englewood Cliffs, NJ: Prentice Hall.

Harris, V. (1995) Moving ahead on cultural change. *People Management*, March, pp. 30–3.

Harrison, A. (1994) Just-in-time manufacturing. In J. Storey (ed.) *New Wave Manufacturing Strategies*, London: Paul Chapman Publishing.

Heap, J. (1992) *Productivity Management: A Fresh Approach*, London: Cassell.

Heisler, W. J., Jones, W. D. and Benham, P. O. (1988) *Managing Human Resources Issues*, San Francisco, CA: Jossey-Bass.

Henderson, R. I. (1984) *Performance Appraisal*. 2nd edn, Reston, VA: Reston Publishing Co.

Hendry, C., Perkins, S. and Bradley, P. (1997) Missed a motivator? *People Management*, May, pp. 20–5.

Heneman, R. L. (1990) Merit pay research. *Research in Personnel and Human Resources Management*, vol. 8, Greenwich, CT: JAI Press.

Heneman, R. L. (1992) *Merit Pay: Linking Pay Increases to Performance Ratings*, Reading, MA: Addison-Wesley.

Higgins, R. L. and Snyder, C. R. (1989) The business of excuses. In R. A. Giacalone and P. Rosenfeld (eds) *Impression Management in the Organization*, Hillsdale, NJ: Erlbaum.

Hinrichs, J. R. (1996) Feedback, action planning, and follow-through. In A. I. Kraut (ed.) *Organizational Surveys*, San Francisco, CA: Jossey-Bass.

Hitt, M. A. and Ireland, R. D. (1987) Peters and Waterman revisited: The unended quest for excellence. *Academy of Management Executive*, **1(2)**, pp. 91–8.

Hogan, R. T. (1991) Personality and personality measurement. In M. D. Dunnette and L. M. Hough (eds) *Handbook of Industrial and Organizational Psychology*, Palo Alto, CA: Consulting Psychologists Press.

Hooghiemstra, T. (1992) Integrated management of human resources. In A. Mitrani, M. Dalziel and D. Fitt (eds) *Competency Based Human Resource Management*, London: Kogan Page.

Hough, L. M. and Schneider, R. J. (1996) Personality traits, taxonomies, and applications in organizations. In K. Murphy (ed.) *Individual Differences and Behavior in Organizations*, San Francisco, CA: Jossey-Bass.

Hubbard, G. (1995) Core competence. In N. Nicholson (ed.) *Blackwell Encyclopedic Dictionary of Organizational Behaviour*, Oxford: Blackwell.

Huber, V. L., Latham, G. P. and Locke, E. A. (1989) The management of impressions through goal setting. In R. A. Giacalone and P. Rosenfeld (eds) *Impression Management in the Organization*, Hillsdale, NJ: Erlbaum.

Hume, D. A. (1995) *Reward Management*, Oxford: Blackwell.

Hyman, J. and Mason, B. (1995) *Managing Employee Involvement and Participation*, London: Sage.

Ilgen, D. R. and Hollenbeck, J. R. (1991) The structure of work: job design and roles. In M. D. Dunnette and L. M. Hough (eds) *Handbook of Industrial and Organizational Psychology*, Palo Alto, CA: Consulting Psychologists Press.

Ilgen, D. R. and Schneider, J. (1991) Performance measurement: a multidiscipline view. In C. L. Cooper and I. T. Robertson (eds) *International Review of Industrial and Organizational Psychology*, Chichester: Wiley.

Incomes Data Services (1985) *The Merit Factor*, London: Incomes Data Services.

Incomes Data Services (1992) *Performance Management*, IDS Study 518, London: Incomes Data Services.

Industrial Society (1994) *Performance Management*, London: Industrial Society.

Industrial Society (1995) *Performance Management*, London: Industrial Society.

Institute of Personnel Management (1992) *Performance Management in the UK: An Analysis of the Issues*, London: Institute of Personnel Management.

Kane, K. (1993) Situational constraints and performance: an overview. *Human Resource Management Review*, **3(2)**, pp. 83–103.

Kane, J. S. (1986) Performance distribution assessment. In R. Berk (ed.) *Performance Assessment*, Baltimore: Johns Hopkins Press.

Kanfer, R. (1995) Motivation and performance. In N. Nicholson (ed.) *Blackwell Encyclopedic Dictionary of Organizational Behaviour*, Oxford: Blackwell.

Kaplan, R. S. and Norton, D. P. (1992) The balanced scorecard – measures that drive performance. *Harvard Business Review*, **69(1)**, pp. 71–9.

Kaplan, R. S. and Norton, D. P. (1993) Putting the balanced scorecard to work. *Harvard Business Review*, **70(5)**, 134–47.

Kaplan, R. S. and Norton, D. P. (1996) Using the balanced scorecard as a strategic management system. *Harvard Business Review*, **73(1)**, pp. 75–85.

Karlöf, B. (1993) *Key Business Concepts*, London: Routledge.

Katz, D. and Kahn, R. L. (1978) *The Social Psychology of Organizations*, 2nd edn, New York: Wiley.

Katzell, R. A. and Guzzo, R. A. (1983) Psychological approaches to productivity improvement. *American Psychologist*, **38**, pp. 468–72.

Kerr, S. (1975) On the folly of rewarding A, while hoping for B. *Academy of Management Journal*, **18**, pp. 769–83.

Kerr, S. (1988) Some characteristics and consequences of organizational reward. In F. D. Schoorman and B. Schneider (eds) *Facilitating Work Effectiveness*, Lexington, MA: Lexington Books.

Kerr, S. (1995) On the folly of rewarding A, while hoping for B. *Academy of Management Executive*, **9(1)**, pp. 7–14.

Kessler, I. (1994) Performance pay. In K. Sisson (ed.) *Personnel Management*, Oxford: Blackwell.

Kessler, I. (1995) Reward systems. In J. Storey (ed.), *Human Resource Management*, London: Routledge.

Kessler, I. and Purcell, J. (1992) Performance related pay – objectives and application. *Human Resource Management Journal*, **2(3)**, pp. 34–59.

Kirkpatrick, I. and Lucio, M. M. (1995) *The Politics of Quality in the Public Sector*, London: Routledge.

Klimoski, R. (1993) Predictor constructs and their measurement. In N. Schmitt, W. C. Borman and Associates *Personnel Selection in Organizations*, San Francisco, CA: Jossey-Bass.

Knights, D. and McCabe, D. (1996) Do quality initiatives need management? *The TQM Magazine*, **8(3)**, pp. 24–6.

Kopelman, R. E. (1986) *Managing Productivity in Organizations*, New York: McGraw-Hill.

Kotter, J. P. and Heskett, J. L. (1992) *Corporate Culture and Performance*, New York: Free Press.

Landy, F. J., Barnes, J. L. and Murphy, K. R. (1978) Correlates of perceived fairness and accuracy of performance evaluation. *Journal of Applied Psychology*, **63**, pp. 751–4.

Larson, J. R. and Callahan, C. (1990) Performance monitoring: how it affects work productivity. *Journal of Applied Psychology*, **75(5)**, pp. 530–8.

Latham, C. and Marchbank, T. (1994) Feedback techniques. In G. Lee and D. Beard (eds.) *Development Centres*, Maidenhead, Berks: McGraw-Hill.

Latham, G. P. and Wexley, K. N. (1994) *Increasing Productivity Through Performance Appraisal*, 2nd edn, Reading, MA: Addison-Wesley.

Lawler, E. E. (1987) The design of effective reward systems. In J. W. Lorsch (ed.) *Handbook of Organizational Behaviour*, Englewood Cliffs, NJ: Prentice Hall.

Lawler, E. E. (1995) Organizational effectiveness: new realities and challenges. In H. Risher and C. Fay (eds) *The Performance Imperative*, San Francisco, CA: Jossey-Bass.

Lawler, E. E. and Jenkins, D. (1992) Strategic reward systems. In M. D. Dunnette and L. M. Hough (eds) *Handbook of Industrial and Organizational Psychology*, Palo Alto, CA: Consulting Psychologists Press.

Lawler, A. (1985) *Productivity Improvement Manual*, Aldershot: Gower.

Lawson, P. (1995) Performance management: an overview. In M. Walters (ed.) *The Performance Management Handbook*, London: Institute of Personnel and Development.

Legge, K. (1995) *Human Resource Management: Rhetorics and Realities*, Basingstoke: Macmillan.

Letza, S. R. (1996) The design and implementation of the balanced business scorecard. *Business Process Re-engineering and Management Journal*, **2(3)**, pp. 54–76.

Leventhal, G. S. (1976) Fairness in social relationships. In J. W. Thibaut, J. T. Spence and R. C. Carson (eds) *Contemporary Topics in Social Psychology*, Morristown, NJ: General Learning Press.

Leventhal, G. S. (1980) What should be done with equity theory? In K. J. Gergen, M. S. Greenberg and R. H. Willis (eds) *Social Exchange: Advances in Theory and Research*, New York: Plenum.

LGMB (1993) *People and Performance*, Luton: Local Government Management Board.

Locke, E. A. and Latham, G. P. (1984) *Goal Setting: A Motivational Technique that Works!*, Englewood Cliffs, NJ: Prentice Hall.

Locke, E. A. and Latham, G. P. (1990) *A Theory of Goal Setting and Task Performance*, Englewood Cliffs, NJ: Prentice Hall.

Lockett, J. (1992) *Effective Performance Management,* London: Kogan Page.

London, M. (1995) Giving feedback: source-centered antecedents and consequences of constructive and destructive feedback. *Human Resource Management Review*, **5(3)**, pp. 159–88.

Long, P. (1986) *Performance Appraisal Revisited*, London: Institute of Personnel Management.

Longenecker, C. O. and Scazzero, J. A. (1996) The ongoing challenge of total quality management. *The TQM Magazine*, **8(2)**, pp. 55–60.

Luffman, G., Lea, E., Sanderson, S. and Kenny, B. (1996) *Strategic Management*, 3rd edn Oxford: Blackwell.

Lundy, O. and Cowling, A. (1996) *Strategic Human Resource Management*, London: Routledge.

Mabey, C. and Salaman, G. (1995) *Strategic Human Resource Management*, Oxford: Blackwell.

Macdonell, R. (1989) Management by objectives. In P. Herriot (ed.) *Assessment and Selection in Organizations*, Chichester: Wiley.

MacKenzie, S. B., Podsakoff, P. M. and Fetter, R. (1991) Organizational citizenship behaviour and objective productivity as determinants of managerial evaluations of salespersons' performance. *Organizational Behaviour and Human Decision Processes*, **50(1)**, pp. 1–28.

MacKenzie, S. B., Podsakoff, P. M. and Fetter, R. (1993) The impact of organizational citizenship behaviour on evaluations of salesperson performance. *Journal of Marketing*, **57**, pp. 70–80.

McAfee, R. B. and Champagne, P. J. (1993) Performance management: A strategy for improving employee performance and productivity. *Journal of Managerial Psychology*, **8(5)**, pp. 24–32.

McConkie, M. L. (1979) A clarification of the goal setting and appraisal processes in MBO. *Academy of Management Review*, **4(1)**, pp. 29–40.

McGregor, D. M. (1957) The human side of enterprise. In *Adventures in Thought and Action*, Proceedings of the Fifth Anniversary Convocation of the School of Industrial Management, Massachusetts Institute of Technology.

McKenney, J. L. (1995) *Waves of Change*, Boston, MA: Harvard Business School Press.

Mager, R. F. and Pipe, P. (1990) *Analyzing Performance Problems*, 2nd edn, London: Kogan Page.

Makin, P. J. and Robertson, I. T. (1983) Self assessment, realistic job previews and occupational decisions. *Personnel Review*, **12(3)**, pp. 21–5.

Management Charter Initiative (1990) *Management Competences: The Standards Concept*, London: MCI.

Management Charter Initiative (1990) *Occupational Standards for Mangers* (Management 1), London: MCI.

Mansfield, R. (1986) *Company Strategy and Organizational Design*, London: Croom Helm.

Marchington, M. (1995) Involvement and participation. In J. Storey (ed.) *Human Resource Management: A Critical Text*, London: Routledge.

Marsden, D. and Richardson, R. (1994) Performing for pay? The effects of 'merit pay' on motivation in a public service. *British Journal of Industrial Relations*, **32(2)**, pp. 243–61.

Masterson, S. S. and Taylor, M. S. (1996) Total quality management and performance appraisal: an integrative perspective, *Journal of Quality Management*, **1**, pp. 67–89.

Masterson, S. S. and Taylor, M. S. (1996) Total quality management and performance appraisal: an integrative perspective. *Journal of Quality Management*, **1(1)**, pp. 67–89.

Martin, J. (1995) Organizational culture. In N. Nicholson (ed.) *Blackwell Encyclopedic Dictionary of Organizational Behaviour*, Oxford: Blackwell.

Meek, V. L. (1988) Organizational culture: origins and weaknesses. *Organization Studies*, **9(4)**, pp. 453–73.

Meyer, M. W. and Gupta, V. (1994) The performance paradox. *Research in Organizational Behaviour*, **16**, pp. 309–69.

Milkovich, G. T. and Wigdor, A. K. (1991) *Pay for Performance*, Washington, DC: National Academy Press.

Mischel, W. (1977) The interaction of person and situation. In D. Magnusson and N. S. Endler (eds), *Personality at the Crossroads*, Hillsdale, NJ: Erlbaum.

Mitchell, T. R. and O'Reilly, C. A. (1983) Managing poor performance and productivity in organizations. *Research in Organizational Behaviour*, vol. 5, Greenwich, CT: JAI Press.

Mohrman, A. M. (1990) Deming versus performance appraisal: is there a resolution? In G. N. McLean, S. R. Damme and R. A. Swanson (eds) *Performance Appraisal – Perspectives on a Quality Management Approach*. Alexandria, VA: American Society for Training and Development.

Mohrman, A. M., Resnick-West, S. M. and Lawler, E. E. (1989) *Designing Performance Appraisal Systems*, San Francisco, CA: Jossey-Bass.

Moores, R. (1994) *Managing for High Performance*, London: Industrial Society.

Moses, J., Hollenbeck, G. P. and Sorcher, M. (1993) Other people's expectations. *Human Resource Management*, **32**, pp. 283–98.

Mount, M. K. and Barrick, M. R. (1995) The big five personality dimensions. *Research in Personnel and Human Resources Management*, **13**, pp. 153–200.

Moyer, K. (1996) Scenario planning at British Airways – a case study. *Long Range Planning*, **29(2)**, pp. 172–81.

Mullins, L. J. (1996) *Management and Organizational Behaviour*. 4th edn, London: Pitman.

Murlis, H. and Wright, V. (1993) Remuneration. *Benefits and Compensation International*, January–February, pp. 5–10.

Murphy, K. R. (1989) Dimensions of job performance. In R. F. Dillon and J. W. Pellegrino (eds) *Testing: Theoretical and Applied Perspectives*, New York: Praeger.

Murphy, K. R. (1990) Job performance and productivity. In K. R. Murphy and F. E. Saal (eds) *Psychology in Organizations*, Hillsdale, NJ: Erlbaum.

Murphy, K. R. and Cleveland, J. N. (1995) *Understanding Performance Appraisal*, Thousand Oaks, CA: Sage.

Naylor, J. C. and Ilgen, D. R. (1984) Goal setting: A theoretical analysis of a motivational technology. *Research in Organizational Behaviour*, **6**, pp. 95–140.

Newell, S. (1995) *The Healthy Organization*, London: International Thomson Business Press.

Nicholson, N. and West, M. A. (1988) *Managerial Job Change: Men and Women in Transition*, Cambridge: Cambridge University Press.

Ogbonna, E. (1992) Organizational culture and human resource management: Dilemmas and contradictions. In. P. Blyton and P. Turnbull (eds) *Reassessing Human Resource Management*, London: Sage.

Ones, D. S., Viswesvaran, C. and Schmidt, F. L. (1993) Comprehensive meta-analysis of integrity test validities: findings and implications for personnel selection and theories of job performance. *Journal of Applied Psychology*, **78**, pp. 679–703.

O'Reilly, C. (1989) Corporations, culture and commitment: motivation and social control in organizations. *California Management Review*, **31**(4), pp. 9–25.

Parasuraman, A., Berry, L. L. and Zeithaml, V. (1991) Understanding, measuring, and improving service quality. In S. W. Brown, E. Gummesson, B. Edvardsson and B. Gustavsson (eds) *Service Quality*, Lexington, MA: Lexington Books.

Parker, S. K. and Wall, T. D. (1996) Job design and modern manufacturing. In P. Warr (ed.) *Psychology at Work*, 4th edn, Harmondsworth, Penguin.

Parker, S. K., Mullarkey, S. and Jackson, P. R. (1994) Dimensions of performance effectiveness in high-involvement work organizations. *Human Resource Management Journal*, **40**(3), pp. 1–21.

Pearce, J. L. (1987) Why merit pay doesn't work: implications from organization theory. In D. B. Balkin and L. R. Gomez-Mejia (eds) *New Perspectives on Compensation*, Englewood Cliffs, NJ: Prentice Hall.

Pearn, M. (1992) A competency approach to role and career management restructuring. In R. Boam and P. Sparrow (eds) *Designing and Achieving Competency*, Maidenhead: McGraw-Hill.

Peppard, J. and Preece, I. (1995) The content, context and process of business process re-engineering. In G. Burke and J. Peppard (eds) *Examinimg Business Process Re-engineering*, London: Kogan Page.

Peppard, J. and Rowland, P. (1995) *The Essence of Business Process Re-engineering*, Hemel Hempstead: Prentice Hall.

Peters, L. H. and O'Connor, E. J. (1980) Situational constraints and work outcomes: the influence of a frequently overlooked construct. *Academy of Management Review*, **5**, pp. 391–7.

Peters, T. J. and Waterman, R. H. (1982) *In Search of Excellence*, New York: Harper & Row.

Pettigrew, A. and Whipp, R. (1993) Managing the twin processes of competition and change: the role of intangible assets. In P. Lorange,

B. Chakravarthy, J. Ross and A. Van de Ven (eds) *Implementing Strategic Processes*, Oxford: Blackwell.

Pfeffer, J. (1994) *Competitive Advantage Through People*, Boston, MA: Harvard Business School Press.

Prahalad, C. K. and Hamel, G. (1990) The core competence of the corporation. *Harvard Business Review*, **68**, May–June, pp. 79–81.

Pritchard, R. D. (1990a) Measuring organizational productivity. In P. J. D. Drenth, J. A. Sergeant and R. J. Takens (eds) *European Perspectives in Psychology*, vol. 3, Chichester: Wiley.

Pritchard, R. D. (1990b) Enhancing work motivation through productivity measurement and feedback. In U. Kleinbeck, H. H. Quast, H. Thierry and H. Häcker (eds) *Work Motivation*, Hillsdale, NJ: Erlbaum.

Pritchard, R. D. (1992) Organizational productivity. In M. D. Dunnette and L. M. Hough (eds) *Handbook of Industrial/Organizational Psychology*, Palo Alto, CA: Consulting Psychologists Press.

Pritchard, R. D. (1995) Productivity. In N. Nicholson (ed.) *Blackwell Encyclopedic Dictionary of Organizational Behaviour*, Oxford: Blackwell.

Pritchard, R. D., Jones, S. D., Roth, P. L., Stuebing, K. K. and Ekeberg, S. E. (1988) The effects of feedback, goal setting, and incentives on organizational productivity. *Journal of Applied Psychology Monograph Series*, **73(2)**, pp. 337–58.

Pritchard, R. D., Jones, S. D., Roth, P. L., Stuebing, K. K. and Ekeberg, S. E. (1989) The evaluation of an integrated approach to measuring organizational productivity. *Personnel Psychology*, **42(1)**, pp. 69–115.

Prokopenko, J. (1987) *Productivity Management*, Geneva: International Labour Office.

Prytz, K. (1995) Modeling in manufacturing enterprises. In A. Rolstadås (ed.) *Performance Management*, London: Chapman and Hall.

Purcell, J. (1995) Corporate strategy and its link with human resource management strategy. In J. Storey (ed.) *Human Resource Management: A Critical Text*, London: Routledge.

Quinn, R. E., Faerman, S. R., Thompson, M. P. and McGrath, M. R. (1996) *Becoming a Master Manager: A Competency Framework*, 2nd edn, New York: Wiley.

Ramsay, H. (1996) Involvement, empowerment and commitment. In B. Towers (ed.) *The Handbook of Human Resource Management*, 2nd edn, Oxford: Blackwell.

Ravlin, E. C. (1995) Values. In N. Nicholson (ed.) *Blackwell Encyclopedic Dictionary of Organizational Behaviour*, Oxford: Blackwell.

Reeves, C. A. and Bednar, D. A. (1994) Defining quality: alternatives and implications. *The Academy of Management Review*, **19(3)**, pp. 419–45.

Robertson, I. T. (1994) Personality and personnel selection. In C. L. Cooper and D. M. Rousseau (eds) *Trends in Organizational Behaviour*, Chichester: Wiley.

Robertson, I. T. and Kinder, A. (1993) Personality and job competences:

the criterion-related validity of some personality variables. *Journal of Occupational and Organizational Psychology*, **66**, pp. 225–44.

Robertson, I. T., Smith, M. and Cooper, D. (1992) *Motivation*, London: Institute of Personnel Management.

Rodgers, R. and Hunter, J. E. (1991) Impact of management by objectives on organizational productivity. *Journal of Applied Psychology Monograph Series*, **76(2)**, pp. 322–36.

Roe, R. A. (1989) Designing selection procedures. In P. Herriot (ed.) *Assessment and Selection in Organizations*, Chichester: Wiley.

Roethlisberger, F. G. and Dickson, W. J. (1939) *Management and the Worker*, Cambridge, MA: Harvard Business School Press.

Rogers, S. (1990) *Performance Management in Local Government*, Harlow, Essex: Longman.

Rosenfeld, P., Giacalone, R. A. and Riordan, C. A. (1995) *Impression Management in Organizations*, London: International Thomson Business Press.

Rummler, G. A. and Brache, A. P. (1995) *Improving Performance*. 2nd edn, San Francisco, CA: Jossey-Bass.

Sadri, G. and Robertson, I. T. (1993) Self-efficacy and work-related behaviour: a review and meta-analysis. *Applied Psychology: An International Review*, **42(2)**, pp. 139–52.

Schein, E. H. (1992) *Organizational Culture and Leadership*, 2nd edn, San Francisco, CA: Jossey-Bass.

Schmidt, F. L. (1993) Personnel psychology at the cutting edge. In N. Schmitt, W. C. Borman and Associates *Personnel Selection in Organizations*, San Francisco, CA: Jossey-Bass.

Schneider, B. (1987) The people make the place. *Personnel Psychology*, **40**, pp. 437–453.

Schneider, B. and Konz, A. M. (1989) Strategic job analysis. *Human Resource Management*, **28(1)**, pp. 51–85.

Schneider, B. and Schechter, D. (1991) Development of a personnel selection system for service jobs. In S. W. Brown, E. Gummesson, B. Edvardsson and B. Gustavsson (eds) *Service Quality*, Lexington, MA: Lexington Books.

Schneider, R. J. and Hough, L. M. (1995) Personality and industrial/organizational psychology. In C. L. Cooper and I. T. Robertson (eds) *International Review of Industrial and Organizational Psychology*, Chichester: Wiley.

Schneier, C. E., Beatty, R. W. and Baird, L. S. (1986) How to construct a successful performance appraisal system. *Training and Development Journal*, April.

Schneier, C. E., Beatty, R. W. and Baird, L. S. (eds) (1987) Introduction *The Performance Management Sourcebook*, Amherst, MA: Human Resource Development Press.

Schriesheim, C. A., Hinkin, T. R. and Tetrault, L. A. (1991) The discriminant validity of the Leader Reward and Punishment Questionnaire (LRPQ) and satisfaction with supervision. *Journal of Occupational Psychology*, **64**, pp. 159–66.

Schroder, H. M. (1989) *Managerial Competence: The Key to Excellence*, Iowa: Kendall Hunt.

Selznick, P. (1957) *Leadership in Administration*, New York: Harper & Row.

Shackleton, V. J. (1992) Using a competency approach in a business change setting. In R. Boam and P. Sparrow (eds) *Designing and Achieving Competency*, Maidenhead: McGraw-Hill.

Sheard, A. (1992) Learning to improve performance. *Personnel Management*, November, pp. 40–5.

Society of Telecom Executives (1992) *Stressing Performance*, London: Society of Telecom Executives.

Spangenberg, H. (1994) *Understanding and Implementing Performance Management*, Cape Town: Juda.

Sparrow, P. (1996) Too good to be true. *People Management*, December, pp. 22–7.

Sparrow, P. and Boam, R. (1992) Where do we go from here? In R. Boam and P. Sparrow (eds) *Designing and Achieving Competency*, Maidenhead: McGraw-Hill.

Sparrow, P. R. (1994) Organizational competencies: creating a strategic behavioural framework for selection and assessment. In N. Anderson and P. Herriot (eds) *Assessment and Selection in Organizations. First Update and Supplement*, Chichester: Wiley.

Sparrow, P. R. (1996) Too good to be true. *People Management*, December, 22–7.

Spencer, L. M. and Spencer, S. M. (1993) *Competence at Work*, New York: Wiley.

Steers, R. M. and Porter, L. W. (1991) Reward systems in organizations. In R. M. Steers and L. W. Porter (eds) *Motivation and Work Behaviour*, 5th edn, New York: McGraw-Hill.

Sternberg, R. J. (1990) *Metaphors of Mind: Conceptions of the Nature of Intelligence*, New York: Cambridge University Press.

Sternberg, R. J. (1994) Tacit knowledge and job success. In N. Anderson and P. Herriot (eds) *Assessment and Selection in Organizations. First Update and Supplement*, Chichester: Wiley.

Sternberg, R. J. and Wagner, R. K. (1986) *Practical Intelligence*, Cambridge: Cambridge University Press.

Stewart, R. (1991) *Managing Today and Tomorrow*, Basingstoke: Macmillan.

Stiles, P., Gratton, L., Truss, C., Hope-Hailey, V. and McGovern, P. (1997) Performance management and the psychological contract. *Human Resource Management Journal*, 7(1), pp. 57–66.

Stone, D. L. and Eddy, E. R. (1996) A model of individual and organizational factors affecting quality-related outcomes. *Journal of Quality Management*, 1(1), pp. 21–48.

Storey, J. and Sisson, K. (1993) *Managing Human Resources and Industrial Relations*, Buckingham: Open University Press.

Streufert, S. and Nogami, G. Y. (1989) Cognitive style and complexity.

In C. L. Cooper and I. T. Robertson (eds) *International Review of Industrial and Organizational Psychology*, Chichester: Wiley.

Stinson, J. and Stokes, J. (1980) How to multi-appraise. *Management Today*, June, 43–53.

Storey, J. and Sisson, K. (1993) *Managing Human Resources and Industrial Relations*, Buckingham: Open University Press.

Swanson, R. A. (1994) *Analyzing for Improving Performance*, San Francisco, CA: Berrett-Koehler.

Taylor, M. S., Fisher, C. D. and Ilgen, D. R. (1984) Individuals' reactions to performance feedback in organizations. *Research in Personnel and Human Resources Management*, 2, pp. 81–124.

Thatcher, M. (1996) Allowing everyone to have their say. *People Management*, March, pp. 28–30.

Thompson, J. L. (1990) *Strategic Management*, London: International Thomson Business Press.

Thompson, M. (1992) Pay and performance: the employer experience. Falmer, Sussex: Institute of Manpower Studies.

Thompson, M. (1993) Pay and performance: the employee experience. Falmer, Sussex: Institute of Manpower Studies.

Thornton, G. C. and Byham, W. C. (1982) *Assessment Centres and Managerial Performance*, New York: Academic Press.

Torrington, D. and Hall, L. (1995) *Personnel Management: HRM in Action*, 3rd edn, Hemel Hempstead: Prentice Hall.

Townley, B. (1994) Communicating with employees. In K. Sisson (ed.) *Personnel Management*, Oxford: Blackwell.

Tuxworth, E. (1989) Competence based education and training: background and origins. In J. W. Burke (ed.) *Competency Based Education and Training*, Lewes: Falmer Press.

Tziner, A., Latham, G. P., Price, B. S. and Haccoun, R. (1996) Development and validation of a questionnaire for measuring perceived political considerations in performance appraisal. *Journal of Organizational Behaviour*, 17, pp. 179–90.

Van Dyne, L., Cummings, L. L. and Parks, J. M. (1995) Extra-role behaviours. *Research in Organizational Behaviour*, 17, pp. 215–85.

Waldman, D. A. (1994) The contributions of total quality management to a theory of work performance. *Academy of Management Review*, 19(3), 510–36.

Walters, M. (1995) Developing organizational measures. In M. Walters (ed.) *The Performance Management Handbook*, London: Institute of Personnel and Development.

Walters, M. (ed.) (1995) Introduction. *The Performance Management Handbook*. London: Institute of Personnel and Development.

Warr, P. (1996) Employee well-being. In P. Warr (ed.) *Psychology at Work*, 4th edn, Harmondsworth: Penguin.

Warr, P. and Conner, M. (1992) Job competence and cognition. *Research in Organizational Behaviour*, 14, pp. 91–127.

Warr, P. B. (1987) Job characteristics and mental health. In P. B. Warr (ed.) *Psychology at Work*, 3rd edn, Harmondsworth: Penguin.

Warrick, D. D. and Zawacki, R. A. (1987) *High Performance Management*, Colorado Springs: Eagle Publishing Co.

Whetten, D., Cameron, K. and Woods, M. (1994) *Developing Management Skills for Europe*, London: HarperCollins.

Wild, R. (1995) *Production and Operations Management*, 5th edn, London: Casssell.

Wilkinson, A. and Willmott, H. (1995a) *Making Quality Critical*, London: International Thomson Business Press.

Wilkinson, A. and Willmott, H. (1995b) Introduction. *Making Quality Critical*, London: International Thomson Business Press.

Williams, A., Dobson, P. and Walters, M. (1993) *Changing culture: New Organizational Approaches*, 2nd edn, London: Institute of Personnel Management.

Williams, R. S. (1989) Alternative raters and methods. In P. Herriot (ed.) *Assessment and Selection in Organizations*, Chichester: Wiley.

Williams, R. S. (1991) Communication in organizations. In M. Smith (ed.) *Analysing Organizational Behaviour*, Basingstoke: Macmillan.

Winstanley, D. and Stuart-Smith, K. (1996) Policing performance: the ethics of performance management. *Personnel Review*, **25(6)**, pp. 66–84.

Winterton, J. and Winterton, R. (1996) *The Business Benefits of Competence-based Management Development*, London: HMSO.

Wood, R. E. and Locke, E. A. (1990) Goal setting and strategy effects on complex tasks. *Research in Organizational Behaviour*, **12**, pp. 73–109.

Woodruffe, C. (1991) Competent by any other name. *Personnel Management*, September, pp. 30–3.

Woodruffe, C. (1992) What is meant by a competency? In R. Boam and P. Sparrow (eds) *Designing and Achieving Competency*, Maidenhead: McGraw-Hill.

Wright, P. (1996) *Managerial Leadership*, London: International Thomson Business Press.

Wright, P. (1996) *Managerial Leadership*, London: Routledge.

Yeates, J. D. (1990) *Performance Appraisal: A Guide for Design and Implementation*, Falmer, Sussex: Institute for Manpower Studies.

Yukl, G. (1994) *Leadership in Organizations*, 3rd edn, Englewood Cliffs, NJ: Prentice Hall.

Zairi, M. (1994) *Measuring Performance for Business Results*, London: Chapman & Hall.

# ──── *Index*